T0284839

FACING
SUICIDE

FACING SUICIDE

Understanding Why
People Kill Themselves
and How We Can Stop Them

James Barrat

Avery
an imprint of Penguin Random House
New York

AVERY

an imprint of Penguin Random House LLC
penguinrandomhouse.com

Most Avery books are available at special quantity discounts for bulk purchase for sales
promotions, premiums, fundraising, and educational needs. Special books or book excerpts also
can be created to fit specific needs. For details, write SpecialMarkets@penguinrandomhouse.com.

Library of Congress Cataloging-in-Publication Data

Names: Barrat, James (Psychologist), author.
Title: Facing suicide: understanding why people kill themselves and
how we can stop them / James Barrat.
Description: 1 edition. | New York: Avery, Penguin Random House LLC, [2024] | Includes index.
Identifiers: LCCN 2023045896 (print) | LCCN 2023045897 (ebook) |
ISBN 9780593539156 (hardcover) | ISBN 9780593539163 (epub)
Subjects: LCSH: Suicide—Psychological aspects. | Suicidal behavior. |
Suicidal behavior—Risk factors. | Suicide—Prevention.
Classification: LCC RC569.B377 2024 (print) |
LCC RC569 (ebook) | DDC 362.28—dc23/eng/20240408
LC record available at https://lccn.loc.gov/2023045896
LC ebook record available at https://lccn.loc.gov/2023045897

Printed in the United States of America
1st Printing

Book design by Patrice Sheridan

**If you are thinking about suicide or if you or someone you know is in
emotional crisis, please call or text 988 at any time to reach the 988
Suicide and Crisis Lifeline for confidential, free crisis support.**

This theory, this day-to-day work really is not about my dad's suicide, anymore. What it's about is the fact that tomorrow in the United States, over one hundred families are going to be bereaved by suicide. One hundred. Just tomorrow. And then the next day. And then the next day after that. And so on and so forth. And that's just in our one country. That's a human tragedy and I want to prevent that.

—THOMAS JOINER, PhD, PSYCHOLOGIST

When you can't look on the bright side
    I will sit with you in the dark.

—UNKNOWN

FOR EVA AND BRODIE,
WITH LOVE

CONTENTS

CHAPTER ONE

WHAT'S SUICIDE GOT TO DO WITH ME?

suicide| \soo-ə-sīd |

noun

the act of taking one's own life voluntarily and intentionally

It's estimated that 85 percent of the people in the United States will eventually know at least one person who killed themselves. Right now you may have a brother, daughter, spouse, or parent who is displaying signs of mental health issues or having suicidal thoughts, right before your eyes. You yourself may have a genetic predisposition for suicide or have one or more stress factors that could put you on the road to self-harm. These signs are not always obvious. But if you do not see the signs that are there, you or someone close to you could needlessly take a step toward catastrophe.

What exactly is suicide? Thomas Joiner, PhD, is a clinical psychologist and researcher who studies the behavior and beliefs of people who die by suicide. He offers this on-the-nose definition of suicide and its aftermath: "Suicide is self-inflicted, purposeful death," says Dr. Joiner. He adds, "Suicide is a catastrophe for families, and I don't think 'catastrophe' is an exaggeration. It just shocks and stuns individuals and families. They are confused, feeling searing emotional pain for months if not years, sometimes even decades, and this reverberates throughout generations."

The American Foundation for Suicide Prevention's Christine Moutier, MD, says, "The CDC [Centers for Disease Control and Prevention] is approaching suicide as a public health crisis because the rate in the United States has been on the rise since about 1999."

Crisis is a heavy-duty word in the world of public health, brought out for only the most serious problems. *Epidemic* has similar punch, and professionals don't like to use it. It refers to "a sudden, widespread occurrence of a particular undesirable phenomenon," usually a disease. In the US the rise of suicide has been widespread, but has it been *sudden*? Yes. Just since 2007 the suicide rate in the US has risen by one-third, to rates not seen since the end of the Second World War. Columbia University epidemiologist Madelyn Gould, PhD, says, "I don't like to use the word 'epidemic' because I don't want to have people get hysterical about the rates of suicide. Unfortunately, suicide can be considered an epidemic. The rates have been steadily increasing over the past couple of decades. Suicide is the tenth leading cause of death across all ages."

On average, about 45,000 people in America die by suicide each year, or 124 every day, a death toll higher than car accidents or homicides. For every person who dies, there is an average of about ten attempts. And every day some 15 million Americans endure suicidal ideation: persistent, agonizing thoughts about taking their lives.

What does that have to do with you?

If someone you cared about were on the brink of having a stroke or a heart attack, wouldn't you want to know *before* it happened? Suicide is no different. Like other health emergencies, its signs are often apparent if you know what to look for. And no one is immune, not even those who we assume are in the prime of life. Suicide is the *second*-largest killer of young people between the ages of ten and twenty-five. It's the fourth-largest killer of men between thirty-five and sixty-four years of age; white men in that age group account for almost 70 percent of all suicides in America.

On average, women attempt suicide three times more frequently than men, but men kill themselves at four times the rate of women. That's largely because men more often use firearms, which are involved in about 52 percent of suicides, more than all other methods combined. In the US each year, about four times as many people die from suicide by firearm than die from homicide by firearm.

The grim statistics around suicide belie a little-known fact: it is preventable. Generally speaking, each death by suicide and the agony it causes family, friends, and colleagues is unnecessary and can be avoided with timely, often low-cost interventions. That it is unnecessary is what makes suicide frightening and different from most other kinds of death. "Normal" deaths, caused by old age, illness, and even accidents, seem to be part and parcel of the natural order of things, jarring facts of life. Not suicide. Like homicide, it is usually unexpected and it is often violent. It has a terrible agency that most other deaths lack. It delivers an awful shock to the systems of the people around it, a shock some don't survive. While we spend so much of our lives coaching ourselves and our children not to be crushed by cars, not to slip off icy roofs, not to be reckless with guns, the fact that some people *willfully* kill themselves challenges us to our core.

Many of us have grieved the "normal" deaths of loved ones; we follow grief's familiar social script and generally emerge bowed but not broken. Grieving a suicide is a whole other kind of grief. On average, each suicide leaves six or more intimate survivors. Besides shock and disbelief, these survivors are accosted by the barbed question *Why?* Why did she do it? Why did she take her precious life? But the *why* is almost always unanswerable, because suicides usually occur at the confluence of many *why*s, which psychologists call risk factors, such as mental health disorders, alcohol abuse, romantic conflict, a family history of suicide, a previous suicide attempt, and many more. Survivors rarely unravel all the *why*s. Almost by definition the dead person is the only one who knows the full breadth of facts and feelings that led to the decision to end their life, and even they may not have been fully aware of the risk factors stacked against them. Into that vacuum of understanding rush the *why*s.

Death by suicide is also different because of blame. Usually when someone dies, we point our finger at the disease or the perpetrator, the heart that stopped working, the driver who was texting, the pharmaceutical company that flooded the town with opioids. But with suicide the victim *is* the perpetrator. Blaming him, who has suffered so much and has now lost everything, feels cruel, and it's not rewarding. The dead will offer no contrition and suffer no punishment. Rarely do friends and family deserve blame for a suicide, but it attaches to them like barnacles to a ship. According to our need to rationalize catastrophes, largely in an effort to push them away, survivors believe they failed to see the signs of the suicide, which only in retrospect may seem obvious, or they failed to support the suicidal person, or they let the victim down in some undefinable way that grows in significance after the loss. In its emotionally tumultuous aftermath, suicide can shatter families in a multitude of ways, but none is as common as blaming oneself or one another. Upon learning that her brother Angelo killed himself, my friend Christina's first words were "We weren't there for him!" Unwrapped, Angelo's story reveals that he suffered from depression, alcohol and drug abuse, chronic pain, failing health, and a failed marriage. Those who loved him had repeatedly urged him to seek professional help. Christina and her family had in fact been there for him as much as they could have been. Angelo's unnecessary suicide was preventable, by Angelo himself.

Blame rarely fits, but it too can kill. Unless treated, some survivors may develop post-traumatic stress disorder (PTSD), and involuntarily relive the trauma. They are themselves at elevated risk for thinking about and planning suicide. It's estimated that the suicide of a loved one increases the chances of survivors' suicide by 60 percent.

There's one more big distinction in deaths by suicide. Stigma. Since biblical times, death by suicide has borne intense social condemnation. Suicide can isolate survivors from their families, communities, and even from their religions, many of which consider suicide a mortal sin. In some twenty countries, attempting suicide is a criminal offense. In medieval Europe, survivors were often punished by *death*. Suicide victims were denied a Christian burial, and worse. Psychiatrist Eric D. Caine, MD, of the University of Rochester Medical Center told me, "A thousand years ago if you died by suicide in, say, Western Europe your body was drawn and quartered and hung by the roadside. Your family was stripped of all its resources and they carried the stain of your death for the rest of their lives. In some societies it's still felt that way."

Survivors may find themselves isolated because they're not comfortable talking about their loved one's suicide, or people in whom they could confide cannot handle the discomfort of talking about it. And isolating yourself is among the worst things you can do if you lose a loved one to suicide.

Survivors are often ashamed and friends rarely know what to say. In the minds of some neighbors, suicide equals crazy or weak. Survivors don't speak honestly because of this stigma and because they don't want to upset anyone. Frequently, a family denies that a suicide even occurred, and claims the victim died in their sleep or suffered a freak accident. Farmers and agriculture workers sometimes disguise their suicide attempts as farming or hunting accidents. Some survivors have to endure hurtful comments from their community or church or school. But keeping suicide a secret can lead to confusion, shame, and isolation that can last years, even generations.

This book, *Facing Suicide*, has three goals. The first is to show you the signs of suicide illustrated by real-life stories of people who killed themselves but, more to the point, people who survived or were stopped in their attempt by someone who saw the signs and intervened. My hope is that once you know the signs of the mental health issues surrounding a suicidal crisis, you may become attuned to them in the people around you, and in yourself. And once you have determined that someone may be suicidal, this book will show you what to do next, for your family member or colleague or for yourself.

Facing Suicide's second goal is to give you a general background in the causes of suicide through true life stories and science. I hope that by doing so, I can help move suicide out of the shadows of its enduring stigma and into the light of public conversation. You probably already know suicide is a national emergency, and the source of untold pain. I hope that by learning more about suicide, you will be more inclined to discuss it as a public health crisis, like COVID or heart disease, and help bring it into the mainstream.

Gathering accurate information about suicide is no small feat, especially when each case is different and each has a distinct constellation of causes. And while the science of suicide has advanced rapidly over the last thirty or so years, much is still unknown. Suicide information is not available from research alone; new insights and theories arise yearly. To learn about suicide, I relied on the ideas and papers of many of the top US psychologists, psychiatrists, neuroscientists, therapists, and social workers, and people who professionally study suicide and provide therapy to people who are suicidal. In each case, early in their careers, they decided that their life's work would be to stop as many people as possible from dying by suicide. For the better part of five years, it was my great pleasure to sit and walk and talk and correspond with these world-class suicidologists, listen to their stories, and pick their brains. I gained this access because I wrote and directed the ninety-minute documentary film *Facing Suicide*, which premiered on PBS in September 2022 and now streams online; many of the experts you'll meet in this book are interviewed in that film.

While I gained the cooperation of the experts, I sought out people whose stories embody the messages of suicide and its prevention: people who had survived attempts to kill themselves, or those who had died and whose relatives and friends could describe the events that led to their deaths. Their experiences with suicide have many things in common, including one or more mental health issues, painful isolation, and a psychological tunnel vision that didn't allow them to perceive alternatives to suicide. Their experiences are also distinct, and have much to do with the socioeconomic and cultural context of their lives. So a Native teenager living through a mass suicide in his region experiences different life stresses than a farmer enduring severe economic uncertainty. And both face life pressures different from those of a black woman living in an underserved community in the American South or a mentally ill white man from Denmark. The stories of their battles with thoughts of suicide contain important lessons. I hope you'll find them illuminating and instructive.

Facing Suicide's third goal is to spread hope. Suicide is a difficult, often dark, and polarizing subject—what role could possibly be played by hope? We learn about hope from happy endings, which, in the case of suicide, are endings in which the subject does not die and ultimately builds a life worth living. Through the extended hands of helpers, through recovery, and through healing, many survivors press on with life, and many thrive. One hundred percent of the survivors I've spoken with are glad they survived. They learned to live and to hope. And hope is powerful medicine.

Christine Moutier, MD, is the chief medical officer of the American Foundation for Suicide Prevention. She believes hope is the antidote to suicide's seemingly intractable grip.

"I'm really filled with hope about not only what's happening right now in the scientific field of suicide prevention and research, but about what's happening in the world," she says. "People are now talking about their experiences of distress, loneliness, hopelessness, when they become suicidal. And talking with others can reconnect them to their healthier selves, and to resources like mental health treatment and peer support and family support. So there are a lot of reasons to hope."

Facing Suicide is a book about hope in the face of suicide.

If you are *thinking about suicide or if you or someone you know is in emotional crisis, please call or text 988 at any time to reach the 988 Suicide and Crisis Lifeline for confidential, free crisis support.*

CHAPTER TWO

THE BALLAD OF GREG WHITESELL, PART ONE

In the winter of 2018, high school basketball standout Greg Whitesell and his team, the Arlee Warriors, felt uncommon pressure to win. For division finals they would play Manhattan Christian, a private school whose team sported new uniforms each year and traveled in private coaches, not school buses. They were white, taller, better fed. The Warriors had beaten them for the 2017 Montana Class C Division title and planned to do it again in 2018. But the Arlee Warriors labored under a weight the private school did not. Between November 2016 and November 2017, twenty people had died by suicide on the Flathead Indian Reservation. A few teenagers died in the fall of 2016, but that wasn't what the community considered the beginning. In the winter of 2017, Roberta Hayes, a foster mother to a houseful of children, a tribal policeman's wife and pillar of Arlee, took her own life. Her death was more than a shock to the team, it was a roundhouse punch. Many of the Warriors, including Greg, called her Auntie, a term of affection for women not related by blood.

It turned out Roberta's death was just the beginning. It was as if a starting gun had gone off in a suicide race.

In April, a former Warrior killed himself, and days later a teen who attended his funeral shot himself but survived. Most Warriors knew both boys intimately. Then the suicides came like clockwork.

Suicide contagion, a particularly frightening facet of suicide, takes some unpacking. Suicide experts define *contagion* as the transmission of suicidal behavior from one person to another, like an infectious disease. By many accounts, one person with a problem, often depression, sees another person with the same problem who is struggling. That person chooses suicide. Since we learn much of our behavior by modeling the behavior of people around us, especially those of higher status or whom we admire, suicide is then seen as an acceptable way to deal with the problem. And the problem is pain. Pain is the dominant theme of every conversation I've had with people who have attempted suicide, and those who knew someone who has killed themselves. Psychological pain is a suicide stressor most experts agree on. It is the main *why* of suicide.

"The people who die by suicide want out of the pain. They want the pain to end and nothing has worked to help them end that pain." Dan Reidenberg, PsyD, is a psychologist and former executive director of Suicide Awareness Voices of Education (SAVE). After more than thirty years of helping those in pain, Dr. Reidenberg has developed a nuanced appreciation for the mental suffering of people who are suicidal.

"The reason it's difficult to understand the level of pain is actually a protective factor for all of us. Because, in fact, if we all felt that level of pain, we'd all be at that same level of risk for suicide. That is what tells us the pain is immense. It is that unbearable anguish, it is beyond what anybody can handle. So it's not just about you get punched in the gut, it's not just about you've lost everything in the world. It's about that magnified a hundred times and a thousand times beyond that.

"Imagine if you had a headache, you'd get through a headache. Imagine if you had a migraine headache, which is debilitating for a lot of people, you might stay home from work, you might not be able to function very well with a migraine, but you can get through it. Imagine having a migraine headache and having a jackhammer outside of your room for an hour and then imagine that jackhammer hammering on your head for an hour. Now multiply that by ten and that's the pain."

This pain applies not just to the original suicide victim but to those who follow their deadly example. Suicide prevention expert Christine Moutier began focusing her psychiatry career on suicide after physician trainees and colleagues in medical school died by suicide. Now she's the chief medical officer of the nation's most prominent suicide reduction organization, the American Foundation for Suicide Prevention. She's quick to point out that people who die following suicide contagion don't kill themselves just because someone else did.

"When a person is exposed to another person's suicidal behavior or death, it can connect to their own sense of suicide, being a solution to the pain that they're in. But they are probably at risk to begin with."

In other words, victims of suicide contagion are usually suicidal before someone else models a "solution" to their pain. Usually, they know the person who killed themselves and come from emotionally and geographically close communities. The closeness to family and community found in Native populations should be a protective force; however, it can undermine safety if individuals come to believe that suicide is a normal, accepted behavior among their peers.

Victims of contagion often share adversities that exacerbate their thoughts about suicide. On the Flathead Indian Reservation, those include depression and drug and alcohol abuse, as well as sources of stress like broken families, unemployment and poverty, and the historical trauma of violent colonization.

Natives have inhabited this part of Montana for upward of 14,000 years. The reservation was born in strife. In 1855 the 2,000-square-mile Flathead Indian Reservation was created by a treaty with a familiar plot—to seize land from Natives in exchange for less land and some cash. The US government immediately reneged and opened the reservation, complete with grants of land, to white settlers. Today, Natives describe the region, an hour north of Missoula, as a checkerboard. A right-hand turn will put you on the reservation—technically a sovereign nation—but a left will take you back to the USA. Today, towns virtually adjoining Arlee are all white, while Arlee is mixed.

Suicide should also be included in this list of adversities affecting the reservation; it's an all-too-common crisis in many Native communities. In 2019, Montana ranked third in the number of suicides per capita in the United States. Natives led that list with 31.39 suicides per 10,000 people, which is almost three times the national average. Before the 2016–17 suicides began, the region had already suffered more than its share. Over the prior decade, suicide was the number one cause of preventable death for *children* between ten and fourteen in Flathead County. After the cluster, in 2018, 11.7 percent of seventh- and eighth-grade students and 12.19 percent of ninth- through twelfth-grade students made one or more suicide attempts.

*   *   *

For suicide contagion to occur, personally knowing the first victim isn't necessary. In 2014, after beloved comedian Robin Williams killed himself, strangers across the country followed suit. David Fink, PhD, MPH, and colleagues at Columbia University found a 10 percent increase in suicides in the United States in the months following Williams's death. The deaths were concentrated in middle-aged men like Williams. Many copied his means of suicide. A large case of contagion like that, influenced by the media, is called a mass cluster.

The deaths following Robin Williams's suicide highlighted failures in media reporting. The internet is a rich source of best practices for handling suicide in print and broadcast media, recommendations that can help avoid suicide contagion and save lives. Yet many media professionals ignore this readily available advice. One of the best information sources for media can be found at reportingonsuicide .org. In Robin Williams's case, reporters broke cardinal rules: describing the place and means of suicide, speculating about motives, glamorizing the victim, displaying sensationalized headlines, and more. It's wrong, in essence, to describe how famous people kill themselves, because others may copy it. It's wrong to make suicide seem like an effective, desirable source of attention.

Instead, it's important to follow a few rules that help reporters deal with suicide as a public health issue in a complete and meaningful way. Some of these include keeping information about the location and means of suicide general; using language that is sensitive to the grieving family; describing risk factors and warning signs for suicide; reporting that many kinds of treatment are effective for most people who have suicidal thoughts; and including information about the 988 Suicide and Crisis Lifeline.

Though it was a fictional series and not news reporting, the creators and broadcaster of the Netflix drama *13 Reasons Why* ignored best practices, and their neglect may have cost lives. In the series, a high school girl leaves thirteen tape recordings explaining her suicide. The series depicts bullying, violent rape, sexual assault, and suicide. Its heroine blames others for actions or inactions that led to her death. What's more, her high school guidance counselor dismisses her suicidal thoughts and seems to blame her for instances of sexual assault.

Dan Reidenberg reflects the concerns the suicide-prevention community has about the series. Besides sending dangerous messages, the series, like the book it was based on, is aimed at teenagers, who are the most at risk for suicide contagion. Reidenberg says, "Young people are not that great at separating fiction from reality. That gets even harder to do when you're struggling with suicidal thoughts." But it was young people who were targeted by the series and young people who were harmed.

According to a study published in the *Journal of the American Academy of Child and Adolescent Psychiatry*—with contributions from several universities and the National Institute of Mental Health—the series was associated with a 28.9 percent increase in suicide rates among US people ages ten to seventeen in the month after its release.

In the study of suicide, the concepts of contagion and cluster are closely linked. A group of suicides, like the 2016–17 Flathead Indian Reservation cluster, that occur within a contained space and time are called a *point* cluster. Christine Moutier says that a point cluster exceeds the usual baseline rates of suicides in an area, and "youth are more susceptible to contagion when it comes to suicide risk." The Flathead cluster had a broader than usual demographic. The National Indian Health Board reported that during the cluster, "Native youth under the age of 18 and ages 18–24 accounted for 34% of the suicides. . . ."

Indigenous communities have the highest suicide rate of any ethnic group in the United States; it's not surprising that they are frequent settings for suicide clusters. During the 2009–10 school year, leaders at Fort Peck Reservation in northwest Montana reported that five children killed themselves and twenty more attempted suicide. In 2019, officials at Fort Belknap Reservation, near Montana's Canadian border, declared a cluster with some twenty deaths and at least fifteen attempts, most among middle and high school students. Across the United States, teen suicides ravage Native populations with grim regularity. Between 2009 and 2011 a reservation in New Mexico and one in Alaska together lost twenty-five young people to suicide with at least twenty-seven other attempts. At Fort Apache Reservation in northeastern Arizona, forty-one Apache tribal members died of suicide from 2001 to 2006. From 2006 to 2012, twenty-nine more died.

Clusters are not restricted to Natives. Between 1966 and 1988, point clusters of non-Native suicides occurred in communities in California, Virginia, Wyoming, two cities in Texas, three counties in New York, Massachusetts, Minnesota, Montana, New Jersey, Nebraska, Colorado, and South Dakota.

Patty Stevens and her husband, Billy, own a ranch house and several sprawling acres along Mission Creek, beneath the towering glacier-capped Mission Mountain Range, about fifteen miles north of Arlee.

The first time I met Patty, an injured great horned owl was hunkered down beside the creek. Before we could call wildlife officials, it hoisted itself into the air, broken leg dangling, and flapped downstream. "That's a bad sign," said Patty, not about the broken leg but about the owl turning up on the day of a powwow. In some Native traditions, owls are connected to night and the underworld. Some consider owls to be the restless spirits of the dead.

In middle age, Patty is an attorney, a former prosecutor, a child welfare court witness, and an active member of the Tribal Council of the Confederated Salish and Kootenai Tribes. She is woven into tribal and community affairs like a bright band in a traditional blanket. In addition to her official roles, she's an aunt, a grandmother, and a foster mom to a houseful of kids, teens and younger. With alcohol and drug abuse rife on the reservation, life is tough on families, and intact families are rare. When a child lacks a meal or a bed, I learned, he or she is quickly gathered up into one of the reservation's extended families. If fate drops you into Patty and Billy's life, you are lucky indeed.

Traditionally, a powwow is a large regional gathering that features feasting, music, and dancing. With just fifty adults and children attending, Patty and Billy's was more intimate. It was the first powwow of any kind to take place after the COVID pandemic, when public gatherings were all but forbidden. And it was one of the first to follow the end of the suicide cluster, in 2017. Although in 2021 when I mentioned that the cluster was over to Anna Whiting Sorrell, MPA, a health official in charge of tribal response to the suicides, and a close friend of Patty's, she said in earnest, "*Is* it over?"

Her remark told me that the cluster—twenty suicides in a two-year span—was not far from the norm. Average numbers for the Flathead Indian Reservation are not available, but for Flathead

County, which contains parts of the reservation, they were even higher, suffering on average twenty-six suicides a year between 2018 and 2020.

At one end of the compound a group of muscular men carved out a thirty-foot-long cedar tree to create a traditional dugout canoe. Nearby, smoked brisket cooled on trays, making mouths water. Across the compound stood an assemblage of teepees, where children and teens prepared their ornate costumes, called regalia, for traditional dancing. At a picnic table in the shade of a pine tree beside Mission Creek, Patty led a group of seven women and teenage girls in making moccasins.

Patty said to the heavens, "Thank you, Creator, for bringing us all together today to make some moccasins." To the moccasin makers, "When we do something like this, we have to do it with really good hearts and good thoughts on our mind because I kid you not, if you start making a design like this and you start thinking thoughts about somebody that aren't very nice, your needle makes knots in about thirty seconds. So have some good thoughts. Good medicine!"

For young people, making moccasins is part of their introduction to their culture. For older women the craft is a traditional way to share thoughts among themselves, away from men. Today's thoughts were about the souls lost during the suicide cluster. Kimberly Swaney, a middle-aged Native woman with a shock of gray-and-white hair and a commanding, gravelly voice, fearlessly launched into her story. She had first endured the grief of suicide when her father killed himself.

"I was probably about ten or twelve when I began to get the understanding that my dad wasn't there because he chose not to be. Because he took his own life."

Her next suicide was just four years ago, the victim her fifty-nine-year-old boyfriend.

"Dave was bipolar and, you know, the Creator put him in our life because he needed to be happy for at least short time. I can remember him saying 'This is the happiest I've ever been.' And he got to experience what it was like to live in an Indian community even though he wasn't an Indian. But when he didn't take his medicine, he just got to be impossible to deal with."

Dave wasn't unusual in the way he died. Suicide results from a mix of causes that are usually different from one person to another. But one factor is present at least 90 percent of the time: a mental health condition, which most of the time is not being treated. Depression, substance abuse disorder, and psychosis lead the way. However, it is important to note that the vast majority of people with mental health conditions do not die by their own hand.

Christine Moutier adds, "There are other risk factors as well, things that relate to impulsivity, aggression, experiences from the past—adversity, trauma, abuse. So it is really important to understand that suicide has multiple risk factors that converge, that come together, and it's not really ever going to be one issue that causes suicide."

Sometimes in dramas or novels, one very bad event—typically a romantic breakup—can propel someone to kill themselves. Think Tolstoy's *Anna Karenina*. Impulsive, one-trigger suicides occur, but they are rare. More commonly a cascade of risk factors comes together. For example, in the United States, alcohol, a common risk factor for suicide, is present in the blood of male suicide victims on average 30 percent of the time, and in some states much higher. Add alcohol abuse to a breakup *and* the loss of a job. Later perhaps the victim is forced to leave their home. And, let's say, she has a history of suicides in her family, and is understandably depressed about the state of her life.

Dave cycled up and down, ecstatically happy one day and sad and quarrelsome the next. After months of instability, which impacted a household made up of other adults and some children, Kimberly called a state hotline that offered one-time emergency counseling. But its staffers would not even provide advice—they insisted that Dave had to make the call. A local health clinic was available to help Dave, but he refused to go to them, and their waiting list for counseling was months long anyway.

One day, Dave had a particularly heated argument with Kimberly's daughter. The two were always at one another. For Kimberly, it was one fight too many. On her way to work she called the tribal police. "You need to go get him," she said. They could take him to a hospital where he'd get a night to cool off and perhaps some treatment. The tribal police visited Dave and determined, without benefit of a psychological evaluation, that he wasn't a threat to anyone. They told Kimberly, "He's fine." She paused in her story to wipe away tears. That afternoon she and her daughter drove home from work. She said, "It was January thirteenth, there was snow on the ground. And I could tell from the tracks in the snow that he had never left the house. I told my daughter to stay in the car. Dave had locked the door, but I managed to get in and I walked down the hall, checking all the rooms."

She found him in their bedroom. Dave had taken his life. She told her daughter to call 911 and keep her grandchildren from going inside when they returned from school. When the tribal police showed up, they didn't want to enter the home. Frightened and superstitious, they left it to Kimberly and a neighbor to cut Dave down.

Throughout David's final ordeal, no coordination occurred among the staff of the hotline, the clinic, and the tribal police. They were the only resources available, but they came from three unconnected jurisdictions. Those seeking help for a suicidal crisis face similar problems across the country.

At this point in the story a young woman holding a smoking bundle of sage wafted it around the table of moccasin makers. It smelled earthy and strong, like pine and herbs. This sacred ritual, called smudging, links smoke to spirituality. It is said to rid spaces of negative energy, and even carry prayers to the spirit world.

Smudging played a part in Kimberly's survival after Dave's suicide. The most potent support came from traditional holy men and women who gave her house a cleansing smudge.

Kimberly said, "I'm just fortunate though that I had Kootenai medicine people around me the entire time and Salish medicine people who really watched out for me and my family and they took care of my house. They cleaned it of leftover energy. We made sure we gathered Dave's things so that he had no reason to come back. I wanted him to have a safe journey because he deserved that."

Engrossed in Kimberly's story, Patty and the moccasin makers had put aside their materials. Patty got back into action and showed her granddaughter Erica how to trace her foot on brown paper and then draw a simple design, including holes for laces, around the footprint. Later she'd trace the paper on buckskin, then cut and sew.

Across the compound, drumming began, and sporadic chanting. There would be feasting soon, and the dancers would take their places.

Michelle Matt, a large woman wearing a beautiful yellow dress with matching butterfly earrings, had opted out of the moccasin activity but listened closely to Kimberly's story. She worked up the nerve to tell her own.

Her younger brother John was a gentle man prone to depression and addiction. He used marijuana and methamphetamine and frequently changed jobs. November 21 had been John's birthday and he had recently finished a stint at a drug rehabilitation clinic. The family celebrated with dinner at their favorite restaurant, Famous Dave's, then saw a movie. At his mother's house the next day, John danced and prayed for snow. Michelle said, "My mom and him were snow people, they loved snow. And they knew winter dances were coming and that was their favorite time of the year."

But just as in Kimberly's story, everything turned on an argument. John and his best friend, who had been living with John and his mother, got into a bitter quarrel. John stormed out into the night. As Michelle told me, her mother phoned her. "'You need to pray hard,' Mom says. 'Your brother's not doing good and he left the house.' I said, 'Well, did he have a gun or anything?' And she said, 'No. I don't think so.' Well, the next day was Sunday, we were gonna go to church. Mom said, 'I'm not gonna go to church. He never come home.'"

This had not been the first anxious morning caused by her kind but unpredictable brother. Michelle feared the worst.

"So we get home, I go and I drive around hoping my brother was maybe walking to my house from the mountains. And um, nothing. I go to Mom's house. I said, 'Anything yet?' We tried calling him. Nothing."

Next, Michelle phoned a friend and asked him to look for John in the hills behind her mother's house. Michelle said, "And it was really weird for him. He said he was driving up behind the house and he saw my brother walking. He got out and he yelled, 'John, where are you going? Where are you going, John?' And John, he said, kept walking. And he kept following him. But when he got there, my brother was already dead."

John killed himself with his rifle, a tool present in every Native home for keeping the freezer full of deer and elk throughout the year. He had been dead all night.

A woman handed Michelle a tissue. Her face folded into grief and her voice keened with pain. "I got there and I walked up to where he shot himself, and I tell you what. That moment I saw him was it just hurt. It hurt so bad." Michelle hit her chest with a fist as her agony erupted in a wail. The moccasin makers put down their work again. "Oh God. It was awful! And at that moment, I just knew I was losing both of them. I just knew my mom and my brother were both gonna leave me and my family was gonna be torn apart."

Because of the endless *whys*—why was he in so much pain, why did he have to perform this irreversible act, why couldn't his family stop what was happening?—grief from suicide is especially difficult. Suicide survivors and those near them should be conscious of its different phases and learn what to expect. Those closest to the victim may first experience what's called *acute grief*, the initial painful response, characterized by shock, disbelief, and blame, as well as the impact of stigma and trauma.

Accompanying the torment will be an unwelcome flood of logistics—paying hospital bills, arranging funerals, notifying relatives, disposing of property, and much more. If the survivor is lucky, acute grief will resolve within several months into *integrated grief*, or adapting to the loved one's death. Survivors return to their lives, to work, and will be able to discuss the loss of their loved one without breaking down. Though grief will linger, life will resume. I've heard more than one suicide survivor say, paradoxically, "I didn't survive. I endured." Most people do endure. They find things to keep their minds off their loss. And with this endurance can come newfound strengths, and new and important relationships.

The third horseman of the apocalypse of sorrow is *complicated grief*. This has all the symptoms of acute grief, but it's not temporary; it moves in to stay. The anguish of the bereaved does not abate. Integration of the death into the rest of the survivor's life, and healing, do not occur. Tragically, the survivor may yearn to join their missing loved one in death. Their own death may seem like the sole path of relief available to them.

John's suicide was one of the first in the Flathead Indian Reservation cluster. Within a month, Michelle's mother died too. Michelle said, "People can will themselves to go. My mom did. When I had to sit there, I'd be so mad. I said, 'Mom, you gotta eat. You can't leave now.' I just laid in bed holding her until she died. I knew she was going to be with my brother so it wasn't as hard as my brother, but that pain was still there."

People who were close to someone who died by suicide within the last year are 3.7 times more likely than average to make a suicide attempt. They're also 1.6 times more likely to have persistent thoughts about suicide and 2.9 times more likely to make a plan for dying by suicide. Relatives and friends of loved ones who have suffered this kind of loss must monitor them closely. At the powwow, I spoke with Patty's granddaughter Erica, a raven-haired nineteen-year-old whose father had killed himself during the peak of the cluster. She told me she thinks about suicide all the time, and the only reason she stays alive is because she knows how much her death would hurt her family. She said something I would hear from coast to coast in the United States.

"Might as well just die," she told me. "If you're not rich you might as well just die."

For suicide attempters or those with suicidal thoughts, most emergency departments will observe them for a night or two. During that time a doctor or nurse may ask if they have plans for suicide, then cut them loose with a referral to a therapist. One problem with this approach is that people who are intent on dying by suicide will say whatever is necessary to gain their freedom and try again. The biggest single indicator of a suicide attempt is a prior suicide attempt. Another problem is if you don't have insurance or if your insurance doesn't cover psychological counseling, you may not be able to afford the referred therapist. And if the therapist comes at no cost, like a handful in Arlee, you will wait months or more for an appointment. On and around the reservation the cost of therapy is prohibitive, so many like Erica who desperately need mental health therapy have one option: wait for months for an appointment with a local, free counselor. In the United States this is the rule, not the exception.

Within a year of her brother John's death, one of Michelle's uncles killed himself and a nephew attempted suicide but survived. It seems likely these acts were connected to John's suicide. But by then the whole Flathead Indian Reservation was in the throes of the cluster.

Amid all the talk of dying and suicide's ongoing presence on the reservation, I found myself questioning Patty and Billy's decision to host a traditional celebration, a powwow. But, as we'll discuss ahead, investing in traditional crafts and music, and sharing stories, is not a luxury at all but a necessity in the face of suicide.

Greg Whitesell was short for a basketball player, just five feet seven, with another two inches added by bleached blond curls that disappeared into a brown fade. He had an open, impish face on the brink of a smile, an athletic, rangy body that could defy gravity, and an irrepressible love of riddles. In the first video clip I ever saw of him, he asked an off-screen teammate, "What do you call a guy with a rubber toe?" The player didn't know. "Roberto," Greg said, to an audible groan.

Greg was a two-sport athlete, great at basketball but also a standout wide receiver on the Warriors football team. For schools as small as Arlee High, full participation in sports is almost a requirement of students, boys and girls alike. Otherwise many sports would have too few players to field a team. During a football game in the fall of 2016, Greg suffered a bruising tackle and a concussion. It wasn't his first. His mother, Raelena Whitesell, an optician and mother of five, told me, "Greg's had many concussions through football, basketball, but the doctors would say, 'Okay, you know, let's let him rest.' Then he would get released but you know as a mom I would always be afraid, scared."

Coach Zanen Pitts, a wiry thirtysomething horse and buffalo rancher, dog breeder, boot-and-hat-wearing cowboy, noticed a change in Greg's mood right away. "When Greg got the head injury, it put him into a state of depression in a really bad way. He always has been a person that can get kind of emotional. He can get really aggressive and really timid in drastic extremes pretty quickly. But he also is super caring and super loving."

Still, to Greg's mom, her son seemed fine. "I didn't know he was depressed. I should have seen the signs because he was always in his room and just kept to himself, but I didn't think anything of it—you know, I thought 'Oh, he's a teenager, just going through it.'"

Greg was displaying signs of distress and perhaps suicidal ideation. Some signs were apparent to his friends and supporters, some flew under the radar, even for his mother. They included more intense mood swings than usual, self-isolation, loss of appetite, depression, and insomnia. And suicide was all around him. According to his own estimate, by the winter of 2016 he knew five people on the reservation who had taken their own lives. It would be safe to say everyone knew someone who had become infected by the deadly contagion sweeping through the community. The victims were dear friends and neighbors. Parents. Schoolmates. Who wouldn't be knocked over by such tragic news day after day?

Now add to Greg's stressors a possible brain injury. Greg had a history of concussions, in addition to the recent one. Athletes, particularly football players, have lots to fear from brain injuries.

John Mann, MD, PhD, is a professor of translational neuroscience in the Departments of Psychiatry and Radiology at Columbia University. As a neuroscientist, Dr. Mann looks into the brain for suicide's causes and cures. Speaking of football, he says, "Every time you see the offensive and defensive line collide, they get a hit from the front. The brain rocks back and forwards on the brain stem and bangs the front of the brain against the skull on the front, and the back of the brain against the back. And it rocks, 'Boom-boom-boom-boom-boom.' Because they're now so athletic, so fast and so powerful, those hits are much worse than they used to be."

The damage is concentrated in the front. "And the front of the brain is involved in mood regulation and in decision-making. So the result is, you have a person who is more likely to act impulsively on decisions and go with their emotions. At the same time, their emotions are now out of control. So they're more likely to experience more extremes of emotion, like depression and distress."

Greg's depression was compounded by a piercing loneliness. Though he had an extensive group of friends and supporters, they were no bulwark against his pain. As he described it, "Lonely. Really lonely, like I knew I had a lot of people on my side, I knew I had a lot of people that cared. But, when you're depressed, man, the only thing you can think about is yourself, and the only thing you can think about is, you know, what's killing you and what's eating you up inside. I did have a lot of people there for me but I was just pushing them away, not even giving them a chance."

Greg developed thoughts of killing himself.

Anna Whiting Sorrell is an outspoken member of the Salish community who has held distinguished positions in public health, including a job as the head of public health for the state of Montana. She was a consultant for the Confederated Salish and Kootenai Tribes Tribal Health Department in Arlee from 2014 through 2018, which put her on the front lines of the response to the suicide cluster. In a conversation at Arlee High school, we hit on the subject of Greg Whitesell.

"Suicide is so prevalent that I wasn't surprised," she said. "Was I devastated? Absolutely. Did I wanna cry? I could cry now thinking about that, because he should have been protected from it. He comes from a great family. He was, you know, this successful basketball player. My husband and I have been in this gymnasium watching him play, and he was my favorite."

Sorrell's lament echoes the heartache that accompanies teen suicides everywhere. Sometimes it seems as if talented and driven adolescents take their own lives more frequently than others. Or maybe
it's that their suicides draw more attention than those of less prominent peers. Experts claim that while the United States does a good
job keeping statistics on suicide deaths, *giftedness* is not a variable
that is tracked. But anecdotal evidence is plentiful. From 2011 to
2014 at W. T. Woodson High School in Fairfax, Virginia, six students killed themselves. Officials looked for commonalities and
found them. Each came from a stable family, earned good grades,
and excelled at sports. The grieving community protested that these
students should have been the least likely to harm themselves. But
scientists point out that gifted adolescents may be more vulnerable
because of the qualities that make them standouts, including per-
fectionism, competitive drive, self-reliance, and hypersensitivity to
criticism. Their go-it-alone style can become too rigid, their mistakes unbearably shameful to them.

Based on journals he has read from gifted teens who died by
suicide, William and Mary University professor Tracy Cross, PhD,
developed a theory about their high rates: gifted teens may be better
at planning and executing their suicides than others, and so accom-
plish them more often.

In late 2016, on a winter night in the tidy clapboard house he
shared with his mother, Greg Whitesell sat alone in his room, unable
to sleep. Team posters and photographs covered the walls. In his
bedroom closet was his hunting rifle. Outside, a howling blizzard
battered the windows and front porch with fusillades of snow.
Around midnight, Greg sent a text, which reached his two closest
friends on the basketball team. It consisted of one sentence.

"I don't want to be here anymore." Then Greg turned off his phone.

Experts say that when teens are suffering, they are more likely to confide their feelings to their friends than to adults, even their parents. Peers have a unique opportunity to step in and make a difference. The two young men tried to reach Greg but got no answer. Minutes later they were racing through the blizzard in an old pickup truck.

As Greg was preparing to kill himself.

CHAPTER THREE

DOWN ON THE FARM

The Catholic University of America's David Jobes, PhD, created an internationally adopted suicide treatment program called the Collaborative Assessment and Management of Suicidality (CAMS). While other therapies address depression and other precursors to suicide, CAMS is one of very few therapies that solely targets suicidal ideation and attempts. Dr. Jobes points out that some 15 million people in the United States suffer from suicidal ideation. "About 1.4 million go on to make attempts. So it's an extraordinary index of misery and despair." He adds that suicide spares no one. "Suicide is ubiquitous. No socioeconomic group, no subculture is immune."

No one is immune, but in the United States the distribution isn't even. Some 70 percent of all suicides occur among white men. The largest number of them are middle-aged. In rural areas, which have a higher rate of suicide than urban areas, many of those middle-aged white men are farmers.

A county fair in America's heartland—ten acres of tents, horse fences, and show barns on a hill overlooking Harlan, Iowa, enjoyed this sunny morning by hundreds of visitors, competitors, and volunteers. Its soundtrack—mooing, squawking, quacking, and snorting, children's chatter, a PA system's cheerful bleat. The smells of manure, overheated bodies, and baked goods greet you before teenage boys and girls direct you to parking. Up ahead on the right, they're giving prizes to exemplary chickens and rabbits; straight ahead, it's bottle calf and breeder beef. Coming up at 10:00 a.m., the Sidney Senior Center Singers. The festivities are under way.

The Shelby County Fair, the closest thing Iowa farmers have to a Hajj, doesn't look like ground zero of an apocalypse, but it is. America's farmers are dying by the hundreds, by their own hands. More than 450 farmers killed themselves across nine midwestern states from 2014 to 2018, according to the Midwest Center for Investigative Reporting. The real total would be higher because not every state provided suicide data for every year. And as we noted, farmers often disguise their suicides as farming or hunting accidents.

Farmers have been among the most-at-risk populations for years. More than 1,000 farmers died by suicide in just five midwestern states during the 1980s farm crisis. The University of Iowa found that from 1992 to 2010, farmers killed themselves at a rate higher than all other occupations. Today, the suicide rate of farmers is six times that of the general population.

Why are farmers dying by suicide?

"What do you think is the most stressful circumstance that can cause farmers the greatest amount of stress? Anybody want to take a crack at that and say what you think?" Psychologist and farmer Mike Rosmann, PhD, stands before a group of about thirty farmers seated on folding chairs and picnic tables, both men and women.

"Lack of rain," says a farmer.

"Financial burden," says someone else.

"Lack of rain imposes a financial burden. So at the top of the list, we have determined that any threat to our economic well-being is the most serious threat that affects farmers. Maybe you receive a letter from the bank that says 'We're going to have to have a forced auction of some of your property, or your equipment.'"

Farmers and spouses emit a collective groan.

Seventy-five-year-old Rosmann resembles the late actor and oatmeal pitchman Wilford Brimley, but he's taller and with an even deeper and gruffer voice. Right now, there's a heat dome over Harlan, and Dr. Rosmann and the farmers fan themselves with leaflets bearing the title of his talk, *Suicide by Farmers Continues to Be a Vexing Problem*. A biography inside declares Rosmann, who once taught psychology at the University of Virginia, the nation's leading expert on farmer behavioral health and America's farmer suicide crisis. He developed that expertise by growing up on a farm himself, and working his way up through academia, copiously publishing on the behavioral health, and particularly the suicides, of farmers. Eventually, Rosmann grew frustrated with writing and lecturing about the minds of farmers from Charlottesville's lofty remove. Forty years ago he returned to Iowa with his wife, Marilyn, took up farming again, and established a practice dedicated to providing therapy to farmers.

There is in every case a host of additional stressors, Rosmann says. The death of a child. Divorce. Your hired help moves away. The ever-present threat of injury. Rosmann admits he walks with a cane because once he tried to kick loose oats that were clogged in a combine. This was before combines had protective cages over the auger. The machine took part of his foot and didn't give it back. His children later found his toes, but they couldn't be sewn back on. Rosmann sums up his point with a flourish. "The farm has become the most stressful setting of any occupation, and has had the highest rate of physical injuries and illnesses and fatalities of any occupational workplace."

Amber and Chris met during high school at a barn dance near Corsica, South Dakota, just north of the Nebraska border. Chris had been the life of the party, but Amber showed "zero interest." Then they both moved to Sioux Falls for college, where Chris persisted. Their courtship moved slow, then fast.

In the twenty-year-old photograph Amber shows me, the wedding party of a dozen are backed up against an altar with a crimson cross looming over the groom's head. Amber glows in a white wedding gown, and Chris, sporting short brown hair and a clipped goatee, manages to look at ease in a stiff white tux. The new husband and wife beam broadly, like they just learned a big secret.

Children soon followed—Kalee, athletic and blond like her mom, then Kahne, born two years later. Red-haired, husky, and a hard worker like his dad, Kahne has a mind of his own and doesn't warm up to strangers right away. Or even later.

"And then it took me some work to convince Chris to have our third child. And Kolbe came in November of 2013."

Kolbe is an instantly likable sprite, always in motion, closely orbiting his mother. "Kolbe just doesn't stop," she said. "He's always bouncing off the walls and into something, whether it be playing his video games, or basketball, or wanting a game of cards. He is very on the go." Kolbe most resembles his dad.

The family lived in Platte, a place with good jobs near where Amber and Chris had grown up. A welder, Chris built box scrapers at a farm supply store. Amber worked in an insurance office and eventually became an agent.

Amber said, "I felt like when we were living in town, my dreams were reality. We had the perfect family. We both had day jobs. We had our evenings, and weekends, holidays free to spend together as a family. Life was great."

But Chris had grown up on a farm, and in his early thirties he had an itch to return to the land. Amber, whose grandparents had suffered financial setbacks at farming, was afraid of its unstable income and days that started before dawn and ended after dark. Weekends, holidays relaxing with the family? Forget about it. Amber said, "It never ends on the farm. There's always work to be done."

At fifty-nine, Chris's father was almost ready to retire. He agreed to hire Chris as an employee with the idea that his son would take over and eventually buy him out. This was basically the deal Chris's dad had made with his own father. Chris would become the third generation of Dykshorn farming land that had become sacred to the family. Together, father and son would handle 789 acres of corn, hay, and soybeans—almost 600 football fields' worth—along with chickens, pigs, sheep, cattle, and goats. In 2015, Chris and his dad began working together. Two years later the family moved to the farm.

Amber told me, "Chris did feel pressure of wanting to succeed, because his grandpa and his dad both had succeeded at farming. But farming was difficult from the moment we started."

At the Shelby County Fair, psychologist Mike Rosmann gets to the heart of his talk. "Worry kills farmers. They're worried their farm operation may become economically unable to continue. They

worry they will lose the farm that's been in their family for generations. They worry there will be no farm to leave to their children.
These are painful, painful things to keep inside your heart. If the
stress does not remit or decrease, then we just completely wear ourselves out to the point that depression sets in."

Every suicide is different. But some suicides, such as those of
farmers and soldiers, occur because of stressors unique to those occupations. They originate differently, develop differently, but tragically end the same. Rosmann had expressed in a nutshell why farmer
suicide is different from all other kinds. Farmers are strongly moti-
vated to work the land and grow food. Often, they are a link in a
chain of land stewardship that has passed from father to son or
daughter, over generations. Failing at farming, and losing the land,
is a hauntingly painful prospect.

Rosmann adjusts his wire-rimmed glasses. His mostly farmer
audience listens, rapt. He's telling the story of their lives.

Farm debt has increased by about a third since 2007, to levels
not seen since the farming crisis of the 1980s. Unless you farm, you
may not know farmers take out loans just to plant for the next sea-
son. Their equipment and land, even their barns and homes, may be
mortgaged to the hilt. Whenever you hear of a farm foreclosure,
remember that the farmhouse is usually included in the mortgaged
property, so the family probably lost their home as well. They may
have had an auction to make the move easier. Tools, craftwork,
furniture, wedding dresses. Keepsakes of generations.

Farmers may carry several lines of credit—they visit bankers like
the rest of us visit barbers. It's common for their partners to have
jobs off the farm and for farmers themselves to have part-time jobs
at a feed lot, or a Home Depot, or someone else's farm, to keep their
operations afloat. Profit margins are low, and the odds of consistent

success are lower. Since 2013, over half of all farmers in the United States have lost money every year.

One big reason is that since 2012, key commodity prices including corn, wheat, soybeans, and milk have fallen by about 50 percent. From 2017 to 2018, soybean exports to China dropped 75 percent amid a disastrous trade war. And in 2019, flooding prevented farmers from planting nearly 20 million acres.

These numbers add up to disaster in the heartland. Between 2011 and 2018, America lost more than 100,000 farms to bankruptcy. Banks foreclosed on 12,000 of those between 2017 and 2018 alone.

The farmers listening to Rosmann nod knowingly. These men and women, or many like them, would quit farming if they could. But even those on the brink of a psychological breakdown feel they cannot. That's because, like Chris Dykshorn, they stand to inherit or have inherited their farms. Some are third- or even fourth-generation farmers. They cannot turn their backs on their heritage or fail to bequeath land to their children. Tragically, dying can come to seem like a better option.

Now Amber is walking around the winding dirt road between barn and chicken coop, tractor shed and hogpen. She coos at the new lambs stumbling gangly in the sunshine. She lingers at the hog's dark sty and a picture-perfect spider's web on which you expect to read "Some Pig." There's equipment everywhere, trucks, hoods open abandoned to the weather, disks, a brush hog, bales of chicken wire, a barn half-full of tractors, too many of them, dating back decades. A sheep's carcass pushed off the path, sunken in like an empty bag, past stinking. Everything clamors for mending, cleaning, paint.

Someone has all but abandoned this farm, but I hear a tractor engine not far away. Probably Chris's father, who had to come out of
retirement to run the operation full time, a workload taken on
single-handedly that had been overwhelming for two. More than a
year ago, Amber and the kids moved off the farm into a house nearer
town and good schools, and far from bad memories. But not all bad.
Back at the lambs, Amber says, "Lots of good times spent with Chris
in here, lots of long days. Just the joy of seeing new life when we
have the baby lambs. That's so much joy."

A farm kitten shyly roams from a barn into the sunlight, spots
Amber, and hides again.

With the heel of her hand she pushes away a tear. "I do feel
Chris's presence when I come here. It can be overwhelming at times.
But other times it brings me joy. And it reminds me of how hard he
worked day in and day out. Such a hard worker."

At the fair, Mike Rosmann has finished tallying the major stressors
aligned against farmers. It made me wonder why anyone would voluntarily farm. Now he turned to countermeasures—how to spot the
signs of extreme depression and possible suicide in those around you
and even in yourself. He says, "So what are the key symptoms that
we look for? For suicide the first is when we become so upset for at
least three weeks that we have not laughed at all. We have not done
anything that gives us pleasure. A second danger signal is a feeling
of hopelessness. 'I don't know how I can keep on doing this, I can't
do it anymore. I'm just overwhelmed, there is nothing that looks
favorable in the future.' That is something to look out for, either in
ourselves or in people that we care about.

"A third, major symptom is when someone starts making

dramatic threats, like, 'No they're not taking my livestock. I'm going to shoot them all before I have to haul them up to the auction.' The fourth signal is what I call the lump-in-the-throat phenomenon. This is an occasion when someone is so down and we say, 'You look like you need to cry,' and if you ask them have you cried, they say, 'No, I haven't, but I wish I could.'"

Rosmann continues. "Other signs are how well the person grooms himself or herself. Have they not shaved in two or three weeks? And profoundly depressed people tend to stay in their bedrooms or at home. They don't go to the Shelby County Fair or to church or to the kids' sports meet. Another thing that happens is sleep disturbance. Profoundly distressed persons either oversleep or can't sleep adequately. And what happens when we can't sleep adequately? We accumulate what we call sleep debt, just like financial debt. Every night you don't sleep seven or eight hours puts you in the red. Did you know that ten hours of sleep debt has the same physiological impact as .08 blood level of alcohol? So we have to manage our sleep hygiene and we have found that nearly always sleep hygiene is poor when farm people end up taking their own lives."

Chris and his father had tied Chris's income to corn production. Chris would plant and harvest corn, store it in their silo, and transport some by truck to the grain elevator—a storage facility in Platte—for sale. The rest would go to feeding their livestock. But the price of corn plummeted, cutting into Chris's already meager income. Then in the spring of 2019, severe flooding made planting corn impossible. The furrows simply filled with rain, washing seeds away. Chris had to work around the clock to be ready when the rain let up. He feared pigs would drown in their pens. When he could get to bed, worry about the weather kept him awake. His sleeplessness left him struggling to make decisions. "I can't think," he told Amber. "I feel paralyzed."

Chris decided to sell corn stored in the silo. But on the rutted farm roads, he snapped an axle on the grain truck and had no money to replace it. Chris's dad arranged to have the corn picked up, for a hefty fee.

Amber said, "Chris started to become very withdrawn. He was very sad. He had stopped fishing, which he loved. His main worry was the finances, and how bills were gonna get paid. He didn't make it apparent to me about being depressed until probably the first part of April 2017."

Sometimes, Chris used his phone to express feelings he had trouble sharing directly. "Chris would send me text messages, Snapchats just about being sad, and how he felt worthless. And he didn't know how things were gonna work. One of the last Snapchats that I received from Chris was a picture of him tightening his belt to the last belt loop." Amber's voice broke telling me this. "He had lost so much weight."

Kahne helped out wherever he could—hooking up tractors, carrying buckets of feed, picking up around the farm. He liked to help his dad and wanted to ease his father's load, but there's only so much a nine-year-old can do. After dinner, Amber helped Chris until nightfall.

Amber told me, "Chris visited with his dad. And his dad actually wrote down a list of all of his assets, and just basically tried showing Chris how he could make things work. How it was gonna be okay. And we had an appointment with our banker, who was working on helping me show Chris that we could make it work. But at that point, Chris was so depressed. I don't think he could really see the light in any situation. The kids could tell he was depressed, because when we would sit down for a meal, he would just be silent. He wouldn't say anything. He just looked down. He was in a lot of pain."

Amber reached out to a nurse who in turn asked the sheriff to perform a welfare check. When the sheriff came by, Chris agreed to go with him to the emergency room for an evaluation. From there Chris was referred for immediate treatment to a behavioral health center. At the live-in facility, he engaged in group therapy and learned coping skills. He discussed what in life was worth living for. When he spoke with Amber on the phone, Chris said he felt great.

Amber felt a flood of relief.

In one sense Chris was lucky. He had found mental health care. Compared to their city counterparts, rural Americans have far less access to mental health services. In rural counties in America, there are on average just 25 mental health professionals—psychiatrists, psychologists, and licensed social workers—per 10,000 people. That's a fraction of those available in urban areas. Most mental health care visits are conducted through primary care providers, not therapists or specialists. And as Rosmann told me, without specialized training, primary care physicians do not adequately understand behavioral health.

Another factor is that rural people are less likely to be able to afford counseling because of poverty and lack of health insurance. Furthermore, for Natives and others in underserved communities, there's a scarcity of culturally appropriate care. Medicaid and telehealth visits have made mental health care more accessible, but they don't impact the shortage of mental health professionals.

And finally, to have an impact, rural mental health professionals need to know about farming. The last thing a farmer or agriculture worker in distress wants to do is explain the problems that are killing him to a counselor who doesn't understand farm life. The counselor might suggest a vacation, to which the farmer would object that his milk cows don't take vacations. Fortunately, in their psychology and social work curricula, many university programs in farm country have begun addressing fluency in agricultural work.

In another sense Chris Dykshorn was very *unlucky*. Somehow after just four days he was able to convince the facility and his wife that he was well enough to go back to the farm. And since he wasn't bound by a legal commitment, he was free to go. Amber drove to bring him home. But Chris was hiding a mountain of anxiety, and it soon came crashing down.

Amber said, "Once we got in the car, Chris's mind started racing. And he's like, I don't even know where to start. I have so much I need to do. And I said, Okay, let's figure it out. What can we do while we're driving home? You can call your crop adjuster. You can make a list of things to do when we get home, that kind of thing. But you could already see how he was starting to get overwhelmed. And he wasn't even home yet."

The next two days passed in a blur. To try to bolster his spirits, Chris's father praised him for the work the two did together. Amber suggested that he might work at a neighbor's farm to increase their income or sell some of their sheep to lessen his workload. Chris remained remote and given to tears. He hardly slept at all. In the field he asked his father to hold his hand.

Had Chris's treatment helped him at all? In the months following their release from a mental health facility, patients admitted for suicide attempts or ideation are at the highest risk for suicide in their lives. Experts are unsure why, but their chances of dying by suicide are 100 times the average for their race and age. This is a period when loved ones must be intensely alert.

At the fair, Mike Rosmann told his audience, "Depressed people do one of three things. One is that they flee from the circumstance by isolating and not talking, refusing to visit with the banker or others. That's called the *flight* response. Two is that they may make broad threats, that's called a *fighting* response."

Chris fell into the third path. "They can't make themselves do things. I have seen farmers so depressed that they couldn't get out of bed to get into the combine and harvest grain in October because they were so encumbered with thoughts of blame and loss. Morbid kinds of thoughts. That is what we call emotional paralysis. Emotional paralysis is probably one of the worst things that can occur to us."

On Thursday, June 13, 2019, Chris got up earlier than usual and was out of the house by the time Amber rose and began preparing for a meeting with their banker.

"I was still in my nightgown at the computer. And at 8:12, my cell phone was ringing beside me. It was Sam, who was our neighbor who lived with Carol in the house Chris's grandparents used to live in. And he said to me, 'Chris's breathing has really slowed down, Amber, but he is still alive.' And I said, 'What do you mean his breathing has slowed down?' And he said, 'Didn't Carol call you?' And I said, 'No, what's going on?' He said, 'Oh, Amber, Chris shot himself.'

"I got in my car and I called our pastor. Our pastor had been meeting with Chris, and he knew that Chris wasn't doing well. And he says, 'I'm on my way out.' So I got over to the farm, and I just, I still have nightmares of him laying on the ground there.

"I remember pleading with him to just hold on, that we couldn't do life without him. And I remember crying to God, I need a miracle. I need a miracle, because I knew he wasn't gonna make it with what he had done."

Chris Dykshorn was strong. He lived all the way to the hospital, where he was pronounced dead. Later, Amber said, "And this was the hardest thing I've ever done in my life to this day, was to tell my kids that their dad was never coming home again. Chris is gonna miss out on a lot of things. Graduations, weddings, grandkids. But I know he's keeping an eye and watching over us."

From the time Chris began farming with his father to the day he killed himself, four years had passed. During that time he faced increasing responsibility as he leased land and took on ownership of cattle. Terrible floods in 2019 slowed all farm operations, bogged down machinery, and cast a sense of doom over everything. There would be no corn harvest that year, and none of its precious income. Though he had probably hidden his depression for a long time, it was April 2019 before Amber realized Chris was depressed. He took his life just two months later. During his troubles, I was told, he never mentioned suicide to Amber or to the mental health professionals he encountered.

Chris Dykshorn, like many farmers, wasn't driven to suicide by one difficult year. Farmer suicides, like suicides everywhere, are complicated. They are caused in many cases by a genetic predisposition compounded by isolation, a shortage of health care, substance abuse, a surfeit of guns, financial pressure, and other factors. But Chris had no suicides in his family history that anyone knew of. He didn't drink or take drugs. It is likely that he had simply suffered from stress and worry for too long. His depression was too severe to be treated in just four days at a mental health facility.

Mike Rosmann preaches a gospel of preemption. Farmers need to look at their emotional health as something to be managed with as much attention as their land. That means doing things that they enjoy—for Chris, fishing, hunting, spending relaxing time with the family. He gave all that up. The stress wore him down. And he only got help when Amber intervened.

What keeps many farmers from getting help? The very qualities that make them good farmers.

Rosmann told me, "Good farmers have the tendency to trust their own judgments, to rely on their own resources, to take risks, to work alone if necessary. They are proud and self-sufficient. Those characteristics work for farmers, but they also work against them during times of stress. Farmers do not reach out for help when they are in trouble. They don't talk about their trouble."

Chris Dykshorn's strengths became his vulnerabilities. And rural, agricultural people have inherent vulnerabilities. They're far more isolated than urbanites and don't have easy access to peer groups with whom to discuss their challenges, if they feel so inclined. And, significantly, rural people have more *guns* than urban dwellers. As we'll see ahead, guns play a devastating role in suicides in the United States. Christine Moutier of the American Foundation for Suicide Prevention outlines the best steps to take with firearms. "If you are in a gun-owning home, a very important aspect of suicide prevention is to think about those firearms and make sure that they're stored safely and securely, ammunition separately. And during periods of crisis, I would even go so far as to say, try to have firearms outside of the home environment."

Amber Dykshorn told me that she had spoken with Chris about giving his guns to his father or a neighbor until he felt better. Chris said he would never shoot himself, and Amber took him at his word. But neither of them knew then the places his illness would take him. In hindsight, getting his guns out of reach might have made a difference. During a crisis, experts say, unload guns and take them to a trusted friend. And don't stop there. Lock up or dispose of prescription drugs and over-the-counter medicines. Lock up or dispose of common household poisons. These are some of the main means of suicide in the United States, and they're simple to address.

Each year, some 15 million Americans think about taking their lives. Many thousands like Chris Dykshorn do. But many thousands *more* are pulled back from the brink by someone who steps in to help.

"And thank you very much and enjoy the Shelby County Fair." Mike Rosmann wraps up his talk about the mental health of farmers and says hello to friends and admirers in the audience.

After a few minutes, he splits off for a visit with David Boettger, a man he's known for more than thirty years. They planned to have a look at stock together. Boettger, like Rosmann, is in his seventies and a retired farmer. He's lean and big-boned, with shoulders and forearms shaped by a lifetime of lifting, pulling, and bending heavy things. From the look of him, he might once have carried a calf under each arm.

Earlier, Rosmann had said to me, "One person I know was so distressed that his wife called me, and she said, 'Can you come right over and help me?'" Rosmann was backing into Boettger's story but wanted to preserve David's privacy. David Boettger and his wife, Nancy, a state politician, had prayed over whether he should share his story with me and the public. Their answer was yes. Later, Boettger himself took up the tale.

"That was the low point of my life. I probably didn't sleep any of the night before. So I was exhausted physically and mentally. I couldn't think straight."

Boettger lives where he was born, on a four-generation farm that was founded in 1890. He doesn't farm anymore but leases his land to a neighbor's son. At his farm, like Rosmann's, all the grass is mown, and the barns, silos, sheds, and fences are structurally sound and painted. It turns out there is a connection between messy farms and mental health conditions. During his talk, Rosmann had asked, "How well is the machinery kept up? Are the farm buildings painted?"

David and Nancy Boettger have four children, sixteen grandchildren, and two great-grandchildren—a blessing, David calls them. But there was a time when a contented old age was unlikely for David and for thousands of other farmers whose lives were overturned by the farm crisis of the 1980s.

For farmers it was a perfect storm, the worst economic crisis to hit farming since the Great Depression. One storm front was, ironically, high farm production, which resulted in a surplus of commodities like wheat, corn, soybeans, hogs, and beef. The surplus drove prices down. Another was the 1979 Soviet Union embargo, which forced a 20 percent decline in exports between 1981 and 1983. Then interest rates on farm loans for equipment and production went up to 21 percent, higher than credit card rates. To counter it, the Federal Reserve System lowered interest rates and, from 1981 to 1985, caused farmland value to drop up to 60 percent in parts of the Midwest. More land was needed to secure loans, which meant you stood to lose more if your farm went belly up.

Low crop prices, a smaller market caused by the trade embargo, crippling interest rates, and low land value put many farms in crisis. Farmers couldn't win for losing. By 1984, farm debt hit $215 billion, almost twice the debt of the early 1970s. Farm foreclosures soared, threatening more than a third of all farmers. In five midwestern states, more than 900 farmers took their lives. Some farmers shot bankers.

It was the interest rates that ate at David Boettger most. "The big kicker was eighteen and twenty percent interest. That's one dollar out of five that goes to pay for interest and that was just devastating because the corn prices were low. The yields weren't anything like they are today. So many people went bankrupt and lost their farms. And farming at least for my generation was a lifestyle, meaning you had failed if you lost the farm."

The Boettgers had two kids in college at the time and were paying 18 percent on equipment and production loans. "We were going backwards every day," said David.

Depression wasn't new to him. Years before, he had been in college for just three weeks when his father died. There were still a lot of gaps in his knowledge of farming, but he left school, took over the farm, and made mistakes. That depressed him. He always felt he was doing something wrong. His depression worsened in the disastrous '80s. Then one of his sons was hospitalized for depression. Boettger lost forty pounds in six months. He couldn't sleep, couldn't focus, couldn't finish a job. He didn't want to be around people. He preferred to stay home.

"My attitude was terrible. I wasn't being a good husband, a good father, or anything else. I just thought, 'I don't know what to do but I got to do something different. I cannot go on this way.'"

Labor Day weekend that year, he was feeding sows in the farrowing house when he had a mental health crisis. "I just remember yelling to myself, 'Lord, I've got to have some help. I've just got to have some help.'

"I would say it was a 10, my mental pain."

Nancy called Mike Rosmann and he came right over. "I think he asked me point-blank, 'Have you ever thought about committing suicide and do you have a plan?' I told him yes, and I told him my plan. And he decided I needed to go to the hospital. Nancy took me down."

David stayed for nineteen days. He engaged in talk therapy with a nurse and a doctor. A social worker conducted group therapy sessions. He did artwork he didn't understand.

"I really had a hard time getting into that. You know I'm making this little painting. And yeah, gimme a break. But I continued to do it. And every part of their plan had some reason and some goal behind it. And I'm happy they insisted. They were the right things for me to do."

David went home for visits, but he would not return for good before he was ready. He called the hospital his safe place. "They told me what to do, when to do it. I was just free to live and not function in the normal way. And that felt safe to me. I had never asked people for help. It's something I just didn't do. So when I had to have it, I got it. And it was freeing. When I think about what would've happened if I had not gotten help, no way would I be alive today. Because I couldn't live with that pain."

David returned to the farm and took it easy for the first few weeks. He began a course of medication he's stuck with for forty years. He still deals with depression, which gets worse in the fall and again in the spring. Nancy keeps an eye on it and he gets his medication adjusted when necessary.

David and Nancy have since read a lot about the neuroscience behind mental health disorders and how they affected famous people, like Abraham Lincoln, who suffered from depression. It helps David to know the condition that once threatened his life has impacted so many and for so long. He keeps an eye out for people he can help.

About his old friend, Mike Rosmann said, "David has learned how to turn his turmoil into an act of benefit to others. He wants as his life's work, partly, to keep other people from becoming so depressed that they contemplate ending their lives."

"If I run into somebody and I'm seeing they have some signs of depression, or any mental health issue," said David, "I try to get them in a personal conversation. And I've led people to that same hospital to do the same things. I don't know how many have done it. But I know a few that had real good success."

If you are thinking about suicide or if you or someone you know is in emotional crisis, please call or text 988 at any time to reach the 988 Suicide and Crisis Lifeline for confidential, free crisis support.

CHAPTER FOUR

THE BALLAD OF GREG WHITESELL, PART TWO

In the winter of 2018, Greg and the Arlee Warriors should have been on top of the world. In 2017 they had taken the Montana Class C Division title, and now they were favored to do so again. But a lot more was riding on the title than just a trophy. The suicides on the reservation numbered in the teens, soon to reach twenty. Watching the Warriors play gave the community a few hours of relief from the ordeal outside the gym. For the players, it raised the stakes even higher.

Their coach, Zanen Pitts, said, "Their success started to excel at such a fast rate, it created a lot of pressure on them. It was hard on those boys. I definitely know that they got to where they didn't want to let anybody down."

Community leader Patty Stevens told me, "I remember the Arlee Warriors right in the beginning of those suicides. And we're trying to encourage and be supportive of the basketball team and support them. And we got to just step out of that, all that sadness, and just be in a place that we could do what we love, and that's watch our Indian kids play basketball."

The Arlee Warriors had become a light against the darkness that was overtaking the reservation. Suicides came faster than caregivers could deal with them.

As a senior consultant for the Confederated Salish and Kootenai Tribal Health Department in Arlee, Anna Whiting Sorrell led the response. But the department was quickly overloaded. Mental health counselors were available, but getting an appointment could take weeks or even months. Those undergoing a suicidal crisis had to make a temporary stop at a hospital in Polson, an hour north of Arlee, which had just eight beds. From there they'd be transferred to clinics in the larger towns of Missoula or Kalispell, but only if those facilities were not already full. Faced with these prospects, people in crisis who were inclined to seek help—and few are—did not.

Sorrell said, "I convened people together in my office, saying, 'What are we going to do?' And then there was another suicide. And then there was another suicide. And I don't even know if we ever said, 'I think we're in an epidemic.' And so, we went from one to two to three, and then I remember seventeen and eighteen coming at the same time. We had to have a more robust response. So we reached out to the feds, we reached out to Indian Health Services, we reached out to the Office of Public Instruction here in Montana, and the Department of Public Health and Human Services. We reached out to the experts and found that there wasn't really much to hang our hat on."

Sorrell and her team devised a two-pronged approach. In the aftermaths of the suicides, they met with the affected families and communities with the goal of preventing more suicides. These "afterventions" were modeled on Western techniques. They were effective but full of *cant*s. "You can't do certain things, you can't open up to people, you can't say that they can get care, they have to go through an assessment and then go to treatment. You know, typical Western protocols."

The second approach emerged spontaneously as Sorrell's group met with people to talk about their shared experiences. These meetings morphed into sewing circles. Sorrell said, "People would come together and sew, and they'd make ribbon shirts, or they'd make shawls, and they would bring their kids, and pretty soon they were talking with each other, and there was peer support happening here in Arlee. So we found there was a way in which we could get people the support they needed, with people to talk to and a safe place to talk."

The moccasin-making session at Patty and Billy's powwow was a long-standing tradition that achieved the same goals. The United States Substance Abuse and Mental Health Services Administration (SAMHSA) leads national efforts to improve behavioral health. In 2015, SAMHSA issued a report about restoring cultural norms to improve mental health in Indigenous peoples. Their conclusion: culture is prevention. What do sweat lodges, language classes, and sewing circles have in common? They are "protective factors" that contribute to lowering Native teen drug and alcohol abuse and delinquent and violent behavior. They improve emotional health, including depression and suicide. And the healing works for adults too.

Gary Door was one of the muscular canoe-carvers at the powwow. A member of the Nez Perce Tribe, he had been separated from his family at age four, adopted by a white family, and sent to a white boarding school. He never saw his parents or siblings again. By his late twenties, he was an alcoholic, a sergeant in the army, and a suicide survivor who was brimming with hatred. Adopting a Lakota motto, *I really want to live,* Door embarked on a fifteen-year spiritual journey comprised of learning Native crafts and languages, taking part in sacred ceremonies, and spending long hours communing with elders. About his innumerable physical ordeals and soul searching, he said, "I was changing and becoming who I'm supposed to be."

At a final ceremony in 2019 he cast off his white name and took the name given to him by the elders. As he explained it, "The bear will tear you apart limb from limb, insides out. Throw you all over the ground. But with bear medicine, the bear puts you back together the way you're supposed to be. And so that's who I've become. I'm not the child taken from his people who held himself in shame. I am this man you see today. Standing Red Bear."

At the powwow, Standing Red Bear put hours into shaving out the inside of a cedar canoe made from a single tree. He had become a master of making and piloting the venerable craft and had accomplished several "firsts" down western rivers thought to be too challenging for the heavy vessels. Standing Red Bear was under contract with Patagonia, Inc., to pilot a dugout canoe down the Flathead River for a photo shoot.

For people in a suicidal crisis, the biggest hurdle to getting help is the reluctance to ask for it. The majority of those who take their lives don't share their intentions beforehand. They have never seen a mental health professional or been diagnosed with a mental illness. Why don't they seek help? A major factor is stigma—the shame and disgrace associated with mental health conditions. SAVE's Dan Reidenberg believes that stigma comes from fear. He says, "Stigma prevents people from getting help because they're afraid that if somebody finds out, they're going to be in trouble. This can happen at work, it can happen in a personal relationship, it can happen in a community, it can happen in the military. Stigma keeps people from help seeking."

Epidemiologist Madelyn Gould, PhD, believes American self-reliance, often a boon, can be a barrier to seeking help. "People want to handle their problems on their own. But if you have a heart problem, you're not gonna handle it on your own. If you break your foot, you're not gonna handle it on your own. Why should we think we can handle psychic pain, depression, serious anxiety on our own? It's putting too much of a burden on ourselves. We're expecting too much of ourselves."

Christine Moutier concurs. "Mental health conditions are health conditions. The same way physical health conditions are. And there is a way to approach them in a proactive manner with self-care strategies. Just like heart disease or blood pressure problems or diabetes. You have to manage it over time and your doctor will adjust the treatment accordingly."

Still, experts do not want to remove *all* the stigma from suicide. Recall that in suicide clusters, there is a danger that suicide can become seen as a "normal" behavior, especially among young people. It's important *not* to make suicide normal. As Reidenberg told me, "We actually need some level of stigma against suicide. We don't want the stigma about seeking mental health but we do want the stigma about the behavior of suicide. We don't want suicide to be seen as in any way good or positive or noble or heroic or anything like that."

*   *   *

After the worst of the suicide cluster in 2016 and 2017, Anna Whiting Sorrell resigned from the Confederated Salish and Kootenai Tribes' Tribal Health Department. She thought she had seen the worst, but the worst was still to come. "In November of 2018, I had a sister die of an opioid overdose. And it devastated me. I just couldn't believe that I couldn't help my own sister, in all that career that I had. So I was ready to move on. I took a couple months off, and applied for a position with Kaufman and Associates (a Native-owned behavioral health consultancy) and I've worked there since. I remember the day I submitted my resignation. I was told there had just been a death by suicide. And I can say I felt a relief in every part of my body that I didn't have to do anything."

Sorrell also felt something else—that she herself had become dangerously vulnerable. "It's an option for me, yes. Suicide is an option for me," she said. And suddenly she was the one who had to ask for help. "All of us have trouble reaching out and asking for help. But I also think for Native people, it's deeper."

She showed me an old black-and-white photograph. Her grandmother, at about twenty-five years old, gazed down at her daughter, a girl of about seven, reminiscent of child star Shirley Temple. Both beamed in matching polka-dot dresses. Sorrell pointed to her glamorous grandmother.

"My grandma had polio when she was young. I loved her. She died when I was five years old. And we have no idea if she died of an intentional drug overdose or not. She was forty-two." Sorrell's finger moved to the little girl, her mother. "My mom died at fifty-seven from cancer. She had been recovering from her own substance abuse for maybe ten years. And I bring that up because I don't think that people really understand the deep historical trauma that Native people have gone through."

Historical trauma is the physical and psychological harm inflicted upon individuals and even whole cultures by harrowing experiences like slavery, the Holocaust, and violent colonization. The University of Nevada's Michelle Sotero, PhD, MPH, describes how, for Natives, historical trauma began when whites committed mass trauma upon Indigenous peoples through colonialism, slavery, war, and genocide. As a result, the affected peoples displayed physical and psychological symptoms. This population passed on those symptoms to subsequent generations, who now show similar symptoms. They consist of elevated risks for alcohol and drug addiction, diabetes, tuberculosis, and a variety of mental health complications, including depression and suicide. Historical trauma contributes to why Natives have a suicide rate up to ten times the national average.

Donald Warne, MD, MPH, of the Johns Hopkins Center for Indigenous Health, calls historical trauma "the collective emotional wounding across generations that results from massive cataclysmic events." Trauma, Dr. Warne contends, is "held personally and transmitted over generations. Thus, even family members who have not directly experienced the trauma can feel the effects of the event generations later."

Trauma's destructive forces can last generations. This is a bold idea that's gaining increasing attention in the scientific community. The mechanism for intergenerational trauma is epigenetics, the way gene activity is changed by behavior and environment. Gene sequences, or DNA segments, are not changed, but environmental and psychological factors can alter the *expression* of genes by switching some genes on and switching others off. Epigenetic changes are also tied to prenatal and postnatal stress, which can program a child's brain for later health issues. Especially catastrophic for Natives was the Federal Indian Boarding School Initiative. Between 1819 and the 1970s, the United States government established 408 federal schools across thirty-seven states. Their goal was to culturally assimilate Natives by removing them from their families and tribes and by preventing them from practicing their languages, religions, beliefs, and customs. Native child removal also demoralized Indigenous peoples during an era of territorial expansion. At the boarding schools, children were forced to perform hard labor. Child abuse was rife. At fifty-three schools and counting, investigators have discovered marked and unmarked burial sites.

Sorrell affirmed the horror of the Boarding School Initiative. "If you can't teach your own kids your own language, think about the trauma in that. If you can't teach them your religion. If you can't teach them your songs or the music that you love, that's our most intrinsic belief system, right?"

She searched my face for answers.

She said, "I would say that returning to our cultural ways is our only way out, to get to the health and healing that we need. And that is really what will prevent the next suicide."

Counting both indoor and outdoor basketball courts belonging to the school system and to public parks, the small village of Arlee boasts twenty courts in all. Greg Whitesell and Darshan Bolen played one-on-one behind the high school on a weather-worn apron of concrete from which there was a clear view of the Lolo National Forest to the west. On the Arlee Warriors team, Darshan played defense, so Greg had a hard time charging the basket without having the ball slapped away. He opted for two- and three-point jump shots, swishes all. But then Dar met him shot for shot, earning grimaces, and compliments, from Greg.

They took a break for water. Dar wandered off to make a call. I asked Greg about the night he almost killed himself. How exactly had he felt? He backs it up a little. He mentions his concussions and the one that preceded his depression. Then he gets to the cluster of suicides.

"I was already kind of in a bad space, you know? I was already going through some things. I knew about ten people who killed themselves. It was just a really hard time going on in my life."

And in everyone else's lives too. But I had heard that there'd been a girlfriend and a breakup as well. I knew that Greg had been close to Roberta Hayes, the foster mother and "auntie" whose suicide had shaken so many. The net effect on Greg was pain and isolation.

Greg insisted the text he sent his friends wasn't a call for help, as some had suggested, but a goodbye note. He had written, *I don't want to be here anymore,* then turned off his phone. And even though a blizzard raged that night, it was funny to him how fast his friends appeared at his house.

"You know, two seconds after I sent that text it felt like my two friends were right there. It's crazy to think about it because I wouldn't be here if they hadn't come through, if they hadn't knocked on my front door."

One of those friends was Darshan Bolen.

That fact that friends came to Greg's rescue would not surprise Christine Moutier of the American Foundation for Suicide Prevention. She says that most young people will talk with their friends about tough issues in their lives, even suicide, before they'll talk with their parents or other adults.

"Peer-to-peer communication can play a really important role in youth mental health and suicide prevention," says Moutier. "Because among youth who are experiencing suicidal thoughts, about half of them are not telling anyone. Among those who do, two thirds of them are only telling a peer. They have a gut feeling about it. Their friends are telling them about the hard stuff going on in their lives."

Often, friends are concerned but unsure how to help. Fortunately, Greg's friends knew they needed to reach him, fast. They woke Greg's mother, Raelena, who wanted to take him to the emergency room, another smart move recommended by experts. Greg resisted, saying again and again, "I don't want to be here!" In other words, leave me to die.

But his friends and mother weren't having it, knowing instinctively another piece of expert advice: you should never, ever leave someone in suicidal crisis alone. Accompany them to an emergency department or to a medical or psychological professional.

Greg was frightened by the ER, where nurses put him in a room with no bed, no table, no fixtures of any kind with which he could hurt himself. He spoke alone with a doctor while his parents learned there were no psychiatric patient rooms available in Arlee, Missoula, or the surrounding area. They had no choice but to take him home. This frightened Raelena.

Her eyes widened as she told me, "I was scared. I was scared because we went home and I think like for a month I could not sleep because I would check up on him. Every night I would look into his room, make sure he's okay. I would set my alarm like every hour so I could go check on him and I would call him, 'Are you okay?' I would ask him every day, 'Are you okay, are you okay?' And then finally he says, 'Mom, quit asking are you okay.' I said, 'I will never, ever stop asking are you okay because I don't want there to be a moment if something happens and I'm not there for you, son.'"

Soon, Greg began regular therapy sessions, which he continues today. It was expensive, but Greg's parents had good health insurance. And now he's grateful for the interventions that saved his life, and happy he did not kill himself as some twenty others on the Flathead Indian Reservation did.

But a question about Greg's good fortune stuck with me. Why had Greg survived when twenty others had not? Why did farmer Chris Dykshorn take his life after four days of treatment, when Greg seemed to begin his rebound after a single conversation with a doctor and a visit to a scary holding room?

There are no easy answers. As suicidologists have repeatedly told me, every suicide and suicide attempt is different, and so are the causes behind them. In the midst of a cluster of suicides, Greg was probably susceptible to suicide contagion. His depression was almost certainly linked to the latest concussion of many he had suffered. But somehow an outpouring of love stabilized him during his most vulnerable days.

Chris Dykshorn had endured extreme anxiety and depression for months before he killed himself, perhaps a more entrenched depression than Greg's. And the source of his pain—the farm, with its endless chores and financial minefield—was waiting for him when he was discharged after just four days of treatment. He never had a true respite from worry, which, according to Mike Rosmann, is what kills farmers. He never found his "safe place," as farmer David Boettger had.

I left Greg at the house he shared with his mother. She had made a lunch of sandwiches and iced tea and they had it on a picnic table on the back porch. They laughed at something and talked about nothing. They had not run out of time.

Greg had told me, "In my head I was only worried about myself, but my mom would be living the rest of her life without me. My pain would just be ending, but everybody else's around me would just be starting.

"If you're thinking about killing yourself, just know that you're loved, know that you're cared for. Today might be hard but tomorrow's a new day. You never know what's going to happen tomorrow."

CHAPTER FIVE

FIRE IN THE BRAIN

Greg Whitesell's and David Boettger's stories, and many like them, show that family and professionals can sometimes identify signs of suicidal behavior and prevent suicides. Scientists hope they can point the way to helping people earlier, before they're in a crisis. It's a complicated challenge because the detectable signs can be subtle, or even hidden by someone who plans to kill themselves. And tragically, few people bent on suicide tell anyone beforehand. Researchers investigate the causes of suicide from different angles—probing human behavior, trauma, and the role of drugs and alcohol. For neuroscientists, there's only one place to start: in the human brain.

Columbia University's Dr. John Mann trained in his native Australia and has the unmistakable accent his countrymen are known for. He's a wry, intellectually exacting scientist, and an aging athlete who has downshifted from running marathons, including six times in Boston, to triathlons. He smiles ruefully as he describes his beef with psychiatrists and psychologists. They think they can understand suicide solely by examining behavior, outward signs, and external stressors in the lives of those who have attempted or carried out suicides. Suicidal thoughts, they claim, can be understood and treated with "talk" therapies like cognitive behavioral therapy and dialectical behavioral therapy.

Mann disagrees. He thinks talk therapies may help people manage their suicidal thoughts, but they take weeks to work and do not get at the basic causes of suicide, which lie inside the brain. He said, "It's a bit like when you take your car to be repaired, the mechanic doesn't listen to the sound of the engine. The mechanic actually lifts up the hood and looks at the engine."

The Molecular Imaging and Neuropathology Division in the Department of Psychiatry at Columbia University occupies a cluster of floors above a vast museum-like lobby of soaring triangular windows and alabaster walls. Mann and his team occupy a warren of rooms whose gleaming stainless steel and glass machinery is designed to store, dissect, and examine human brains. In two rooms, row upon row of freezers contain just that: nearly one thousand brains of people who have died by suicide. What prompted Mann to collect brains?

"We started out a number of years ago by principally examining mood disorders. And in order to understand what was fundamentally wrong with people who suffered from mood disorders, we began collecting brain tissue from suicide decedents at the medical examiner's office. We did that because we understood that about half those patients suffered from a major depressive episode at the time of death. We began to think about what was wrong with the other half of the folks who died by suicide."

Mood disorders are specific types of psychiatric illness that primarily affect an individual's emotional state. Mood disorders include conditions such as depression, bipolar disorder, and symptoms of depression that are caused by drug and alcohol abuse and sometimes medicine or medical conditions.

Mann decided to treat acquiring brains like acquiring organs for donation. Early each morning he would find out from the medical examiner who had killed themselves in the past twenty-four hours and which of them required an autopsy.

"I would then call the families, express my condolences, and talk to them at this very difficult moment in their lives. I would ask them if they would be willing for us to have the brain donated to us for research after the medical examiner had finished their examination, and if they would be willing to talk to us about the circumstances of the suicide. Three quarters, on average, of these families agreed that their loved one's brains could be given to our laboratory in order to figure out why their loved one may have died. Just about every person welcomed the chance to talk to us so we could understand the circumstances of the suicide of their loved one. People understood that in this way maybe we could learn something that could help prevent future individuals from dying by suicide."

Mann and his team also collect brains from controls, people who died suddenly but from other causes, not suicide, and did not have a known psychiatric disorder. They meet with both the families of the suicide decedents and those who died of other causes. With each family they conduct what is known as a *psychological autopsy*: a profile of the psychological state of someone who has died. Sometimes law enforcement and insurance companies carry out psychological autopsies to determine whether a death was caused by suicide, homicide, natural causes, or an accident. With a battery of questions, Mann and his colleagues gather information about each donor. Mann especially wants to know about stresses the decedent lived with, their childhood, history of drug or alcohol abuse, and suicides in the family.

Mann and his team quickly learned that although 95 percent of the people who died by suicide had a psychiatric illness, only half suffered from a mood disorder. Therefore, a great number of people who did not have a mood disorder were dying by suicide. "So we gradually diverged onto two parallel but somewhat independent paths. One was the study of the biology in the brains of people with mood disorders and the second was a study of the biology of the brains of people who died by suicide. It had not occurred to scientists that there could be two separate sets of abnormalities."

Mann's team quickly realized something else. While suicide impacts people of all ages, Americans who die by suicide generally have a psychiatric disorder that begins in their teens or early twenties. These disorders include schizophrenia, bipolar and anxiety disorder, and major depression. "A significant proportion of the risk is genetic," said Mann, "but a significant proportion of the risk is also environmental, due to childhood experiences that modify their genes in a process that we call epigenetics—a chemical modification of their genome due to life experience."

Not surprisingly, the same epigenetic modifications that scientists found in Native populations occur in people everywhere. But Native populations record higher instances of epigenetic problems, including suicide, because in most cases they've suffered these problems and accrued their damage over generations.

To learn about the brains of people who killed themselves, and the controls, our journey began in a room where medical freezers stored a large collection of brains. One had been prepped for dissection—a slice the size of a hockey puck lay in a plastic tub. It was taken from the prefrontal cortex, the part of the brain involved in regulating emotion, decision-making, social cognition, and working memory.

Mann said, "We cut the brain into slices about the thickness of my hand and then we cut those slices into very fine slices that we mount on a slide." A technician carried the tub from the freezer room down the hall to a dissection area that was as spotless as an operating room. Mann's colleagues were clad in personal protective equipment from hairnets to plastic booties. One technician placed the section of brain into a small machine consisting of stainless steel and sharp edges. A long, flat blade shaved a paper-thin slice from the segment. With a brush the tech nudged the slice onto a slide about the size of an index card. The damp brain tissue, barely one cell thick, clung to the dry glass. She put the slide on a tray under warm air.

Mann said, "So, the tissue dries on the slide. And then we can do a variety of things in order to study structural and functional changes in the slice of the brain of [a person who has] depression and who died by suicide in order to determine exactly what's wrong."

Mann and his team apply chemical stains to the slices to determine the kinds of cells they contain, the biochemistry across the brain in the same section, and the function of the genes in that section. On a table an array of slides held brain slices that had been stained different colors. Slides dyed blue showed the cellular structure of the tissue. Other slides indicated the presence of serotonin.

Mann's team focuses on serotonin, sometimes called a "happy hormone." Of the many chemical compounds found in the brain, it's the one most closely linked with suicide. Serotonin is a neurotransmitter—a chemical that carries messages between nerve cells in the brain and throughout the body. These messages tell the body how to get things done. Serotonin is the Swiss Army knife of neurotransmitters, regulating, for starters, cardiovascular function, sex drive, digestion and bowel movement, even bladder control. While it's associated with the brain, only about 10 percent of serotonin is produced there. The rest is made in the cells lining the gut.

In the brain, serotonin regulates a whole other gamut of processes, including sleep, decision-making, and mood, three important components of suicide. Low levels of serotonin in the brain contribute to mental health issues that show just how essential the chemical is to well-being: depression and anxiety, PTSD, panic disorders, and phobias. Excessive serotonin activity can contribute to psychoses like schizophrenia.

Specialized nerve cells, or neurons, release serotonin into the brain. Too few of these neurons, scientists once thought, make depression and even suicide likely. Mann and his team made a surprising discovery—it wasn't true.

Mann says, "For years we thought that depression is due to a deficit of serotonin in the brain. What we find now, as we learn more about it, is that actually there's plenty of serotonin in the brain and plenty of serotonin neurons. The problem is not having too few neurons or not having enough serotonin. The problem is that there's an abnormality in how those neurons are controlled and they don't fire enough so the serotonin isn't released."

In other words, the serotonin is present in the neurons that produce it, but not enough is available to the brain.

"When we actually counted the number of neurons and looked at the amount of serotonin that was in those neurons, we found to our surprise, it's the opposite. Depressed people have more serotonin producing neurons than the average person."

But why do these brains have *more* serotonin neurons? And why are more serotonin neurons associated with depression instead of the opposite?

"We speculate that this overabundance of serotonin neurons

could be a compensatory mechanism," said Mann. "When the brain lacks something, it tries to compensate. This may be that kind of scenario."

It seems the brain creates a surplus of serotonin-producing neurons in order to overcome a deficit of the "happy hormone" that could result in depression or suicide. But in depressed and suicidal patients, the strategy doesn't work. The serotonin-producing neurons in their brains don't function correctly. Mann says they fire, but then they prematurely *stop* firing. They don't release enough serotonin.

Mann showed me serotonin-producing neurons from a microscopic image blown up on a monitor. The image was taken from the brain of someone who had died by suicide. It showed a section of the brainstem called the raphe nuclei, the main location for the production of the brain's serotonin, which is distributed throughout the brain and spinal cord. The image was covered by ant-like black spots, which are serotonin-producing neurons.

When they counted the neurons, Mann's team found there was a surplus of serotonin neurons. Then, when they examined the feedback autoreceptors on those neurons, which control the neurons' firing, they found depressed suicide decedents had an excess of them as well. As a result, their serotonin neurons don't fire for long enough, and they release insufficient serotonin. Their entire brain suffers from a serotonin deficit. In a large part of the brain, that deficit is related to depression. In another, smaller and more specific part, the deficit is connected to suicide attempts.

When these two deficits, or abnormalities, exist together, contributing to depression *and* suicide attempts, Mann's team found danger. The combination indicates the brain of a person who is at increased risk for suicide. In fact, the two brain abnormalities are found in most people who die by suicide.

How do the abnormalities promote self-harm?

Acting together, they distort one's emotional perception of the world. People in a suicidal crisis suffer from a kind of tunnel vision. They see fewer reasons for hope, and few options other than suicide. As Mann explained, "The world is more threatening, more critical, and less helpful and understanding. And they are more vulnerable to criticism, which is why you see reports that bullying or critical comments at school have driven somebody to try to take their own life. And you may think, 'Why would they have done that?'

"It's because what you see is not what they see."

In one taut phrase, Mann put into words why so often friends, colleagues, and loved ones do not see a suicide coming. It's why we're so often perplexed by the desire of another person to leave this world. We simply cannot see what people in crises are seeing. Their suicidal brains have presented them with a "tunnel" vision of a different, hostile, painful, and hopeless reality. And that inhospitable landscape contributes to searing emotional pain. I thought of Greg Whitesell, a young athlete for all appearances on top of the world. He texted to his friends, *I don't want to be here anymore.* And Chris Dykshorn, father of three beautiful children and husband to a devoted wife, up early one morning convinced that his only option was to die. And David Boettger at his chores, yelling, "Lord, I've got to have some help." As their emotional pain reached critical mass, Greg, Chris, and David could not see what others saw in themselves and the world.

Mann discovered other important features of the pain suffered by people who kill themselves: they feel more emotional pain and they feel it more intensely than depressed people who do not attempt. Mann uncovered their depth of suffering by asking attempters to rate their pain on a subjective scale. He then corroborated their assessment with positron emission tomography (PET) scans.

These showed more intense brain changes in the brain areas that convey subjective emotion in depressed patients who made suicide attempts compared with depressed patients who never made suicide attempts. PET scans can measure metabolic activity—chemical reactions within the cells of the body. PET technology can detect both normal and abnormal activity, including the presence of diseases such as cancer, and the overall function of organs like the heart and brain. Mann's goal is to pioneer an outpatient procedure using PET scans that can detect the same two abnormalities he found in the brains of suicide decedents. But he would find them in the clinic, before the patient attempted suicide.

Mann said, "After several years of discovering a lot of interesting and important abnormalities in the brain of folks who had died by suicide that were related to depression and suicide, we became determined to try and translate our findings into the clinic to try and help patients. PET was attractive as a method of brain imaging because unlike practically any other method, it detected biochemical or neurotransmitter abnormalities."

When Mann's team scanned people who made serious suicide attempts but survived, they found what they were looking for. "To our amazement, we found the same kind of abnormalities in their brains as we found in people who died by suicide. When we scanned the brains of depressed people who didn't die despite a suicide attempt, through the good fortune of being found in time or because it was a lower-lethality suicide attempt, we found the same sort of biochemical abnormalities as in suicide decedents. But the extent of the abnormality was in proportion to the lethality of the suicide attempt. When we followed our patients for two years, we found the PET scan abnormality also predicted the medical lethality of future suicide attempts. This indicated that such PET scans can help identify patients at higher risk for future suicide attempts and can stimulate better prevention."

The implications for future clinical work are profound. Mann hopes we will be able to scan a patient in crisis and determine how severe his or her condition is, and what course of treatment to pursue. Perhaps more important, he hopes to be able to estimate by a brain scan the level of risk of some patients who aren't willing to discuss their pain or their suicidal ideas.

"In the office, I have to rely on what the person tells me and what I see. But sometimes the most suicidal patient does not wish to reveal their true intent. Patients have their own agenda, and that might be a very bad agenda. They might want to kill themselves and they don't want to be dissuaded. That's why we're interested in brain imaging, because we seek to determine what's wrong with the patient even when they don't tell us themselves. The doctor is a detective."

After their suicidal crisis has been treated, many patients benefit from a variety of talk therapies, such as cognitive behavioral therapy, dialectical behavioral therapy, CAMS (collaborative assessment and management of suicidality), and other suicide-focused interventions. Mann interviews patients to understand their pain and its sources in their lives, but his expertise is in prescribing medicines such as ketamine and SSRIs (selective serotonin reuptake inhibitors). Ketamine quickly reduces suicidal ideation by improving thinking and reasoning in some people who are considering dying by suicide. But it has not been tested in preventing actual suicidal behavior. SSRIs treat depression and prevent suicide attempts and go to the source of the serotonin deficit present in both the brain abnormalities Mann studies.

After the neurotransmitter serotonin carries a message, it is mostly reabsorbed by nearby neurons. SSRIs block that reuptake, leaving serotonin around for longer to pass messages between neurons. It normally shuts off its own release by stopping serotonin neuron firing. Over weeks this feedback-autoreceptor effect on firing progressively diminishes and firing rates increase, normalizing serotonin release and relieving depression. To Mann, medicines like ketamine and SSRIs are treatments that target a basic cause of depression and suicide risk.

He said, "People who suffer from depression suffer from a real illness. And unless you have a treatment for the real illness, you're just holding their hand and being supportive and sympathetic. With therapies you teach them ways of coping with the negative thoughts and feelings, and that can help, but it is not the same as directly relieving the depression. You wouldn't dream of doing that to somebody who fractured their leg. You would take an X-ray, get an orthopedic surgeon to examine them and set the bones. In psychiatry, we have people who have real illnesses. Depression is an example. When we actually look into their brains, just as if we were doing an X-ray of a broken leg, we find abnormalities."

But as Mann admits, talk therapy helps. He said, "Cognitive therapy is a form of brain exercise or practice which changes how we react to negative emotions and can change negative thoughts and negative perceptions into positive ones. As a consequence, it changes how we make decisions based on those positive thoughts."

For people who are at risk for depression and for those who are at risk for suicidal behavior, talk therapy reduces the risk of suicide attempts. Talk therapy just takes longer than some medications, like ketamine, but is more comparable with SSRIs in affecting the onset of measurable benefits.

Mann is well on his way to applying his discoveries with PET technology to save lives. He hopes to catch abnormalities in the brain before they can develop into a mortal threat. His PET detective technique isn't available now chiefly because PET scans cost on average $5,000 per scan, and provide good information only in patients not currently on antidepressant medications. As the price of PET technology goes down, and as newer PET tracers are developed, this form of detection will become more available to people at risk. Until then, there's still much that can be done to reduce suicide rates.

Mann believes the federal government will have to step up in two key areas. The majority of people who die by suicide have never seen a mental health professional or been diagnosed with a mental illness. But up to 90 percent of those people see a health care professional in the year before they kill themselves. Most often it's their primary care physician for issues not related to mental health. If these professionals were trained in detecting depression, the psychiatric illness most closely connected with suicide, a great number of suicides could be prevented.

Mann said, "We could educate non-psychiatrists, like general practitioners, primary care physicians, internists, OB-GYN doctors, in the recognition of depression, and how to treat it. We could do this in an analogous way to how we reacted to the opioid epidemic. We required every doctor in the country to take a course online on how to prescribe opioids more safely and treat addiction problems more effectively. We can do the same thing for depression. We could treat this as an urgent problem requiring a national effort."

Parkland Health and Hospital System in Dallas is one of the largest public hospital systems in the country. It treats more than one million patients every year. In 2015, Parkland became the first health system in the United States to implement a universal suicide screening program in its facilities. Among the adult and child populations screened that year, 96 percent did not report symptoms that would indicate they were at risk for suicide, and 97 percent did not need any further action from their health care provider. However, the screening protocols did find elevated suicide risk in about 2.3 percent of patients seeking nonpsychiatric care, and those patients would not have been found if universal screening had not been put in place. These findings back up other research that suggests a lack of universal screening is a risk factor for suicide.

Mann indicated another commonsense approach to suicide prevention that touches Americans in a sensitive spot—firearms. Firearms are involved in about 52 percent of suicides, more than all other methods combined. The states that have the highest suicide rates in America—Wyoming, Montana, and Alaska—have the most firearms per capita. It's no coincidence.

Mann said, "Make it harder to access the method that half of all American suicide decedents use to kill themselves. Reduce access to firearms. If people who are suicidal have less access to firearms, they will be forced to use less lethal methods. They'll have more chance of surviving. Why allow people to use the most lethal method to kill themselves? Safer storage of guns and ammunition prevents suicide."

Mann's research proves that suicide has its origins in the brain. Not one neurological disorder but two must be present before the risk of suicide becomes critical. These disorders can be influenced, even created, by genes and by early life adversity. But big questions remain.

Even in the absence of epigenetic influences, can suicide be passed down through genes? Can we be born with a brain bent on suicide?

Suicide is sometimes called a *disease of isolation* because isolation and loneliness are major risk factors for suicide. It's not surprising, then, that families play an important role in keeping suicide at bay. Strong family ties and other dynamics, like having living parents who are together, being married, and having young children, all make suicide less likely. But as scientists have long suspected, suicide runs in families. How do they know? By studying twins.

The annual Twins Days Festival is held in—where else?—Twinsburg, Ohio, which was founded in 1819 by the twins Moses and Aaron Wilcox. About two thousand pairs of (mostly) identical twins from around the world come together for events like the Double Take Parade and a talent show. Twins dress up in matching outfits, and to see them is to experience a glitch in the matrix; there's something a little unearthly about twins, and a crowd of them makes you distrust your eyesight. For science researchers, the festival is a bonanza—the relationship between twins allows them to probe the roles of genetic and environmental influences on physical and psychological development. For two centuries, twin studies have been important in exploring mental health disorders and other diseases.

Between 1812 and 2006, scientists conducted thirty-two studies of twins and suicide. Many examined pairs of twins in which one or both died by suicide. The majority found that the risk of suicide is higher in identical, or monozygotic, twins, who have almost identical DNA. That means these twins developed from the same egg and sperm that came from their mother and father. If one twin kills himself, the other has a better than average chance of following suit. These findings can mean only one thing—some of the risk of suicide involves genes.

David Jobes, who developed the Collaborative Assessment and Management of Suicidality (CAMS) treatment, finds evidence in an

American dynasty. "You look at the Hemingway family, for example, and the genogram of that particular family, and there's depression and suicide and alcoholism. A family just plagued with tragedy and way too many suicides."

Ernest Hemingway wasn't the only family member to kill himself, just the most famous. His father, two brothers, a sister, and a granddaughter, supermodel Margaux, also died by suicide. Christine Moutier notes that you can have a genetic predilection for suicide and not even know it. "If you are someone who has a family history of suicide, you may have a genetic loading for suicide and not realize it. We haven't become very sophisticated yet as a society about recognizing it, the way we do for heart disease, for example. We're much better at that."

Most people with a family history of suicide never try to take their lives. But those who have inherited a risk must be vigilant about additional risks in their environment. Scientists know that it's genes plus life experiences that add up to suicide. SAVE's Dan Reidenberg summed it up for me. "There are a number of risk factors that are both internal and external: family history of suicide, a prior suicide attempt, substance abuse. And then there's these other pieces like unemployment, economic problems, financial problems, relationship problems, legal problems. All of these put you at greater risk of suicide. Again, it's important to remember that most people can survive and live through those. Some can't."

Recently, 260 researchers from twenty countries completed a large-scale study to try to find a distinction between mental health risk factors for suicide, such as depression, and an independent genetic risk that contributes to suicide. They concluded that there is such an independent risk located in the human genome. DNA variants in a region of the genome on chromosome 7 increase the risk of a suicide attempt. Not only that, when researchers eliminated mental health disorders from the study, they found that the risk was still significant.

This finding doesn't mean that there's a suicide gene, however; the risk is significant but not determinative. Instead, it means that even when the specific gene or genes are discovered, it will still be true that a combination of risk factors, not one, leads to suicide.

If you are thinking about suicide or if you or someone you know is in emotional crisis, please call or text 988 at any time to reach the 988 Suicide and Crisis Lifeline for confidential, free crisis support.

CHAPTER SIX

FONDA BRYANT

Gastonia is a satellite city of Charlotte, North Carolina, and though it is contained within the official Charlotte Metropolitan Area, you have to drive thirty minutes west on an interstate (85) to reach it. Its old neighborhoods favor expansive shade trees and quiet streets, which give Gastonia an easygoing Southern vibe. Its hip downtown scatters gastropubs, BBQ joints, and live music among bookstores and consignment shops. Gastonia is less cosmopolitan and more relaxed than Charlotte, and that's why North Carolinians like it.

Fonda Bryant grew up in a number of places, but a quiet street at the intersection of Winget Street and Memory Lane in a mostly black neighborhood holds memories of a childhood spent running free with her cousins. An athletic woman in her fifties, Fonda strolls beside her towering son, six-feet-four Wesley, and smilingly tries to make him feel the magic of her home. In his early thirties and a sports broadcaster, Wes was an offensive lineman at Wake Forest University a dozen years ago. While he's lost some of the three hundred pounds he carried on the gridiron, he's no less imposing.

Fonda finds the house she's looking for, a simple wood-sided cottage in a line of cottages, all in need of fresh paint, with an ample yard and a sampling of trees. She tells Wes, "This is where many a day that me and Spankie and Tut would come when we were just little kids. And we'd come up here and hang out with Great-Grandma. That was your great-great-grandmother."

In an old black-and-white photograph Fonda produced from her purse, she, Spankie, and Tut beam with mischief. At six, Fonda hugs a cat while Spankie, about eight with wild hair, holds on to Fonda's brother, Tut, a toddler whose suspenders keep his short pants up. Just three years older, Spankie is Fonda's aunt, but they look like sisters. I'm reminded of *To Kill a Mockingbird*'s Scout, Jem, and Dill adventuring through an endless summer. Fonda's gang had milder escapades but enduring bonds nonetheless.

"Which grandmother?" Wesley said, trying to place the house's owner. "Nanny Cooper?"

"No, she was your great-grandmother," said Fonda. "This would be your great-*great*-grandmother. And we'd come up and sit on the porch and talk. But we would just run around and play a lot of times. Grandma would still chop wood. And she did something that you would've loved—she fixed biscuits *every day*." Her voice is full of emphasis and punctuation, her phrases never resting on one octave when three will do.

"Yeah? Why'd she make biscuits every day, though?"

"Because back in the day, that's what they *made*," Fonda laughed. "She still had a wood stove. And I never will forget one time she tried to put a TV dinner in a wood stove and burned it slap up!" Fonda smacked her hip and laughed. "Her name was Lizzie. But we called her Great-Grandma."

The pair follow a path made of paving stones to a backyard in need of a gardener.

Wesley said, "I've never been back here."

"This yard needs a fix-up."

Fonda rounded the house cautiously, like an explorer. She had already warned Wes about snakes.

"Great-Grandma had a well back here which she didn't allow us to play around cause they were worried one of us would fall in." Fonda's voice was hushed, as if the old matriarch still stood vigil on the back porch. "And when we used to hang around up here, they didn't even have indoor plumbing."

"Hm."

"You had to go outside."

Fonda closed in on the well. It was covered by a weather-beaten wooden box held shut with an ancient padlock.

"But that well water was really good. Better than any store-bought water."

"Water is water," said Wes. "Unless it's dirty."

A shake of her head and a tolerant smile. "You are always knocking it but I'm telling you it was totally different. I miss my childhood. You know, being able to just come up here and play and be kids, and nobody was bothering you, and your great-grandma would give you food to eat. And if you got a quarter, you were really something. Because you could buy bubble gum, a cookie, chips, and a soda, and still have some money left. Can't do that with a quarter now."

"What's that?" said Wes, pointing at the well cover. Below the lock hung a metal sign with an engraving.

Fonda moved nearer and read it aloud. "Be happy. For every minute you are sad, you lose sixty seconds of happiness." She took out her phone and opened the camera app. "Man, I didn't know that was back here. I'm gonna take a picture of that. That is really something. It will remind me of doing better when I'm not having a good day."

*   *   *

Fonda's mother had four children, two while married and two while single. She had Fonda when she was just seventeen and not married. Fonda's brother Tut followed, then two more girls years later. She worked at a Wix Filters factory, which made oil and air filters, but money was tight. Fonda's father was the late Blues Hall of Fame singer Johnnie Taylor, dubbed the Philosopher of Soul, and best known for the 1976 hit "Disco Lady." Taylor fathered nine children with three women and never acknowledged Fonda's existence or contributed a dime to her upbringing. Recently in court, Fonda and her half siblings forced a royalties payment out of Sony Records. But that money hadn't been there when Fonda needed it.

Fonda began a story with a smile. I imagined like many of her tales of childhood it would be funny or whimsical, but it wasn't. "When I was growing up in Gastonia one of my classmates, Lisa, never will forget her, I had on some shoes that had holes in the soles. And I had put some cardboard in them to keep the dirt out.

"So Lisa thought it would be funny to make fun of my shoes. She asked me to walk in front of her. Well, you know, when you walk, your whole shoe comes up and kids could see the holes in my shoes. And I could hear them behind me laughing and that really, really hurt me. It hurt me for the fact that I had to go to school like that and it hurt me because I felt like my mom was doing the best that she could. Because I was very attached to my mother. And the fact that Lisa, who lived on my street, would even act that way, you know? She thought it was funny.

"I tell people now, be careful how you treat each other. Because when you're in elementary school, middle school, high school, you think it's no big deal. You think that what you say is not going to affect the person as they get older." Fonda's smile slipped, then was gone. "But it does."

It is unlikely that there is a direct line between Lisa's cruelty and Fonda's later suicide attempts, but the bullying she suffered probably played a contributing role. Bullying is more dangerous than it was previously thought and far more dangerous now than it has ever been before.

Dr. Madelyn Gould, professor of epidemiology in psychology at Columbia University, studies youth suicide. About bullying, she told me, "Thirty years ago, we did not recognize how devastating bullying could be. People thought, well, kids get bullied, right? And then the research started coming out that showed that being bullied increases the risk of dying by suicide. Now, the vast majority of young people who are bullied will not engage in suicidal behavior. But if you have underlying vulnerabilities, whether it is a family history of suicide or the propensity to be depressed, or you're coming from a family who may not have as many resources as other families, that's already putting stresses on you. And then when you're bullied in school, that can become devastating."

Bullying takes many forms, none of them good. Physical bullying can cause immediate injury and result in long-term effects such as headaches, poor sleep, and physical symptoms related to stress. If bullying persists, young people can develop feelings of insecurity and hypervigilance. They can become angry and isolated. They can also suffer lifelong health problems associated with chronic inflammation caused by stress. For reasons that are not yet clear, girls who are bullied report more anxiety and health problems than boys.

As Gould said, bullying is particularly harmful to those who already suffer from underlying mental health conditions. People suffering from depression and suicidal thoughts—as noted by John Mann—react more strongly to criticism of all kinds, including criticism from teachers and authority figures.

Angelo Bavetta was an acquaintance of mine, a business owner who worked with his hands. He killed himself at age fifty-three. Angelo had always struggled with his weight. In elementary school, he suffered an unconscionable amount of bullying in what should have been a safe environment. His sister Christina told me, "We went to this little Catholic school first to eighth grade. Angelo was tortured in school because he was heavy. For years they tortured him, the same mean kids grade after grade. Even the nuns were mean to Angelo. *Tease the fat kid!*"

Angelo suffered from a number of risk factors, including alcohol abuse disorder and a recent divorce. But according to his family, the bullying he endured in elementary school was never far from his thoughts.

No amount of bullying should be tolerated in school or any environment; besides being cruel and emotionally grueling, it has the epigenetic power to switch genes on or off to increase the probability of suicide and other maladies. One mechanism involves the chemical cortisol, one of the "fight-or-flight" hormones. The natural daily production of cortisol in the body increases during times of stress. Cortisol elevates blood sugar, suppresses the immune system, and speeds the conversion of food into energy. But preparing to fight or flee over a long period of time can switch off the gene that inhibits cortisol production, resulting in surplus cortisol. This abnormality has been found in the brains of people who have died by suicide.

Fonda suffered more than one episode of bullying due to poverty. But the torment she suffered might have been much worse for her had she been a child today. That's because Fonda didn't have social media to contend with. Social media is a bullying multiplier. Because of the vast networks of users on Facebook, Snapchat, Instagram, and other platforms, incidents that begin as petty insults balloon overnight into overwhelming assaults. And the assaults are magnified and perpetuated.

On February 1, 2023, fourteen-year-old Adriana Kuch was attacked by a group of her New Jersey high school classmates. They kicked, punched, and pulled her by her hair in the school hallway. A video of the assault circulated over Twitter and TikTok. To continue their harassment, classmates mailed the video and screen grabs to Adriana, along with ugly comments. Two days later, Adriana killed herself. Forensic psychologist Tristin Engels, PsyD, commented, "When [a video] is circulated in uncontrolled and unregulated environments like social media, it opens up the victims, families, teachers, and communities to more forms of cyberbullying. That's traumatizing."

"Online bullying is so quick and it's so big," says SAVE's Dan Reidenberg. "So whereas twenty or thirty years ago when bullying occurred in a school or on a playground, that was one against one or maybe three against one. Now it's three hundred against one or three thousand against one. And because it's so broad and so diffused, it can happen across the state or across the country, whereas instead it used to happen in a parking lot."

Not only are the bullying numbers magnified but their intensity is also magnified because of the anonymity granted by the internet. Reidenberg says, "People feel far more emboldened to say things that are far more hurtful than they would in person. So there is this connection between what happens with bullying and social media that we didn't have twenty or thirty years ago."

"Social media can be used for good as well," counters Christine Moutier, chief medical officer of the American Foundation for Suicide Prevention. "Social media can provide connections for people when they don't feel connected, it can provide support for people when they don't feel supported. Social media can provide resources and good information for people when they need it."

Clearly, social media is a double-edged sword, but aspects of it are indisputably harmful, making it hard to gauge whether its benefits outweigh its risks. One negative phenomenon is called FOMO, short for "fear of missing out." Those who post on sites like Instagram and Facebook typically share images and stories that portray a life crammed full of vacations, family gatherings, new homes, cars, clothes. Social media consumers experience feelings of social anxiety based on the conviction that other people are having better, more rewarding lives.

Moutier says, "There is a large body of evidence that shows that for many, many people, let alone youth, there can be a negative impact on their mental health from using social media—really just endless scrolling and feeling like you're missing out. For kids who have any level of preexisting anxiety or family history of mood disorders, there needs to be a lot of caution and guardrails around social media use, and particularly the age at which kids get access to a smartphone."

Between 2000 and 2007, suicide rates were almost stagnant for young people between the ages of ten and twenty-four. Then they began moving steadily upward. By 2018, suicides in this age group had increased 57.4 percent from 2007 levels. An economic crisis darkened that period, and according to online posts, some seventeen- and eighteen-year-olds felt like a burden because their families were overwhelmed by household expenses and had too many mouths to feed.

But something else was happening in the background. Social media was gaining a real foothold.

In the past ten years, social network platforms have more than quadrupled their number of users—from 970 million in 2010 to 4.48 billion in 2021.

"Youth suicide rates turned upward at a time when social media were becoming more available," psychiatrist Eric Caine, MD, of the University of Rochester Medical Center told me. In 2018 an academic review of literature supported this alarming correlation, stating that the "increase in suicide rates paralleled the increase in social media use." In 2019 the American Academy of Pediatrics reported the astounding fact that mental health disorders have surpassed physical conditions as the most common complaints causing "impairment and limitation" among adolescents. That same year the United States Surgeon General expressed alarm about the devastating mental health epidemic affecting American teens.

But was social media to blame? At least in part. A ten-year study of five hundred teens conducted by Brigham Young University beginning in 2009 showed that girls who used social media for two to three hours a day and increased their use over time developed a higher risk for suicide. An independent survey of US teens in grades eight through twelve and national statistics on suicide deaths for those ages thirteen to eighteen both showed that depressive symptoms, suicide-related injuries, and suicide rates all went up between 2010 and 2015, especially among girls. Teens who spent more time on new media, like social media and electronic devices such as

smartphones, were more likely to say they had mental health problems. Teens who spent more time on non-screen activities, like in-
person social interaction, sports/exercise, homework, print media,
and religious services, were less likely to say they had mental health
problems.

How else do social media and new media contribute to suicide?
The ten-year study of five hundred teens suggested that young people who harm themselves are more active on social networks than
young people who don't engage in self-harm. Self-harm generally
consists of cutting, burning, or hitting oneself, often without the
intent to die. However, those who engage in self-harm are at significant risk for suicide. As Moutier says, some may be seeking help
online and are rewarded with supportive messages. But the opposite
can also be true. Online help-seeking is often met with derision,
which can fuel self-harm. And young people engaging in self-harm
find messages that encourage their behavior and even copy the
dangerous actions of others shared in messages or videos.

Danish suicide expert Annette Erlangsen, PhD, who studies suicide in Denmark and the United States, observed darker online connections. "We do know suicide pacts that have been established
through Facebook or groups forums, where people are discussing
thoughts of suicide and maybe even trying to promote or trigger
others to carry out suicidal acts. So we have examples where we can
clearly see that social media has had a bad impact."

At least one social media giant has studied the life-threatening
impacts its sites cause and has done nothing about them. In 2021,
The Wall Street Journal reported that internal documents prepared
by researchers at Facebook showed that the company had long been
aware that it contributed to mental health disorders in young people. They found that Instagram, its photo-based site, made body-

image problems worse for about 30 percent of female teenage users and added to depression and anxiety. Another internal report showed that among teens who reported suicidal ideas, 6 percent of American users and 13 percent of British users traced the desire to kill themselves to Instagram. These revelations came courtesy of whistleblower Frances Haugen. In May 2021, she quit her job as a product manager at Facebook and took tens of thousands of internal papers with her. The records, made public in newspaper articles, have led to a flurry of accusations and lawsuits from eight states.

Meta Platforms, the company that owns both Facebook and Instagram, is in the crosshairs of litigation that accuses it of causing eating disorders, despair, and even deaths among adolescents and teenagers. In 2021 the parents of Englyn Roberts, a Louisiana teenager, brought a case against Instagram. According to their suit, Englyn was "bombarded by harmful photos and videos," including "violent and distressing content celebrating self-harm and death."

As Englyn interacted with these images and videos, carefully crafted algorithms offered up more and more similar content, trapping the teenager in a dangerous cycle. Englyn began sharing films of herself and her friends committing self-harm. In August 2020, copying a video she had seen online, Englyn tried to take her life in the same manner. After days on life support, she died.

Her parents' suit alleges her death was the direct result of psychic damage brought on by her compulsive use of social media, particularly Instagram. Englyn Roberts was just fourteen.

When Fonda Bryant turned fourteen, social media and smartphones hadn't yet complicated the landscape for teens, but she nevertheless contended with serious sources of stress. She worked two jobs to help her mother make ends meet. After classes she filed papers in an administrative office at her high school, and on nights and weekends she waitressed. The jobs irked her, but the family had new additions. "I'd work like forty hours a week and still go to school. And I resented that because we were already struggling and my mom had two more children. I loved my brother and sister, but it fell on me to help take care of them and sign my checks over to my mother to pay the bills. I knew it wasn't right. Being a kid and working like that. I think the onslaught of depression started when I was around fifteen or sixteen."

But Fonda isn't exactly sure—she thinks her depression might have begun much earlier. She attributes her lack of awareness to her culture and an enduring stigma about mental health issues, particularly in her church. "When I started feeling real depression, I didn't know what it was. Because black people didn't talk about mental health, we didn't know what the signs were. The racial difference with mental health among black people, and people of color in general, is how we were raised. Pray about it. Don't claim it. Give it to God. But I know I was probably dealing with depression all my life."

Sean Joe, PhD, MSW, an authority on suicide among Black Americans, concurs with Fonda's assessment of church attitudes. "For some the Black Church has not always been helpful. They say you're not faithful enough, you're not prayerful enough. That if you were a stronger Christian and turned your life over to God, that would heal you. But in the last fifteen to twenty years, more Black Churches and leaders are making sure they encourage people to seek mental health services."

But while the church hasn't always been helpful at providing counsel or advice, it has indirectly protected black women from suicide. Dr. Joe says, "A connection with the church brings social and emotional support, and that has an impact. There is the idea that black women in the United States are more orthodox in their religious views, so individuals who have a negative attitude toward suicide are less likely to engage in suicidal behavior. If your doctrine is that suicide is a sin, that's one component of the protective factor that might be at play."

But Joe thought there had to be more protective factors. That's because when he explored suicides among black men and women, he found a large difference in suicide rates that could only be partly explained by churchgoing. Averaging all ages, non-Hispanic black women die of suicide at *one-fourth* the rate of non-Hispanic black men.

Joe says, "When we started to understand that suicide was increasing among younger generations of black men—and this has been happening since the 1970s—we never saw the same increase in suicide among black women. And that posed an interesting question. If the generations of child slavery, Jim Crow, mass incarceration is impacting the black population, what is unique among black females and their experiences that they don't engage in the same levels of suicidal behavior as black males?"

For starters, black women tend to be the primary caregivers for children, which means they cannot solely think about themselves when they're considering the consequences of suicide. Children can also be shields against solitude and loneliness, major risk factors for suicide. And culturally, black women are able to express themselves more frequently and completely than black men. Joe says, "Black women, unlike black men, are more likely to be allowed to express their emotions and find social connections and spaces to get support. And black males and males in general are not allowed to emote or find those sorts of spaces because of the idea it's not masculine."

In the bigger picture, protective forces make black women less likely to kill themselves than other minority American women—Natives, Asians, Latins, and Pacific Islanders. In the United States in 2019, the last year for which data is available, non-Hispanic black women had less than half the suicide rate of non-Hispanic white women. However, in recent years the suicide rate for black girls has steadily increased, particularly among adolescents and children under thirteen. From 2003 to 2017, the suicide rate went up by an average of 6.6 percent *per year* for black girls.

On average, suicide rates among black youths are lower than those among white youths, but variations occur depending on age, gender, and other factors. According to the Centers for Disease Control and Prevention (CDC), between 1999 and 2018, the suicide rate for black children and adolescents from ages five to seventeen was lower than the rate for white children and adolescents. However, currently the suicide rate for black males ages fifteen to twenty-four is higher than that of white males of the same age group.

Not so fast, says Sean Joe. The rates at which black people of both genders and all ages kill themselves may be inaccurate, and greatly undercounted. Undercounting casts doubt on many conclusions we may draw from statistics about black suicides. Joe first encountered this problem when he began exploring suicides among black children.

He says, "We suffer from a lack of attention to specific ethnic groups in the United States. There's been no real research on black children. When children are studied or treatments are developed, black children are not included in those studies." Why not? For Joe, the problem is tied to institutional racism. "If you never develop black scientists, then you don't get individuals who are likely to ask the question. The reason that we're talking today is because someone invested in me, and I asked a question. And if they didn't invest in me, who would have asked some of the questions that I'm asking?"

West Virginia University's Ian Rockett, PhD, MPH, also studies black suicide and asked a broader question: Why is the rate of suicide among Black Americans recorded as one-third of that among whites? According to his 2010 study, Black American deaths are 2.3 times more likely than white deaths to be labeled as "indeterminate." Dr. Rockett discovered reasons for this. Chiefly, coroners and medical examiners have less information to work with when examining black deaths. That's because black people are less likely to acquire a mental health record due to their lack of access to medical specialists. Consequently, black people may not have a history of mental health issues or prior suicide attempts, both of which can add to a determination of suicide when they die.

"When there's less psychological documentation," says Rockett, "they're more likely to be labeled as undetermined intent. This leads to suicide misclassification."

Rockett knows a lot about suicide misclassification. His studies show that suicides among *all races* in the United States are underreported, and he asserts the true body count is at least 30 percent higher than its 2020 accepted number of 45,979. That would make suicide three times more common than murder. In another recent study, Rockett and coauthors showed that suicide has become the leading cause of "injury deaths," which are those deaths such as car accidents in which people harm themselves.

A pair of black platform shoes with a glittering silver band. Huge-heeled open-toed shoes in two colors—sapphire and red. "This pair is kind of self-explanatory," said Fonda about some elegantly decorated black pumps. She beamed at the design. "They have flowers. Thank God they were marked down." Then her favorite, a pair of translucent green T-straps. Fonda said, "The color green for mental health stands for hope, so I had to have a pair of shoes in green."

At her cozy apartment in Gastonia, Fonda sat on a well-padded brown sofa in the living room surrounded by a small mountain of shoeboxes. They are a fraction of her collection. She said, "Nothing makes me feel better than for somebody to look at my feet and say, 'You got on some bad shoes,' because I love that. And I don't go spend a ton of money on my shoes, but I do have a lot of nice shoes. And I love for people to look at them and say, 'Oh, where'd you get those shoes?'

"Automatically my brain goes all the way back to when I was a kid in elementary school. It all comes back to Lisa. So it really does go to show that words can hurt and being bullied can affect you for the rest of your life. It took me years to realize why I love shoes so much."

In her teen years before her passion for shoes took hold, Fonda enjoyed one of the protective forces that benefit anyone with a large, loving extended family. During most of her childhood she was surrounded by close relatives—grandparents, aunts and uncles, and cousins. Still, her family's warm embrace didn't protect her from depression she seems to have been born with. Like so many of those afflicted with severe depression, she medicated her dark feelings. Her medicine of choice wasn't alcohol, drugs, or food. It was sex.

She said, "I started being promiscuous very early, at thirteen. That's why I tell people all the time I can understand addiction even though I've never done drugs, even though I've never done alcohol. Whether it's eating, or working out excessively, shopping, gambling, sex. It's not healthy, but it's a coping skill. And if you don't realize that and get help for it, that coping skill can spiral out of control. And it did for me. I just became a wild child. I was just wild. And I had no idea that it had anything to do with my mental health."

A rough definition of sexual addiction, or compulsive sexual behavior, is an impulse control condition that persists despite unfavorable consequences. Studies about compulsive sexual activities indicate shortages of serotonin, norepinephrine, and particularly dopamine, all neurotransmitters. Sexual addiction begins, on average, at eighteen years of age. Some 88 percent of sexual addicts have a history of other mental health conditions, including severe depression, like Fonda. In addition to depression and compulsive behavior, Fonda probably had another brain abnormality, the one that John Mann claims causes suicidal ideation and which, combined with depression, increases chances for suicide. Fonda's future behavior would seem to bear this out.

Fonda's mental health threw a monkey wrench into her adolescent years. She had her first child as a single mother at age sixteen. After just thirty days the infant died in the hospital from undiagnosed medical conditions. The event traumatized Fonda and worsened her relationship with her mother, who was angry her daughter had become an unwed mother, as she had twice been herself. Fonda finished high school and a year of college, then began a series of retail and secretarial jobs, one, significantly, as a pharmacy technician. At age twenty-three she had a second child, Wesley. But throughout, besieged by mental health issues, her life spun out of control.

"To be honest I attempted suicide four times. Two times where I just thought this would be the best way for me and two times where I actually had a plan."

The first time, in the middle of an argument with her mother, Fonda swallowed a handful of painkillers she'd taken from the pharmacy where she worked. Instead of going to the hospital immediately, as she should have, she went to bed. "I thought I was gonna die. But I woke up the next morning, I was scared and I was like, 'Oh my God, am I gonna die?' So I called the paramedics, they came, they asked me did I need to go to the hospital and I told them no. And after that, I went back to work and just kept working. But I knew I needed help and I remember my mom did take me to a behavioral health clinic." She spent a few hours at the clinic, had a perfunctory therapy session, then was sent home. There was no follow-up.

Fonda's experience with thwarted suicide is not unusual. In the United States, women attempt suicide three times more often than men, but men succeed more often, about 70 percent of the time.

Why? Men more often use firearms.

Dr. Sean Joe observes, "The thing that we understand is that a suicidal crisis is usually one to ten minutes. One to ten minutes." It may come back, to be sure, within hours, days, or months. But the crisis itself has a short duration. "In a suicidal crisis, if you have a lethal means, it's more likely to result in death, so if you have a firearm, you have a ninety-five percent chance of dying. If you don't have a firearm and you use some other means, right? You only have about a five to ten percent chance of dying. So the means matter."

Men, compared with women, appear to be less fearful of death and more able to endure physical pain. As a result, they may be more likely to use more violent means of suicide, such as shooting themselves, hanging, or jumping from a high place. About 60 percent of men use a gun, compared to over 30 percent of women, whose most favored means of attempt include overdose, suffocation, hanging, self-piercing, and burning. Less than 10 percent of these cases result in death.

The means of death men choose also impacts how many attempts they make compared to women. Around 62 percent of men die from their first suicide attempt, whereas about 38 percent of women die after their first attempt. While more than 50 percent of women who die by suicide have previously attempted, less than half of men who die by suicide have a history of one or more prior attempts. Dr. Thomas Joiner's interpersonal theory of suicide, which offers precise ideas about how the desire and capacity for suicide develops, is based in part on the notion that suicide is difficult and painful and therefore more often completed by men. We'll discuss the interpersonal theory of suicide ahead.

As we've seen, the common denominator in almost all suicides is an excruciating amount of mental and physical pain that is almost indescribable. Of the people I've spoken with who have attempted suicide, Fonda did the best job of putting that pain into words. She described it as we drove across Gastonia to visit her aunt Spankie, who figures prominently in Fonda's closest brush with death.

Fonda said, "The best way for people to visualize the pain, it's from the top of your head to the bottoms of your feet. I've had wisdom teeth removed, an abscessed tooth, open-heart surgery, given birth twice, hysterectomy, knee surgery. You could put all the pain together and it would not touch the pain that I felt on February fourteenth, 1995."

At the time, Fonda was thirty-five years old and living in Gastonia with Wesley, then twelve.

"I had just had it. And my mind was telling me, you know, if you just take these pills, if you just go to sleep, everything will be over with. It's amazing how strong our mind is. It guides everything.

But when it's sick, it can make you do stuff you never thought you would do. And so my mind was telling me, you know, kill yourself. Your son would be better off. Nobody's going to care. And that's how I felt." Fonda looked down at her hands. Then she looked at me.

"In my heart, I still knew I was a good mom. I was doing the best that I could, but in my mind, it was telling me, you know, just chunk it in. It'll be better for you. So I had that plan that I was just gonna take some pills, almost like Sleeping Beauty, where your house is immaculate and you're just gonna lay down. I had it planned out to look a certain way. I didn't want them to find me like some people who shoot themselves. Some people hang themselves. That's traumatic on top of it being traumatic. I didn't want that. I just wanted to go to sleep."

We turned into Spankie's neighborhood, a middle-class suburb on Gastonia's outskirts with midsize brick homes surrounded by neatly kept yards and chain-link fences.

"But before I took the pills I said man, somebody's got to know about my pain. And I called my aunt Spankie. We grew up three years apart, always been close, she was always getting us out of trouble. I reached out to her and I simply said, you can have my shoes. That's all I told her. And I think we talked a little bit more, but I don't really remember what I said."

At Spankie's door a flurry of cheerful greetings as Fonda and Spankie embrace. Spankie is a head shorter and more soft-spoken compared with Fonda's forceful, expressive self. Spankie's husband had recently died and she was renovating their home. Fonda didn't miss a detail. "I knew you were gonna do that, I knew it!" Their smiles and laughter said loud and clear that the man who was gone might not be missed all that much and these two weren't mere relations but closer than sisters. Aunt Spankie fussed over the flowers Fonda had brought and ushered us into the screened back porch. Just outside, a huge purple and orange buddleia bush attracted a kaleidoscope of colorful butterflies.

Fonda caught Spankie up on what we were talking about.

"During the course of the conversation," said Spankie, "she said, 'You can have my shoes.' That was an instant indication that there was something wrong. 'Cause we are serious about shoes." She gave me a look. "And I eventually asked her was she planning to hurt herself and she said yes."

Fonda said, "She called me back and she asked me, 'Are you going to kill yourself?' And I said yes. And then she went into action like a superhero. She took out the papers for me to be involuntarily committed."

The same day a policeman came calling.

Fonda said, "There was a knock at the door and there was this big black Charlotte-Mecklenburg police officer. He said, 'Are you Fonda Bryant?' And I said yes. And he said, 'I came to take you to a mental health facility.' And I'm like, oh no you're not!

"And I got scared," said Fonda. "And I went up the stairs to the bedroom thinking if I went up there, he'd just go away. Which they don't do if you're being committed. They come after you. And he came upstairs and things started escalating. And he put his hands on me. And I scratched him. And when I scratched him, he grabbed me by the back of my neck. He shook me extremely hard and he put me in handcuffs."

Even cuffed, Fonda fought on. But twelve-year-old Wesley, who had followed the policeman up the stairs, pleaded with her. "Momma, you need help!"

As Fonda tells it, she was saved twice that day. Once by Spankie, who had had her committed, and again by her son, Wesley, whose plea worked magic. Fonda surrendered. "My son kept me from getting seriously injured by a police officer because we hear all the time where people who have mental health issues have been killed by police officers. So it was very fortunate that my son was up there that day because I could have gotten seriously injured or killed."

An expert on black suicide, Sean Joe puts the scene into context. "There used to be two service providers Black Americans did not want showing up to their doors. One was a psychiatrist, the other one was a police officer. And the concern was, they can both lock you up. Then you have the history of violence among Black Americans in police custody, where police suggested they hung themselves, they killed themselves. So, this sort of history plays out into the common experience of Black Americans and has an impact on their perceptions about mental health services."

For Joe, Fonda's confrontation combines two elements that are important to consider—stigma about mental health issues, and violence against black and mentally ill people by law enforcement. First, the stigma. As we saw earlier, black people tend not to have mental health records because they don't seek out services, and that's owed chiefly to cultural stigma and therapy's steep price tag. Another disincentive—people of different races and cultures are often driven to suicide by different risk factors. Mental health services don't often make adjustments for cultural differences. One size doesn't fit all.

Joe says, "If the services do not work for the population, were never designed for the population, that also impacts the stigma related to mental health services. So if we never invested in making sure that the treatments work for Black Americans, which we did not, and on top of that, it can lead to some level of involuntary incarceration, naturally people developed concerns around mental health and mental health services."

If these services fail black and underserved communities, who do they serve? Psychological therapy is challenging to obtain in the United States unless you are financially well-off and white. Money alone won't cut it. White culture brings with it familiarity and acceptance of psychiatrists, therapists, and medicines that treat depression. Joe parses the demographic even further. "Our mental health services, our efficacious treatments, were designed for middle-aged, middle-class white *women*." That's because, according to Joe, men of all races have traditionally frowned upon mental health services. "It was primarily middle-aged white women who can afford therapy and have the time to go to therapy. So our system of mental health services was really designed around them."

I've heard more than one expert assert that the popular and effective therapy modality cognitive behavioral therapy (CBT) was designed for white women. I thought this was hyperbole until I read that CBT trials included primarily white populations.

Joe agrees that access and cultural sensitivity have improved, but not much. "I'd say in the last fifteen to twenty years, some of that has changed. There are now more intentional efforts to design services for specific populations because we know the risk factors vary."

Next there's the police violence component of Fonda's commitment. In the United States, there is a long and well-documented record of police killing black people and others with mental health disorders. Black people are killed by police at more than twice the rate of white people, even though they make up only 13 percent of the US population. A vast majority of the black people who are killed are male, and half are younger than thirty-five years. But age is no protection—police are five times more likely to shoot and kill unarmed black men over age fifty-four than unarmed white men in the same age range. Regarding black men with a mental health disorder, police are more apt to shoot and kill unarmed black men who exhibit signs of mental illness compared with white men with similar behaviors.

In fact, people with mental disorders of any race have much to fear from police contact.

A 2022 *Washington Post* investigation reported that at least 25 percent of those who are killed by police officers in the United States have a severe mental health disorder at the time of their death. According to a study by the national nonprofit Treatment Advocacy Center the same year, people with untreated mental illness are sixteen times more likely to be killed during a police encounter than other civilians.

Most shockingly, from 2019 to 2021, law enforcement officers shot and killed 178 mentally ill people *they were called upon to help*. Many of the callers—worried family members, friends, or neighbors—told authorities that someone was having a mental health crisis, or someone was planning to kill themselves. None of these callers expressed concerns about anyone else's safety.

"It should horrify but not surprise us that people with untreated mental illness are overrepresented in deadly encounters with law enforcement," said John Snook, lawyer and coauthor of the Treatment Advocacy Center study. "Individuals with untreated mental illness are vastly overrepresented in every corner of the criminal justice system. Until we reform the public policies that have abandoned them there, these tragic outcomes will continue."

Police understand that they don't have many good ways to deal with people who are mentally ill. A recent survey by the Police Executive Research Forum found that new recruits spend about sixty hours learning how to use a gun, but only eight hours learning how to de-escalate tense situations and eight more learning how to deal with people with psychological disorders.

In interviews, current and former police chiefs said that these deadly encounters will keep happening if police aren't retrained on a large scale and mental health services aren't expanded across the country. But in recent years, some states have cut their budgets for psychiatric services by as much as 30 percent, leaving a gap that local police aren't willing or qualified to fill.

In response to the United States' growing need for suicide and mental health crisis support, SAMHSA (the Substance Abuse and Mental Health Services Administration) set up the new 988 Lifeline for voice and text to make it easier for people to get appropriate help in a crisis. The 988 Suicide and Crisis Lifeline is modeled after 911. It's intended to be a rapid and memorable number that links people who are experiencing suicidal thoughts or any other type of mental health crisis with a qualified mental health practitioner. The 988 initiative aims to eventually decrease run-ins between the law and mentally ill people, and to connect those in need of immediate assistance. At the federal, state, and local levels, considerable capacity investments have made it possible for the 988 Lifeline to assist a lot more people in need. August 2022 showed a 45 percent increase in the volume of calls compared with August 2021. September calls increased by about 32 percent over calls from a year before.

Tipped off by Fonda's remark that she would leave Aunt Spankie her shoes, Spankie took an impressive step: she filled out court papers to have her niece Fonda committed to a behavioral health center. Spankie told me, "I just did what I did, I didn't stop to think about who would be affected or who would be mad, I guess I didn't care."

State laws vary greatly, but generally speaking, a person must have a mental disorder to be forced into psychiatric hospitalization by a probate court. Probate courts handle cases involving wills and estate administration. In a majority of states, but not all, they demand that an individual be committed if they pose a clear and present risk to themselves or others. In some cases, whether or not a person is deemed dangerous, involuntary hospitalization may take place if they refuse necessary care.

There's no doubt Spankie deserves credit for acting quickly and decisively. It's no small feat to have anyone involuntarily committed to psychiatric care, much less someone to whom you are related and emotionally close. But what exactly did Spankie do right?

First of all, Spankie saw one of the signs of impending suicide: giving away prized possessions. Giving things away isn't the most common sign by far, but a meaningful one nevertheless. SAVE's Dan Reidenberg says, "We know anecdotally there are a lot of people, especially young people, that will give away prized possessions. They'll leave a book that they borrowed from somebody in a locker or they'll give a trophy that they earned to somebody else as a goodbye present. But if you look across the span of those who died by suicide, not everybody gives things away."

The stories of Greg Whitesell and Chris Dykshorn show more common signs we should all look out for: isolating oneself, pushing loved ones away, giving up treasured pastimes, feeling like a burden, and talking about dying. Reidenberg further describes the impression people who are suicidal make upon others. "They have a sense of being hopeless, like there's no future for them, or that there's no reason for them to be alive, no sense of purpose for them—they don't have anything left to contribute to their family, to their friends, to society, or to the world."

In many ways, people on the verge of killing themselves are pulling back from everything that attaches them to life. The changes in their demeanor and what they talk about should be easy to detect, but often they are not. Some people display no signs before dying by suicide. And recall that most people who die by their own hand don't tell anyone about it, nor do they seek professional help. Some deliberately hide their intentions so their plans won't be interrupted. But if you know what to look out for, you have a better chance to save a life.

The American Foundation for Suicide Prevention points out additional signs of suicidal thinking, which we can organize into three categories—talk, behavior, and mood. Does the individual talk about killing themselves, or say they feel trapped? Do they complain of unbearable pain? Are they visiting people to say goodbye, or increasing their use of drugs or alcohol? Do they search online for methods to kill themselves? Have they bought a gun or are they stockpiling pills? Do they display unusual anger, anxiety, irritability, feelings of shame, and sudden *improvements* in mood? Sometimes when people who are suicidal have conclusively decided to kill themselves, they become almost euphoric; they've made up their minds, their pain will soon be over.

Dr. Sean Joe frames a concise portrait of someone on the brink. "We see people start to change their behavior. They start to not eat. They don't sleep right. They start to express thoughts like 'I don't want to be here,' or they might even say, 'I want to die' or 'Life is too difficult for me, I can't go on.' It's important that we pay attention to these sorts of expressions. In addition, we can see those individuals who are suicidal really start to close themselves off. All the things that used to bring them joy don't bring them the same level of joy and at all times, they might begin to express, and this is important, 'I'm fine. I'm fine.'"

One theme I've often heard is that people in an emotional crisis have a strong desire to talk about it but at the same time are afraid or ashamed, so they may have their guard up. You do not need special training to have an open conversation about mental health; you just need patience and a few guidelines. The American Foundation for Suicide Prevention suggests that you let the person know that you are open to a conversation about how they are really doing by casually initiating a discussion. You may say, simply, "Are you feeling okay?" Or "I care about you. Can we have a conversation about how you've been feeling?" Or "You seem stressed lately. Is there something going on in your life that's making you feel a little overwhelmed?" If it's appropriate, you could even share your own experiences with emotional issues as an introduction to the subject. You may say something like "I've had challenging times in my life and I've found that talking to someone really helped me."

If the person isn't comfortable talking with you, don't be insulted. Ask if there's someone else they'd feel at ease talking with. This gentle approach accomplishes a few things. It lets the other person know you care and that you are open to talking about mental health issues. It tells them you're not judging; again, you're coming from a position of caring. Make sure you make time to really listen. You might be surprised at how productive and rich the conversation you prompt becomes.

If you have reason to believe that the person is a danger to themselves, ask this specific question: "Are you thinking about killing yourself?"

There's a long-standing hesitation to ask this because of fears it will plant ideas in the distressed person's mind or spark suicidal behavior. Studies have shown that it won't. Researcher and clinician Jane Pearson, PhD, of the National Institute of Mental Health wants to put this myth to rest. "We've learned over time it's okay to ask somebody if they're suicidal. People are often concerned you'll put that idea in their head, and for adolescents and adults we know that that is not the case. So, people will tell you if they're suicidal or not, but you're not creating a problem that way."

Not only are you likely to get a straight answer, but offering an opportunity to talk about suicidal feelings may reduce the risk of acting on them. Combined with a gentle introduction to a conversation about mental health, the question will increase the individual's sense of connectedness. Isolation or lack of connectedness is a major risk factor for suicide. Your question might illicit a simple yes or no, but it may also begin an outpouring of information about the individual's state of mind and intentions.

Remember that asking the question is effective only if you actively listen. Take their answers seriously, especially if they say they are thinking about killing themselves. Take care to learn why they are in such emotional pain. Listen for reasons why they may want to keep on living. Encourage them to think about why they want to live.

Aunt Spankie instinctively did the right thing and asked Fonda, "Are you thinking about killing yourself?" Fonda answered yes. Aunt Spankie completed the process to have Fonda committed to a psychiatric hospital. Between their phone call and when the policeman arrived, Fonda was alone with her twelve-year-old son for a few hours at most. The policeman's arrival must have seemed dizzyingly fast, which prompted Fonda to call Spankie a superhero.

The American Foundation for Suicide Prevention advises you to quickly get to the person and stay with them. Never leave someone in a crisis alone. If you are nearby, go and be prepared to spend time. Help them remove lethal means from their home, such as firearms; medicines, including over-the-counter painkillers; household poisons; and sharp knives or tools. As we've discussed, the best option for firearms is to make sure they are unloaded and then taken somewhere else—the home of a friend, for example—for safekeeping. Some police departments will hold on to guns if they present a danger to a citizen. The second-best option—lock the guns in a gun safe and lock up ammunition separately. It's best of course if the suicidal person does not have the combination or key to the safe.

Restricting access to lethal means accomplishes a couple of things. First, it prevents the person in crisis from immediately using those means to harm themselves. Second, if people who are suicidal cannot access their primary means of self-harm, they may not look further. They may give up their suicide attempt for that day, or forever. For this reason, barriers on bridges and high buildings have been particularly effective in stopping or dramatically reducing suicides at those locations.

Next, if the individual has a mental health counselor or therapist, contact them to see if they are available to meet with their patient. If the individual does not have a counselor, or if theirs is unavailable, escort the person in crisis to mental health services or a hospital emergency department. Again, do not leave them alone until they are under the care of a medical or mental health professional.

If you are not nearby and cannot take these actions with the individual in crisis, your job will be more complicated. Find out if the person can depend on someone close by to visit them. Ask the individual to call or text the 988 Suicide and Crisis Lifeline. There they'll be connected to trained counselors at one of over two hundred crisis centers nationwide. Studies have shown that talking to a Lifeline counselor makes people feel less suicidal, less depressed, less overwhelmed, and more hopeful. At any time, whether or not you are nearby and you would like information about how to handle someone in crisis, you may also call or text 988.

Finally, follow up. Though you'll want to do something more than send a postcard, studies have shown that hospitals that sent a regular postcard expressing concern improved patients' mental health and decreased later suicide attempts. This shows the efficacy of even the simplest follow-up steps. Once you are involved in the suicidal crisis of a friend, loved one, or colleague, following up should come naturally. Check and make sure their crisis is over. Make sure they have a plan for continuing care. And keep checking up. Getting quality care is challenging in the United States, especially for people of limited means. Perhaps your friend, colleague, or loved one could use your help penetrating the often dense bureaucracies.

After Fonda was taken from her home, she spent a week at Cedar Spring Hospital in Pineville, North Carolina, where she received inpatient psychiatric care. At first she was angry and resistant to help. But during group therapy she turned a corner. "I first learned about self-care when the therapist asked me, 'Who do you put first,

Fonda?' And I said, 'My son, Wesley.' And she told me that was the wrong answer. She said, when that oxygen bag drops in an airplane, what are you supposed to do? Put it on your face first, so you can help someone else. And that's self-care because if we don't put ourselves first, we can't help anyone. I couldn't help myself that day. I couldn't help anyone that day."

Fonda followed up with regular therapy and eventually a regimen of self-care. She told me, "We have so many things that can help us now. Exercise—I hit the gym three to four times a week. That gets my serotonin going no different than if I was taking medication. You also have walking in nature, being among trees, vitamin D from the sun, that's a great help. Adult coloring books are great because they're very intricate. And when I color, I can feel the anxiety leaving. You have to eat right. Who would've thought that eating has anything to do with our mental health, but it does. Eating blueberries, strawberries, raspberries, they contain antioxidants. Getting enough sleep and music therapy helped me. So we have all these great things now that can help us. It's not just about medication and talk therapy."

But medication and talk therapy are important tools for those suffering from mental health conditions. Fonda has received behavioral therapy since 1995. Insurance through her employers paid for some of it. Later a benefit offered by her son Wesley's employer called the Employee Assistance Program (EAP) helped with the cost. Many employers offer EAP, which supports the wellness of employees and family members as they navigate life stressors, including mental health issues, divorce, recovery from substance abuse, job transitions, and more. Fonda also got involved in Mental Health America (MHA) and the National Alliance on Mental Illness (NAMI). MHA is a community-based nonprofit founded to address the needs of those living with mental health issues through services, education, research, and advocacy.

NAMI is a nonprofit that provides access to support groups and educational programs that help individuals and families living with mental health conditions. NAMI is active in every state in America, as well as Puerto Rico and the District of Columbia.

CHAPTER SEVEN

THE INTERPERSONAL THEORY OF SUICIDE

We have explored suicides and near-suicides and identified common risk factors, such as substance abuse, mental health disorders, and access to lethal means. We've learned how suicide can be contagious and develop into a cluster, and how a propensity for suicide can be passed down directly through genes and also through the modification of gene expression, called epigenetics. We've explored many of the signs of suicide, and learned the importance of opening a conversation with those we fear are at risk. We've seen that one should remain with those in a suicidal crisis, remove lethal means from the environment, and accompany them to safety.

Taken together, we can't help but reach the same conclusion experts do: suicide is highly complicated. And no part of suicide is more complicated than predicting who is planning to kill themselves. The warning signs are almost all we have, but they are not enough. Promising technologies such as PET scans may in the future make anticipating suicidal behavior routine, at least among psychiatric patients who make themselves available for treatment. But for the time being, if a patient makes it to care at all, clinicians have little chance of determining whether they will kill themselves. To say nothing of the majority of suicide victims who neither tell anyone of their plans nor seek medical help.

With a team of researchers, Joseph Franklin, PhD, associate professor of psychology at Florida State University, studied 365 suicide case studies and found that the traditional risk factors we've discussed, such as depression, substance abuse, and previous suicide attempts, are not solid predictors of suicide. He said about clinical forecasting, "Nothing was better than luck. Guessing or flipping a coin is as good as the best suicide expert in the world who knows everything about a person's life. That was a wake-up call for us and for the field as a whole, because it showed that all the work we've done over the past fifty years hasn't led to any real progress in terms of forecasting."

In fact, in the last half century, scientists, physicians, and therapists in the United States have made little sustained progress in either forecasting or preventing suicides. Crisis hotline centers have been set up in most American cities and a whole new generation of antidepressants has been invented. Yet in 2008, at the start of a national recession, the suicide rate in the US was almost exactly what it was in 1965: eleven deaths per one hundred thousand people. And between 2007 and 2018 the numbers have grown on average by about 35 percent, and about 57 percent for young people between the ages of ten and twenty-four. There was a brief dip in rates in 2019, but by 2020, suicide was back on the rise. Experts agree that in the United States an annual increase in the number of suicide deaths is all but certain for the foreseeable future.

Ahead we'll look into the possible sources of this crisis, but disturbing trends appear when you examine the rates of major causes of death—suicide, murder, and car accidents—over time. In the 1970s, you were more likely to be killed by someone else or die in a car accident than to kill yourself. Today you are much more likely to kill yourself.

In an auditorium in the psychology department at Florida State University, a seventy-inch projection screen plays an interview with Fonda Bryant. The big screen and speakers amplify her already supersize personality. She's talking about her four suicide attempts and the pain she felt prior to each.

With uninhibited candor she says, "It feels like a bear is squeezing the life out of you. Your brain, the most powerful organ in your body, is saying you're a loser, kill yourself, nobody's gonna care."

Watching Fonda, at my request, is an athletic middle-aged man with a shaved dome who though sitting down looks large in every dimension, like the college football player he once was.

Thomas Joiner, PhD, the Robert O. Lawton Distinguished Professor of Psychology at FSU, is a rarity among suicidologists—a celebrity. He achieved this status by developing a unified field theory of suicide, a theory he claims explains "all suicides at all times in all cultures across all conditions." Called the interpersonal theory of suicide, it ought to be one of the Rosetta Stones suicidology has been looking for—a general model that explains suicides and may be able to help anticipate which patients are going to kill themselves.

Joiner's bona fides include hundreds of published papers, several books, a Guggenheim Fellowship, and a tragic origin story befitting the hero he's become in the world of suicidology. When he was a twenty-five-year-old graduate student in psychology, his father killed himself. For Joiner it was foremost a tragedy and later a puzzle. Then, suicide was seen as a weak person's out, an escape from the vicissitudes of life for those not strong enough to weather its storms. But Joiner's father was a former marine, an outdoorsman, a successful businessman—a man who didn't shirk from hard work and physical challenges. In Joiner's eyes his dad was immune to pain or frailty of any kind. He was anything but weak.

His death stirred Joiner personally and professionally. He recalibrated his academic focus and, to quote one writer, began "interrogating suicide as hard as anyone ever has, to finally understand it as a matter of public good and personal duty."

Joiner felt that suicidology needed organizing principles to make sense of its overwhelming complexity. When he and a colleague sat down to count risk factors for suicide—things like genetic loading, alcohol abuse, and childhood trauma—they recorded *hundreds*. Academically, this was interesting, but for someone who treated patients on a daily basis it was "a chaotic mess." How could a clinician track patients' risk factors and figure out which ones might add up to suicide? Joiner realized that risk factors are relevant, but the field needed to discover broader psychological patterns in the lives of people who died by suicide. And the patterns, which Joiner calls processes, should allow his model to help predict lethal outcomes. He created the interpersonal theory of suicide to fill the gap.

In the FSU auditorium, Joiner left his seat and took a stance at the whiteboard up front, a spot where he exuded ease. In his long career, he had probably spent months of his life at boards like this one.

"The interpersonal theory of suicide points to three processes that are key, and the idea is that when those three processes all converge in the same individual, that's when death by suicide becomes likely." Joiner drew a large circle and labeled it *Perceived Burdensomeness.*

"The first process is perceived burdensomeness. That's the idea that one's death will be worth more than one's life to other people. The perception of this feeling is true, though in reality it is almost never true."

Being a burden to others is a powerful idea but not quite as simple as it seems. What constitutes burdensomeness in the context of a family? Of a community? One might be a financial burden by not helping to support oneself or family members. One could be an emotional burden by consistently engaging in arguments or demanding attention. On the Flathead Indian Reservation, Kimberly Swaney's boyfriend, Dave, was an argumentative, disruptive force within Kimberly's household, so much so that she asked the police to remove him for treatment. Whether or not Kimberly and her daughter would have agreed, Dave might easily have viewed himself as a burden before he killed himself.

Michelle Matt dearly loved her brother, John, and would never have labeled him burdensome. But he was addicted to drugs, had clocked at least one stint in rehab, and often changed jobs. It's not hard to imagine that he thought of himself as someone who contributed nothing but disorder to his loved ones before he too killed himself. A burden.

In his seminal book *Why People Die by Suicide*, Joiner more closely defines "burdensomeness." One feels like a burden, Joiner writes, when one feels incompetent and ineffective, and worse, unfixable. In other words, we have a deep need to be competent and effective—to be good and impactful at our work, at our caretaking, at key aspects of our lives. Our competence permits us to contribute to our social group emotionally and materially. When none of this is true, and there's no way to repair it, we feel like a burden. It bears reiteration that the perceived harm to others is magnified by irregularities in the brain, as described by Dr. John Mann.

What happens then? In this merciless view of yourself in these circumstances the only alternatives are to continue sapping the love and energy of those around you, making them and you feel even worse, or taking your own life. Getting help and recovering aren't on the table.

Fonda Bryant claimed that she was doing her best as a mother but reasoned that if she killed herself, "My son would be better off." Generally, being a good mother and suicide are not compatible, but as Mann might argue, these sorts of ideas make sense to a mind reconfigured by suicide-grade depression. I found Fonda Bryant to be a doting mom to her son, Wesley. Wes is the too-rare son who genuinely enjoys hanging out with his mother. Their loving banter is life-affirming. As a boy of twelve, would Wesley have been better off if Fonda had suddenly taken her life, leaving him to be raised by members of their extended family? The pain he would've felt at his mother's suicide isn't hard to imagine. It would have been crippling and disorienting and it would probably have never really gone away. The impact on his development, and how he might have fared within a family of relatives, is impossible to gauge.

Greg Whitesell never discussed feeling like a burden to me. But after he was prevented from killing himself, he recognized that his death, not his life, would have imposed a burden on the lives of his friends and family, particularly his mother. He said, "I was only worried about myself, but my mom would be living the rest of her life without me. My pain would just be ending, but everybody else's around me would just be starting." As we've noted before, the catastrophe of losing a loved one to suicide dramatically increases the odds of taking one's own life.

Joiner holds that perceived burdensomeness is the idea that you strongly believe "everyone would be better off if you were gone." He said, "It's important to underline that word 'perceived,' because the idea is not that suicide decedents are actual burdens. I would never say such a thing, that is not my take on it. My take, rather, is that the soon-to-be suicide decedent has misperceived things. They think they're a burden on others and reason that 'if that's true then it follows that if I die I would remove the burden from everyone.' But they're mistaken about that. The tragedy of suicide is they don't realize that they're mistaken and they die on that basis."

However, in the past some people who killed themselves were not quite mistaken. Joiner points out that some historical cultures considered elderly people an excess cost to be respectfully done away with. These individuals may view their death as a way to alleviate their burdensomeness on others. Eskimo, ancient Scythians, and many other peoples separated by geography and time practiced versions of "senicide," or the killing or abandonment of the elderly, and enacted them especially during times of famine.

Senicide is connected to the concept of *altruistic suicide*, which occurs when people are so integrated into social groups that they lose their sense of individuality and are willing to give up their lives for the good of the group. Military history records many instances of soldiers falling on time-fused grenades to save their comrades. Joiner's theory holds that a sense of obligation to others—not the goal of killing oneself—is a form of extreme burdensomeness that drives altruistic suicides.

With regard to Fonda Bryant, Greg Whitesell, and others we've discussed, it's important to point out how *internal* the feelings of burdensomeness are, that being an unredeemable burden deserving self-execution is a construct of an unwell mind. In Joiner's model, burdensomeness brings about grueling psychological pain and shame. But it is not sufficient to bring about death. Suicide has two more formidable weapons in Joiner's model, and it needs all three to kill.

At the whiteboard, Joiner drew another large circle, which overlapped the first in an almond shape. He labeled the circle *Thwarted Belongingness.* He said, "Thwarted belongingness is really just a long way of saying loneliness. And mainly it's the subjective element of loneliness, not the objective one. The idea is not so much that people's worlds are literally unpeopled but they feel subjectively their internal world is unpeopled."

Loneliness, or lack of belongingness, also calls for fleshing out. In Joiner's view, like burdensomeness, loneliness reflects the absence of a bedrock need: to frequently interact with those who care for you. What's more, those interactions should be positive ones, and the people who care for you should represent stable relationships, not "a changing cast of relationship partners."

Joiner told me, "Say for instance there are popular high school students or college students who are objectively popular and yet they feel very lonely despite their popularity. Internally they feel alienated and lonely and die by suicide at times, leaving everyone so puzzled. 'How could that be?'" Joiner looks legitimately confused. "They were popular. And yet they didn't feel that way about themselves. They felt lonely."

No one better epitomizes a popular high schooler than Arlee

Warrior Greg Whitesell. Describing his feelings on the night he almost killed himself, he said, "Lonely. Really lonely, like I knew I had a lot of people on my side, I knew I had a lot of people that cared . . . but I was just pushing them away . . ."

It has become a cultural cliché that popular personalities who are much loved and presumably have no shortage of friends nonetheless die by suicide. Loneliness imposed by fame is often implicated. "I have very few friends," Marilyn Monroe once told an interviewer. And about her childhood, "I often felt lonely and wanted to die." In 1963 she died by overdose. Shortly before his 2018 suicide, author and TV celebrity Anthony Bourdain texted to his wife, "I hate being famous. I hate my job. I am lonely and living in constant uncertainty."

If loneliness kills, connections can keep us alive. As you may recall at the powwow on Patty and Billy Stevens's spread in Montana, Patty's granddaughter Erica told me she thought about suicide every day. She said only the pain it would cause her family keeps her from killing herself. And that's a feeling she knows well—her father had killed himself just three years before.

As we've seen, for people like Fonda Bryant the connections conferred by church membership and having children are protective. Connection, or *belongingness* in Joiner's terms, is a persistent protector that reduces the odds of suicide. On the other hand, thwarted belongingness is an odds-raising condition.

For example, being married is a protective buffer, but being single nudges your odds in the other direction. Getting divorced is a double whammy because it supports feelings of incompetence as a spouse and can cost the divorced their primary social connection and potentially children and friends, to say nothing of adding a possible financial strain. Generally speaking, being pregnant is a plus. Interestingly, so is being a fraternal or identical twin (but parents of multiple births are more likely to be depressed or anxious). Conjoined twins should be the exemplar of connectedness, but they haven't been studied.

Suicide rates tend to fall after big events experienced together by a lot of people. This is called the *pulling-together effect.* It helps explain why there are fewer suicides on Thanksgiving, Christmas, and Super Bowl Sundays, when groups of family and friends get together for a common purpose. The suicide death rate dropped by 5.6 percent between 2019 and 2020, when the COVID-19 pandemic struck. For 180 days after the 9/11 terrorist attacks, suicide rates in New York fell "significantly."

Now two ominous circles dominate Joiner's whiteboard—Perceived Burdensomeness and Thwarted Belongingness. Joiner gives a name to the almond-shaped oval where the circles overlap. He writes *the Desire to Die.* In other words, when these two psychological states exist in someone, they want to die but they do not necessarily kill themselves. Dr. David Jobes, who created the suicide prevention strategy CAMS (Collaborative Assessment and Management of Suicidality), cowrote a paper with Joiner that concluded that each year, there are on average 50,000 suicides in the United States and about 1.5 million attempted suicides, but there are about 15 million people who suffer from suicidal ideation—persistent, agonizing thoughts about killing themselves. Jobes says, "That's a lot of unnecessary suffering."

In Dr. John Mann's view, these individuals probably suffer from the brain abnormality that causes depression, plus the abnormality that causes suicidal ideation. But while their chances of suicide are dramatically enhanced, they don't kill themselves. In Dr. Joiner's view, these sufferers lack a psychological state that everyone who kills themselves has, including his own father. Joiner calls it the Capability for Suicide. He draws and labels the Capability for Suicide, the third and final circle in his suicide model.

While the other two processes set the stage for suicide, and untold suffering, it's the capability for self-destruction that completes the lethal puzzle.

Joiner said, "The capability for suicide has three elements and one of them is the fearlessness of death itself. The way I think about it is that it's natural to fear death. Creatures the world over avoid and fear death. We have brain circuits that lead us to avoid states like physical pain and illness and death itself. It's natural. And so one of the puzzles of suicide is that people are approaching death largely without fear, or at least they're able to stare down that fear."

Capability also requires tolerance of physical pain. Joiner said, "A lot of suicide methods are painful, not all but most. People imagine overdose scenarios won't be painful, then get surprised by the ordeal of it. So there are three elements of capability—fearlessness of death and physical pain tolerance, and finally pragmatics. How do you do it? A lot of people don't know how to operate a firearm, for example. An insight of the theory is that if you don't have the capability, it really doesn't matter how much desire for suicide you have, you're not going to be able to actually die. You'll feel a lot of anguish and that's an important thing in its own right, but you'll be protected from the worst outcome of all, death, because that final piece is not in place."

This strikes me as cold comfort. To have all the agony of suicide while desperately sought relief is out of reach. It almost seems like cruelty heaped upon cruelty. But of course this is shortsighted thinking. There are solutions for suicidal ideation, and we'll explore some.

People with all sorts of mental health issues do get better and go on to live satisfying and happy—yes, happy—lives. Greg Whitesell and Fonda Bryant are two such people, and I've spoken with others. The relief that death would bring is no relief at all but a transferal of pain, like waves in a lake caused by an asteroid, not a pebble. Waves that will cripple or even hasten the deaths of those closest to you.

How, then, does one acquire the cornerstones of capability, fearlessness of death, and tolerance for pain? As it turns out, mostly by practice.

In *Why People Die by Suicide*, Joiner writes, "A main thesis of this book is that those who die by suicide work up to the act. They do this in various ways—for instance, previous suicide attempts. . . . They get used to the pain and fear associated with self-harm, and thus gradually lose natural inhibitions against it." A prior suicide attempt is the leading indicator of suicide for this reason—individuals often try repeatedly and gain proficiency.

Recall that Fonda Bryant said, "To be honest I attempted suicide four times. Two times where I just thought this would be the best way for me and two times where I actually had a plan."

The fourth time, in 1995, Fonda had fine-tuned her approach for conclusive results. She never got that far because her aunt Spankie saw the signs and had her committed. But what about Greg Whitesell and Chris Dykshorn? Neither had a history of suicide attempts. Neither worked up to the act. But as we'll see, in Joiner's view preparing for suicide is a big tent that contains those who grow accustomed to pain but also those who inflict pain and violence on other beings. Take people who've grown accustomed to pain and experience higher suicide risk than average. They include athletes, intravenous drug users, prostitutes, tattoo aficionados, bulimics, and those who engage in self-cutting. They are people to whom pain doesn't have the customary sting. Studies have shown that people who are suicidal have higher tolerances for extreme temperatures of heat and cold and for electrical shock, and can endure more pain as the result of traffic accidents. Even preschoolers who have displayed signs of wanting to kill themselves show less pain and crying after getting hurt than a control group.

Hunters, physicians, and military personnel become habituated to acts of physical intrusion and violence, and also suffer from higher than average suicide risk. Both Greg and Chris hunted and came from hunting cultures. In Greg's case, hunting deer and elk is a deeply embedded feature of Native life in Montana. It's not a stretch to say most adolescents and adults on the Flathead Indian Reservation are familiar with firearms and with hunting and butchering animals to fill their freezers. Hunting is also a big part of rural life, and as a farmer, Chris Dykshorn was accustomed to slaughtering farm animals and game for the table. And he was an avid fisherman. Chris killed himself with the rifle he had used to hunt deer. Greg planned to shoot himself with his hunting rifle, but fortunately he was interrupted.

In Joiner's view, people get used to the pain and fear associated with self-harm in other ways besides hands-on experience. Joiner reports that rock icon Kurt Cobain obsessively watched a video of a politician shooting himself to death on live TV, perhaps preparing for his own suicide by gun. He was reportedly afraid of needles, heights, and firearms; however, he gradually trained himself to inject drugs, climb high above his stage on scaffolding, and recreationally shoot guns.

Joiner isn't quite finished with the whiteboard yet. Overlapping in a textbook Venn diagram are the three circles of the Interpersonal

Theory of Suicide: Thwarted Belongingness, Perceived Burdensomeness, and Capability for Suicide. The first two intersect in an oval shape labeled *Desire to Die*. Now Joiner labels the small triangle where all three circles converge. If Hell has a center, this is it. He labels it *Lethal or Near-Lethal Suicide Attempts*. It is here at the convergence of three psychological processes that attempting to kill yourself becomes at least very likely, at most a certainty.

Since Joiner first introduced it in 2005, the interpersonal theory of suicide has become psychology's most debated and commented-upon suicide model, though to be fair, there aren't that many. Joiner has rebuffed many critics, acknowledged others, and revised the theory as it garnered adjectives from the psychology community such as *elegant*, *insightful*, and *effective*. It has fans and detractors around the world, but it's been thoroughly tested and generally found to measure up.

The theory's major achievement is that while it acknowledges

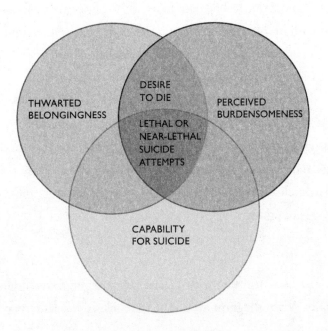

the risk factors that have been linked to suicidal behavior, it doesn't get bogged down in them. It suggests that we instead take a step back and focus on the impacts of those factors on the mental state of individuals. What's happening in their internal, subjective reality? For therapists, that's an invaluable tool. Broadly, it permits them to determine which patient has a foot in any of the circles. Who is challenged by feeling like a burden? Who is painfully lonely? Who has both feet planted in the center circle and probably won't live long without speedy intervention? Interestingly, of all the links offered by the theory, it's the one between feeling like a burden and having capability that critics find most persuasive. Apparently, extreme loneliness doesn't hurt us as much as burdening others.

If therapists can anticipate with only 50 percent certainty which of their patients will kill themselves, it would seem certain that applying the theory would tip the odds toward identification and survival. Despite how robust his theory has proven to be, however, Joiner doesn't fully buy this conclusion.

"You're asking yourself the impossible—to try to identify up front who will kill themselves and when. It's beyond us. What you can do is have a sense of where people are on a spectrum of risk. And once you know that, there are actionable things that you can do as a consequence. It's still very challenging because the array of risk factors is so variable. But I think the value of the theory I've developed is that it tries to boil that down a little bit and make it more manageable."

Joiner's life's work has grown beyond his landmark theory to training future clinicians and researchers. What began as a quest to understand his father's self-destruction has grown into a mission to help prepare the next generation of suicidologists to take on America's least understood and most painful epidemic.

Joiner told me, "This theory, this day-to-day work really is not about my dad's suicide anymore. What it's about is the fact that tomorrow in the United States, over one hundred families are going to be bereaved by suicide. One hundred. Just tomorrow. And then the next day. And then the next day after that. And so on and so forth. And that's just in our one country. That's a human tragedy, and I want to prevent that."

If you are thinking about suicide or if you or someone you know is in emotional crisis, please call or text 988 at any time to reach the 988 Suicide and Crisis Lifeline for confidential, free crisis support.

CHAPTER EIGHT

STABILIZATION AND SUICIDE-FOCUSED INTERVENTION

Emergency treatment of people who are suicidal in the United States is a patchwork of services that differ from state to state and even county to county. There is no working national policy in place for suicide treatment or prevention. This is in part because the US Constitution does not explicitly delegate health care concerns to either the states or the federal government. The Tenth Amendment holds that powers not assigned to the federal government are reserved for the states or the people. Suicide treatment therefore varies, depending on what state you're in. Presumably the federal government *could* take control of suicide prevention just as they've taken charge of monitoring workplace safety standards through OSHA (the Occupational Safety and Health Administration) and the production of drugs through the FDA (the Food and Drug Administration). But federal powers are more likely to leave specific decisions to the states. For example, during the COVID-19 pandemic the CDC, a federal agency, issued guidelines, but decisions about mask wearing, social distancing, and school closures were made by the states.

As it stands across the nation, a suicidal person might expect one or two nights in an emergency department under observation, and a therapy session that may or may not be conducted by a mental health professional. Before the patient is released, he or she may receive a referral to a professional, but once released, hospital staff generally will not follow up to inquire about how they are feeling or if they are receiving therapy. Once discharged, many patients do not engage in follow-up care, which puts them at a greater risk for suicide. As we've discussed, there is a dangerous gap between emergency psychiatric treatment and vital follow-up therapy.

But whether those follow-up therapy sessions are weeks or months away may make no difference if the patient has no health insurance or cannot afford their prohibitive cost. As we've learned, there are paths to low- or no-cost mental health care, and we'll discuss one ahead. However, with few exceptions, they are complicated for anyone to navigate, more so for someone in the aftermath of a suicidal crisis or who lacks funds. As Erica told me on the Flathead Indian Reservation, "If you're not rich you might as well just die."

That's the tragic state of affairs for many people suffering a suicidal crisis, to say nothing of other mental health conditions, here in the nation with the world's largest economy. Again, in some states and some counties within states, the situation is better, sometimes much better. But generally speaking, a deficit in mental health care costs the lives of countless Americans. Their families, friends, and loved ones subsequently bear suicide's traumatic aftershocks.

Fortunately, a new kind of help is on the way in every state. Sponsored by US senators Roy Blunt and Debbie Stabenow, the Excellence in Mental Health and Addiction Treatment Act in 2014 provided funding for Certified Community Behavioral Health Clinics (CCBHCs) around the country. Every state receives money for mental health clinics in their communities, paid for by Medicaid and the Substance Abuse and Mental Health Services Administration (SAMHSA), a branch of the US Department of Health and Human Services. The money comes with strict conditions. CCBHCs are required to provide a comprehensive set of services, which include 24-7 crisis support, outpatient mental health and substance abuse treatment services, immediate screenings, risk assessments, and diagnoses, care coordination, and partnerships with emergency rooms, law enforcement, and veterans' organizations.

What this can mean for individuals in suicidal crisis is breathtaking. Any adult or child who walks through clinic doors can receive care whether they can afford it or not. For homebound patients who have a CCBHC in their region, a mobile crisis team will be dispatched to provide care. People in urgent need but not imminently suicidal will receive an appointment within twenty-four hours. For more routine mental health needs, patients can get an appointment within ten days. Currently, there are 480 CCBHCs across forty-nine states and territories, with plans to add more centers every two years until at least 2025.

David DeVoursney, MPP, a division director at SAMHSA, heads a department with hands-on input into CCBHCs. "I'm really excited," he told me. "This effort is really hopeful. Since the 1960s, there's been a long narrative of taking mental health patients out of institutions and serving their needs in outpatient facilities. The second part of the plan never happened. Finally it's coming about. And CCBHCs are our best hope of developing those services.

"To be able to solve this decades-old problem with the mental health care system is amazing."

If CCBHCs sound too good to be true, they kind of still are. While the clinics number in the hundreds, they're not evenly distributed across the country, and for many people, care can be prohibitively distant. The federal government has had trouble consistently funding the clinics, which are often run by local governments or nonprofits. This has made it hard to keep staff and pay for services.

Nevertheless, CCBHCs are a welcome bright light in our nation's murky patchwork of suicide and mental health interventions.

Fortunately, there is a tool that is available to almost everyone in a suicidal crisis who reaches care, and it doesn't suffer from funding or staffing problems. This simple intervention is used in emergency departments and clinics across the United States and abroad and has saved innumerable lives. It even meets Denmark's laudably high standards for mental health care and is used throughout that country. It's called the Safety Planning Intervention, and it was developed in 2008 by clinical psychologists Drs. Barbara Stanley and Gregory Brown. They explored the critical flaw in suicide care—the time gap between a patient's visit to an emergency department and the initiation of critical therapy sessions—and found it to be a dangerous place indeed. A 2017 study concluded that during the first three months after discharge from a psychiatric hospital, a patient's suicide rate is about 100 times greater than average. A 2019 study showed that for a year after their visits, Californians treated at an emergency department for deliberate self-harm had a suicide rate 57 times higher than average.

Barbara Stanley is a gifted psychologist and professor who told me, "The Safety Plan Intervention came about because there was a huge dearth of evidence-based interventions to prevent suicide.

Which is really surprising because there is no problem in psychiatry that has greater mortality than people who become suicidal." She added, "There was a lot of room for a brief intervention that clinicians could use and make accessible to many people."

To fill that empty room, Stanley and Brown created the Safety Plan Intervention, a list of strategies that will help people who are suicidal get through a suicidal crisis. The intervention involves the clinician and patient collaboratively completing a safety plan form to identify coping strategies and resources that can be used whenever they feel like a suicidal crisis is emerging. It works like this.

At a conference table in the department of psychiatry at Columbia University Irving Medical Center, Stanley and Ron Joss are deep in conversation. Joss is a real estate agent in his forties with salt-and-pepper hair and a hangdog demeanor. Yesterday he tried to kill himself by overdosing on pain medication. Stanley assesses his suicidality by having him reveal the facts of his attempt.

Distracted by his recent divorce, Joss has seen his home sales slip and his boss told him his job was in jeopardy. On top of that, his ex-wife moved out of state with their two children, and he'd had painful knee surgery, which had not healed well. He's also in recovery for alcohol abuse. In tremendous emotional distress, Joss tried to take his own life. When he missed a scheduled phone call with his children, his ex-wife intervened.

Stanley listened carefully to Joss's story about how the crisis unfolded and then resolved. It escalated to the point of overdosing and then diminished once Joss was rescued by his ex-wife and brought to the hospital to see Stanley.

"Things really snowballed for you, didn't they?" said Stanley. She tells Joss she's sorry he felt so bad that he wanted to end his life but is glad that he is willing to discuss what happened. "Would you be interested in learning about a tool that could help you through rough times?"

Joss answered, "Absolutely. I didn't want to die. I just wanted to stop the pain."

Stanley said, "That's good to hear that you actually didn't want to kill yourself. It sounds like it would be helpful to discuss some strategies to get through a crisis without acting on the urge to die." Stanley went on to tell him, "There are six steps on the safety plan, and the first step is to identify warning signs. Warning signs are thoughts, feelings, or behaviors that tell you you're headed for emotional trouble. So now we're gonna identify your warning signs so that you know when you need to grab the safety plan and start using it. We don't want you to make another suicide attempt, okay?"

Joss nodded.

"And what are some of your warning signs? What made you think about hurting yourself?"

"My boss. When he threatened to fire me. It brought up everything else that had been going wrong. And it just made me angry at myself and it kept building up."

"How did that feel?"

"It was tight and numb at the same time. It's like a ball of numbness in my chest, a ball of darkness. And an overall feeling of dread."

"And that happened at work?"

"No, when I got home. I was trying to figure out what I could do to make myself feel better. And the more I thought about how to get out of the funk I was in, the hole I had dug for myself just kept getting deeper."

"How awful."

"And it just got to the point where I thought my kids would be better off without me. I couldn't think of a single person in my life who wouldn't be better off if I was just not around."

Both doctor and patient fell silent. Even the seasoned Stanley seemed at a loss over Joss's bleak assessment of his own value.

"So I swallowed the pills."

Stanley had Joss's full attention as she drew a simple axis graph in her notebook. She labeled the horizontal axis *Time* and the vertical axis *Risk*. She drew a line shaped like a hill. It began at the bottom left, went upward, then curved back down again on the right.

Stanley said, "This is the suicidal risk curve. We want to try to get you off this curve before you get to the top." Stanley tapped her pen at the top of the hill. "But the other part that is really important to notice is time. You are not having suicidal thoughts now, right?"

Joss shook his head. "Absolutely not."

Stanley tapped the lowest part of the hill on the right. "That shows that suicidal thoughts do come down and it's really important

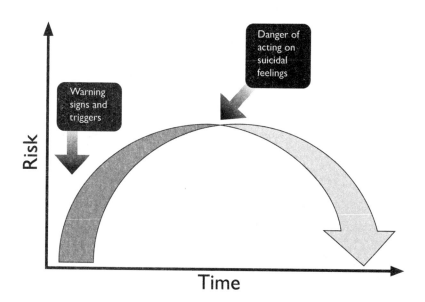

for you to remember that fact. Even without the safety plan, the passage of time enables you to become less suicidal. Nobody stays suicidal forever. And if you don't act on your suicidal feelings, they eventually come down no matter what."

Joss looked relieved. "Okay."

"The passage of time is your friend. And I'm not as interested in what your boss said as I am about how it made you feel. How did you feel when he told you he might have to let you go?"

Joss thought about it. "Helpless. I hadn't known my sales numbers were so bad. I didn't know that I was that far behind and I felt helpless about how to get the numbers back up."

Stanley drew a line near the start of the curve and wrote *Helplessness*. She said, "I don't want to put words in your mouth but I'd say feeling helplessness is one of your warning signs. Later you said you felt a tightness in your chest and you felt numb, right?"

Joss nodded.

Stanley drew another line above the first and wrote. *Numbness in chest.*

"Then you said something very striking that you felt right before you took the pills. Remember?"

"Everyone would be better off without me."

"Exactly." Stanley wrote that down at the highest point of the curve, the top of the hill. "And that to me is like, wow, you're very close to doing something to hurt yourself."

Stanley reiterated an important point about warning signs. They may begin with an emotional event, such as Joss's talk with his boss or an argument with a spouse. But what's important is the person's internal reaction to that event.

Stanley's position is consistent with what Drs. Mann and Joiner assert about the internal state of people who attempt to kill themselves. Events in life might objectively be bad, but in the internal life of persons in crises those events feel much, much worse. Academia has a phrase for it—the "diathesis-stress" model of psychological disorders. *Diathesis* comes from the Greek word for "disposition." The model holds that everyone has a certain amount of natural disposition for developing a disorder, such as thoughts of suicide. Some have a greater disposition than others, and these are the people whose feelings are more intense and who tend to kill themselves. Stress triggers, such as a fight with a spouse or a threat from a boss, can make their inclination grow.

And therein lies an insight into one of the major *Whys* of suicide. When someone we care for takes their life, we're saddled with a lifetime of *Whys*. Why did they do it? This answer is painfully simple; we cannot really know what someone else is feeling, especially someone in suicidal crisis. To quote Dr. John Mann, "It's because what you see is not what they see." We cannot know this major *Why*.

Fortunately, the safety plan can stop a suicidal urge in its tracks.

Dr. Stanley had Joss write his warning signs on the safety plan template. Having the patient fill in the plan increases his or her buy-in to the intervention and the likelihood they'll follow it.

And it's important to note that the safety plan is designed to be completed with a mental health professional who is competent in the intervention. Their training ensures that the rationale for the plan is thoroughly explained, then collaboratively filled out with the patient to identify the most helpful and feasible strategies, with no omissions or shortcuts. People who are given a blank safety plan and told to fill it out on their own often don't, and if they do, they're not always likely to follow it. Completing a safety plan with a loved one is not optimal but it's better than winging it on your own. That said, some particularly disciplined people have been known to download the safety plan from the internet, where it is easily found, fill it out, and work it to a T on their own.

If Joss experienced any of the warning signs, he would grab the completed safety plan and follow it by proceeding to step 2—internal coping strategies. Stanley told me, "We have them identify the things that they can do just by themselves because a lot of the times people get suicidal at night when they are alone. Something that will engross them even for a little while from their suicidal thoughts. Really simple things—this is not rocket science." Stanley suggest playing with your dog or watching favorite programs on television. "Like *The Simpsons* for example," she said. "Comedies are good. Have them record their favorite comedies in advance so they don't have to go searching for these things when they're suicidal." Video games can be good, but long, dense books—probably not. Dostoevsky, for example, isn't guaranteed to make you feel better. And music. "If they want to listen to music, we work with them to identify what kind of music is certain to not make them feel worse and, hopefully, makes them feel better."

Ron Joss volunteered that he liked to run. "You know, usually when I'm running, I'll put on a podcast and no matter what's going on, I'm kind of in a zone."

"Okay," said Stanley, "but we'll put a couple of cautions on that. One, pick what you're going to listen to very carefully because we want to make sure it's not something that's going to make you feel worse. And second, it's fine to put down running with your headphones on, but you're not gonna do that in the middle of the night should you get suicidal."

"No."

Stanley helped Joss think of another activity to keep his mind occupied, then they moved on.

"Okay," said Stanley. "So now we have three distracting activities that you can do on your own without contacting anybody else. These activities may help you not become suicidal. They may just take you right down. And so you put the safety plan away and you go on with whatever you are doing. If it doesn't work, then you go on to the next step."

Step 3 is writing down people and social settings that provide distractions. Stanley issued more cautions. Call people you should speak with, such as old friends and relatives. Don't call your ex-wife and inflame your feelings. Don't phone your boss and give him a piece of your mind. Included here are visits to social settings such as a friend's house or a park or a gym but probably not a bar, for obvious reasons. Find places where you feel at home and engaged and, most of all, distracted. Interestingly, with these people and places, you *don't* talk about your suicidal feelings. As Stanley says, "Sometimes people have a hard time telling other people that they are feeling bad or that they're feeling suicidal. But social support and social engagement are really helpful at taking a person outside themselves. So, at this stage, you're just seeking interaction."

So far the safety plan has relied on self-help measures, but now it shifts gears. If the suicidal crisis has *still* not passed, the plan starts pulling out all the stops. In step 4, you ask for help from family and friends who you think would be helpful to you. Stanley told Joss, "The next step is people who you could turn to and say, 'I'm in trouble. I'm having a crisis.' Or, hopefully, you could say, 'I'm feeling suicidal.'" Joss was instructed to come up with three people closest to him. And he will have to tell them they are in his safety plan. That is so they won't be unprepared should he call. And that means telling them he's made a suicide attempt. That's a big step.

Stanley shared the tough news. "That would mean having a conversation with that person and letting them know what's been going on underneath and whether you could rely on them. And often the people you would use as distractions are not gonna be good for telling them you're in a crisis."

Going over these steps is not for the squeamish, but patients understand their lives may hang in the balance. The temporary discomfort is worth it.

Now, at this point, despite your best efforts with all the earlier steps, your crisis may *still* threaten your life. Step 5 is where you talk to a professional, a therapist, a pastor or other spiritual adviser, or call or text the Suicide and Crisis Lifeline at 988 for confidential, free crisis support. Step 5 may lead you to an emergency department or a psychiatric hospital, but if that's the advice of professionals, that's where you need to be. In this step and others it's important to write down relevant phone numbers because a person in a suicidal crisis should not face additional complications such as locating telephone numbers.

The importance of the last step of the safety plan cannot be overstated. By now we know that ridding the environment of deadly means of suicide is vital in the treatment of a person in crisis. Step 6 is called making the environment safe.

Stanley said, "What we mean by that is how do we put time and space between the suicidal person and the means they would use to kill themselves? It's with the same idea of why we use the safety plan to begin with.

"On the risk curve, suicidal urges don't last forever—they're relatively short lived. This is why it is very, very problematic if there is a suicidal person in the home and there are loaded guns around the house. We know that more than ninety percent of people who use a firearm in a suicide attempt die. So, they are extraordinarily lethal and often readily available. This is very difficult especially with firearms because people are very attached to their guns and they don't want to give them up."

Locking up guns and ammo separately is generally not optimal because the person in crisis may have the combination to the gun safe or keys to gun locks and may be tempted to use them if another suicidal crisis occurs. It's better to temporarily store firearms with a friend or with a local police department. Patient Ron Joss volunteered that he's a member of a gun club that will store firearms for members. He owns a rifle; he agreed to take it in. Stanley will contact him after he leaves the hospital to check on whether the firearm is safely stored.

Stanley told me, "Another big one is pills. A lot of people have lots of extra medications lying around the house. We talk with them about disposing of those medications. If somebody is on a psychotropic medication like an antidepressant or an antipsychotic medication, we talk with them about limiting the number of pills they have in their possession at any one point in time. But that often means having a trusted person in their life with whom they feel comfortable saying, 'I have a month's worth of medication; I'm gonna keep a week's worth; can you hold the other three weeks for me?'"

Over-the-counter pain and cold medications should not be overlooked. In sufficient quantities, medicines containing ibuprofen, acetaminophen, and aspirin can kill you. Advil and Tylenol are trade names for ibuprofen and acetaminophen, respectively. Some cough and cold medicines can cause extreme harm too.

Stanley said, "That's another good reason to have a clinician help a patient fill out the safety plan. The clinician has a lot of experience with trying to figure out in a creative and respectful manner the ways that we can limit the patient's access to medicines for a relatively short period of time."

At the bottom of the safety plan is a later addition that is perhaps its most potent step. It's a kind of safety net hanging beneath the whole strategy. It asks about reasons for living that are important.

Back in the conference room, Stanley asked Joss, "So what is that for you when you think about it?"

Joss answered, "My kids. Jack and Sarah. They just moved out of state with their mom, but I talk to them a lot."

"So it sounds like they're very special to you. Very important. Okay. So why don't you write them down?"

Of course many people don't have children, but many people have beloved brothers and sisters and other relatives and friends who'd grievously suffer should they die. Some have pets that are dependent upon them. Others have lifetime goals they have not yet achieved, or a spiritual faith that is the one thing they live for. There are many good reasons to stay alive.

In the big picture the safety plan does not substitute for prompt, ongoing therapy following a suicidal crisis. But it has been proven to be a durable stopgap and even a kind of therapy on its own to be used until alternatives are available. Patients have dubbed its list of things to do "working the plan," after the Alcoholics Anonymous saying "working the program." One military veteran told Stanley, "This is really helpful to me because I've had many suicidal crises where I feel like I just had to white-knuckle it through. Like, just hang on 'til the crisis passed. And now I have something to do instead." Many thousands of individuals share this sentiment.

Stanley said, "The whole idea behind the safety plan is that we want people to learn how to cope on their own as much as possible. Of course, we want them to reach out when they need to reach out, we have people on their plan they reach out to, but it's on their own initiative."

Joss would take his safety plan with him as his appointment with Dr. Stanley came to a close. But as a final measure, Stanley had him take a photo of the plan to keep on his smartphone so it's never far away.

What happens to Ron Joss, then? The safety plan is what's known as a "stabilization plan." It is meant to prevent another suicide attempt, but it doesn't address psychological disorders or risk factors that led to his attempt in the first place. In a perfect world, Joss would quickly begin therapy through his employee health benefits plan. His hospital would follow up with messages of interest and care, which are proven to reduce suicide attempts. Or, if he isn't covered by insurance or doesn't have the means, he might get himself to a CCBHC, if one is close by.

Joss might benefit from talk therapy such as cognitive behavioral therapy (CBT) or dialectical behavioral therapy (DBT). According to research, CBT is typically the more successful treatment for conditions like post-traumatic stress disorder, obsessive compulsive disorder, phobias, depression, and anxiety. DBT is frequently the best option for treating borderline personality disorder and self-harming behaviors. Both therapies are effective in reducing suicide attempts. Until therapy begins, Joss can ward off additional attempts by "working the plan."

Many studies have tried to determine which interventions are most successful against suicide. Therapists have created versions of both CBT and DBT that are customized to address suicidal behavior. And there are other stabilization plans and therapy types as well. A quick method called the Crisis Response Plan (CRP) is a calming technique developed by a suicidal person in collaboration with a trained clinician. It's often handwritten on an index card for easy access. Collaborative Assessment and Management of Suicidality (CAMS) builds a therapeutic alliance with suicidal patients from a place of empathy.

Some interventions are good at stopping suicide attempts but don't reduce suicidal ideation. If you treat people who attempt suicide, you may fail to address the causes of their underlying ideas and thoughts about killing themselves. But if you could treat sufferers of ideation, you'd generally get fewer downstream suicide attempts.

Each year in the United States some 15 million people suffer from suicidal ideation—persistent, agonizing thoughts about killing themselves. About 1.2 million of them attempt suicide. About 47,000 of those individuals end their lives. What moves those who suffer from suicidal ideation to go further and make a suicide attempt? As Thomas Joiner observes, the capability for suicide is what separates the thought from the act. And that capability can be learned. Far better to start upstream and attack ideation before suicide's progression goes any further.

In a classroom a youthful middle-aged man with styled white hair said, "With patients I'm really transparent and I'll say things like *of course* you can kill yourself. But is that the best thing to do? Since you're here with me and I'm a licensed therapist, I'm thinking a part of you is not quite prepared to terminate your biological existence.

And if that's true, then we should consider what we can do together to make your life more worth living. You have everything to gain and nothing to lose. And the fact of the matter is, you can always kill yourself later."

You can always kill yourself later. That floored me. Even though he said it in a matter-of-fact way, the statement seemed at odds with the warm, optimistic demeanor of David Jobes. But the Catholic University of America professor was making a point about the therapy he created, CAMS. At thirty-five years old, CAMS is a relative newcomer in the therapeutic world, but its ability to reduce suicidal ideation is backed by randomized controlled trials and the enthusiasm of some thirty thousand clinicians around the world who have been trained in CAMS. I encountered CAMS in use everywhere from Charlotte, North Carolina, to Copenhagen, Denmark. It has achieved success because it reduces symptoms of depression and hopelessness *and* suicidal ideation in six to eight sessions. When you consider that some suicidal patients have been hospitalized for years on end and some undergo CBT and DBT also for years, CAMS is a breakthrough.

The point Jobes was making was about CAMS's radical honesty. Honesty is perhaps the most important of the therapy's four guiding principles, or "pillars," as Jobes calls them. The point of honesty is to pull down the wall separating therapist and patient, to put all your cards on the table. In most places by law, if a therapist thinks you're an imminent danger to yourself, they can put you in a hospital. Jobes puts that card on the table. You are a free individual with your own volition—you can go kill yourself if you want. That card goes on the table. Radical honesty helps neutralize the traditional power dynamic between patient and therapist, in which the therapist has all the power—including the ability to have you committed to a psychiatric hospital—and the patient has none, except to take their own life. In Jobes's experience, dispensing with the power dynamic strengthens the therapeutic alliance needed for treatment.

And honesty helps patients keep their sense of autonomy. Someone willing to tell you "You can always kill yourself later" is more invested in your free will than someone threatening to put you in a hospital. And one of the carrots Jobes dangles is that with CAMS you don't have to go to a hospital at all. With CAMS the emergency-department-therapy-session-referral pipeline doesn't exist. You go straight from suicidal incident to evaluation and CAMS. No hospital and usually no medicines. What have you got to lose? *You can always kill yourself later.*

Jobes told me, "From a clinical standpoint, we wanna hit the pause button and say, 'Before you kill yourself forever, have you turned over every stone? Can we help you do that to see if there's a way to make this life livable?' And I think that's a compelling argument since we're talking about forever. We all get to be dead soon enough, what is the hurry?"

In tens of thousands of rooms all across America, therapists and patients talk about forever. We are familiar with the traditional couch and chair, the two facing chairs, the two chairs with a table between—variations on the static geography of most therapy rooms. Butts planted, nobody moves. But as I witnessed a CAMS therapy session with an undergraduate student, Maggie, it wasn't static. There were three chairs in the room, one for Maggie, one for Jobes, and an empty chair beside Maggie. Maggie was a student in her early twenties, a brunette athlete whose face reflected abject pain.

The session began much like the safety plan, with Jobes gaining a baseline understanding of Maggie's situation in her own words. In brief, Maggie's boyfriend, Tyler, suddenly died of an undiagnosed heart ailment. Both were on the university swim team and had many friends in common. Upon her boyfriend's death, Maggie sank into depression. Her roommates were cruelly unsympathetic.

"Nobody really wanted to be around me because I was so sad. My roommates kicked me out. They said they didn't want to room with me because I was too much to handle, so I got moved to another room. And this whole time I've been so alone in this grieving process."

One night, Maggie set a timer for ten minutes and texted her team group chat. "Somebody help," she said. She decided that if nobody came within ten minutes, she would swallow medication she'd been prescribed for depression. Fortunately, two women showed up to talk. She was referred to the counseling center and given an appointment with Dr. Jobes.

Jobes expressed heartfelt sympathy and concern, then introduced CAMS by saying, "I suspect there are things on your mind that we can address together. I've found that going through a written assessment together can help us understand the nature of those things. It's a tool that I've used many times and it kinda helps me understand what you're going through."

"Okay."

"And we fill it out together, if that's okay."

"All right."

"And to do it, I could take a seat next to you if you don't mind."

Then it happened. The action. With Maggie's assent, Jobes rose and took the seat next to her, bringing along his clipboard and papers. It was like a chess move. Now they were close together but not too close. This therapy jujitsu accomplishes a couple of things. Like

Stanley and Brown's safety plan, it pulls back the curtain on what the therapist is writing and thinking about, because therapist and patient fill out the document, called the CAMS Suicide Status Form, side by side. No secrets, and that reinforces buy-in and collaboration. Second, it promotes another one of CAMS's primary principles—empathy. Empathy doesn't mean as much coming from the other side of the room. Empathy needs proximity.

Jobes told me, "We used to have a different approach. At school in the eighties and nineties, the bulk of inpatient psychiatry was like, Have you thought about suicide? *Yes I have.* You can't kill yourself. *Oh yeah? It's my life, I can do what I want.* No you can't! *Yes I can.* Wanna bet?"

Boom, off to the psychiatric hospital.

"And that's the dynamic we're trying to avoid," said Jobes. "Because one of our pillars is empathy. But when you think of empathy with people who are suicidal, there are some issues around it. Why would it be difficult for clinicians to be empathic of suicidal risk?"

First, therapists are afraid they might lose a patient who, despite therapy, kills themselves. Jobes has lost patients. Many therapists have lost patients. It's devastating. Therapists either shoulder the risk of attaching to somebody and possibly having them take their life, or they keep a "professional" distance and neglect empathy.

And second, lawsuits. "There's a tremendous fear of malpractice," said Jobes. "And for some clinicians it's just paralyzing. Because they're afraid if they lose a patient, the family is going to sue them. So even though the patient is not extremely suicidal, it's better to put them in the hospital. Better safe than sorry. Have your rear end covered, so to speak, right?"

But with rear ends covered, empathy will have flown, and with it honesty and the kind of alliance Jobes and Maggie are beginning to forge. Three pillars come into play now, with honesty and empathy supporting collaboration.

Maggie fills in the CAMS Suicide Status Form and together she and Jobes build a baseline for her condition. On a scale of 1 to 5 they rate feelings like psychological pain, agitation, and stress, and indicate the source of those feelings. For example, Maggie's psychological pain is a 5—the worst—and its source is "not being able to talk to Tyler," her deceased boyfriend. She rates her agitation level as a 5 too. She writes the source of this stress is when she's in the pool because it reminds her of Tyler.

Next the plan addresses Maggie's reasons for wanting to live. But unlike the safety plan, CAMS also takes onboard her reasons for wanting to die. In order of importance, Maggie's reasons for living are to honor Tyler's memory, to graduate from university, and to get a dog. For dying, Maggie cites that she's alone now, she cannot have fun, and she feels useless. Then, alarmingly, she rates her desire to live a 2 out of 8. Not very high. But she rates wanting to die as a 2 also, which is at least better than a 3 out of 8.

Jobes learns Maggie's suicidal ideation appears as soon as she wakes up in the morning. She remembers Tyler is gone and she wants to die. This rumination lasts for two or more hours. She's thought about how she might kill herself. She's a frequent metro train rider. There's a station on campus.

Maggie says, "I think if I really wanted to go through with it, I could just jump in front of the metro." One night she thought about going to the metro station, but she learned it was closed.

It all goes down on the form in Maggie's hand, along with more of what we recognize as risk factors and warning signs. Maggie's been drinking alone, she's sleeping poorly, she feels like a burden, and she's suffered two significant losses. Tyler of course, but also her lifetime joy, swimming. And her friends have abandoned her.

In Thomas Joiner's interpersonal theory of suicide she's got both feet firmly planted in Thwarted Belongingness (Loneliness) and Perceived Burdensomeness. Does Maggie have the Capability to kill herself as well?

From an observer's perspective, Maggie is lost deep in the woods. The CAMS Suicide Status Form breaks down her suicidal ideas into precise, painful parts. In total so far, they are alarming, almost like a psychological autopsy of a suicide that's already occurred. And you can understand why some therapists might get her to a hospital pronto. Not Jobes. In his view, hospital treatment would not save her from suicide and CAMS is focused on suicide, as he put it, "like a dog with a bone."

In fact, the laser focus on suicide means there's much that therapist and patient will not talk about if it is not connected to suicide. No one's going to ask about your relationship with your parents. Your birth order among your siblings isn't very important here either.

Jobes says, "We're not going to talk about a whole lot of other things while you're engaged in this intervention because we're trying to take suicide off the table. Now, here's the thing, for some people that's good news. You know like 'Phew, I really don't want to have these feelings anymore. I can't go to sleep at night.' For other people it's kind of like, 'Uh, this is my thing. This is actually a way that kind of keeps me alive. This is sort of like my warm blanket and you're trying to take it away from me.'"

Is this Maggie? No, while she has evaluated her own risk for suicide as a 3 out of 5—bad news—she's also told Jobes that her suicidal ideas frighten her. They don't bring her comfort. And Jobes indicates on the form that in his view Maggie is not in imminent danger of suicide.

On the other hand, he understands those who find suicide comforting. For them, it represents the promise of relief from the pain of depression and suicidal thoughts. In a 2014 study of 217 patients with a history of recurrent depression and suicidality, 15 percent reported feelings of comfort from thoughts of suicide. CAMS may not be the answer for these patients or for the chronically suicidal. And it may not be as effective as more traditional approaches to deeply entrenched conditions. "So this addresses the idea that if you've got a hammer, all the world's a nail," Jobes says. "CAMS isn't always the best therapy. What we really need are different tools for different kinds of needs."

CAMS brings a large toolbox to its treatment plan that may include elements of behavioral therapies. Its forte is bringing the tools to bear on someone who's having their first or second phase of persistent thoughts about suicide, and who finds that ideation disturbing. Like Maggie.

Contained within the CAMS Suicide Status Form is a stabilization plan that covers now familiar ground. Maggie agrees to remove lethal means from her room, which means giving her medication to a friend and having the friend dispense one pill at a time. It also means avoiding the metro, going on the metro with a companion, or taking a taxi. It means getting rid of ropes and knives.

Jobes tells her, "The thing about lethal means is that when they're available, they're a temptation. And this intervention is designed to save your life. But to save your life, we've got to keep you alive and not have you tempted by other means."

Maggie thinks up coping activities, things to keep her mind off suicide, including watching a movie, working out in the gym, journaling, and listening to music. She writes down people she can contact to decrease her isolation as well as the 988 Suicide and Crisis Lifeline, which she can call or text anytime for confidential, free crisis support. Jobes gives her his personal cell number in case of an emergency.

Maggie plans to stay away from the pool for the foreseeable future because of its painful associations.

The collaborators have one more task to complete—a treatment plan. Jobes proposes six sessions. "Most people respond to this intervention by six sessions. And that may seem crazy, but that's what the research shows." Jobes then asks Maggie to identify two problems that have the most potential to her for self-harm. He calls them drivers. "These are the things that made suicide become an option for you."

Being alone has come up repeatedly as a source of agitation and suicidal ideation. Jobes says, "There's a number of things that we can do to attack this particular issue. We want to decrease your isolation and increase your social support. We're going to do something called behavioral activation, which is a part of cognitive behavioral therapy. Behavioral activation helps us understand how behaviors impact emotions."

The second big driver is Tyler being gone. For that, Jobes prescribes grief therapy. Maggie needs to grieve her loss. "I'd like to learn more about Tyler," says Jobes.

Maggie nods her assent.

"And about your relationship. And there's some bibliotherapy for grief too. I'll prepare some readings for you."

Maggie looks a little wiped out. Jobes says so far what has only been implied. Her stabilization plan will help keep bad thoughts at bay until their next session. And with each session as they address her feelings, her overall ratings of risk should go down. As treatment of her drivers evolves, overall distress will decrease along with her suicidal ideation. Toward the end of CAMS she can look forward to meaningfully reduced suicidal ideation, an increased sense of hope, and a gradual reconsideration of a life worth living.

Maggie smiles hopefully. "That would be nice."

Jobes says, "Most people do get better with this intervention. It's very focused on suicide but it's also focused on what's on your mind. We're going to see what fits and tailor your treatment as we go. Every session, we'll update the treatment plan to make sure we're getting at the drivers that put your life in peril."

It's been a productive albeit emotional meeting of the minds over the sources of Maggie's crisis. A majority of CAMS patients report that they enjoy the therapy. In a final collaborative act, Maggie and Jobes sign and date the CAMS Treatment Plan, along with copies that patients take from every session.

Jobes notes, "CAMS does not eradicate every vestige of suicidal thoughts and feelings; instead, it helps patients better manage such thoughts and feelings while becoming more behaviorally stable. The single biggest effect of CAMS from clinical trials is that it increases hope and decreases hopelessness, and to me that is the secret sauce of lifesaving work!"

STANLEY & BROWN SAFETY PLAN

STEP 1: WARNING SIGNS:

1. _____

   _____

2. _____

   _____

3. _____

   _____

STEP 2: INTERNAL COPING STRATEGIES—THINGS I CAN DO TO TAKE MY MIND OFF MY PROBLEMS WITHOUT CONTACTING ANOTHER PERSON:

1. _____

   _____

2. _____

   _____

3. _____

   _____

STEP 3: PEOPLE AND SOCIAL SETTINGS THAT PROVIDE DISTRACTION:

1. Name _____

   Phone_____

2. Name _____

   Phone_____

3. Place _____

4. Place _____

STEP 4: PEOPLE WHOM I CAN ASK FOR HELP DURING A CRISIS:

1. Name _____

   Phone_____

2. Name _____

   Phone_____

3. Name _____

   Phone_____

STEP 5: PROFESSIONALS OR AGENCIES I CAN CONTACT DURING A CRISIS:

1. Clinician/Agency Name_____

   Phone_____

   Clinician Pager or Emergency Contact #

   _____

2. Clinician/Agency Name_____

   Phone_____

   Clinician Pager or Emergency Contact #

   _____

3. Local Emergency Department

   _____

   Emergency Department Address

   _____

   Emergency Department Phone

   _____

4. Suicide Prevention Lifeline Phone: 988

STEP 6: MAKING THE ENVIRONMENT SAFE (PLAN FOR LETHAL MEANS SAFETY):

1. _____
2. _____

STEP 7: LIST THE REASONS FOR LIVING THAT ARE MOST IMPORTANT:

1. _____
2. _____
3. _____

CHAPTER NINE

IS THE FUTURE OF SUICIDE PREVENTION DIGITAL?

Back before artificial neural networks, deep learning, and large language models sucked up all the oxygen in discussions about artificial intelligence, there was a simpler, faster, and less complicated machine learning technique called logistic regression. LR is a Big Data approach to data mining, or learning a lot about a lot of data. Logistic regression is often used to provide yes or no (binary) answers to simple questions; for example, whether a certain job candidate is the best choice among many, or whether a high school student should be admitted to a particular college. By training an algorithm on data such as grade point averages, test scores, and extracurricular involvement for thousands of students, logistic regression reveals patterns in the data and provides useful information. The better the data—the better it is labeled, the more there is, the less bias it contains—the better able the algorithm is to yield useful information.

Now imagine that scientists trained an algorithm with the medical records of thousands of patients who had killed themselves.

Later, when it evaluated a new patient's records, the algorithm would indicate whether this patient was or was not like the others—whether he or she might make a suicide attempt. Ultimately, with a machine learning upgrade, the algorithm would automatically run this diagnostic, and others indicating ailments like heart disease, cancer, prediabetes and more, whenever a new patient's records entered the system. These are some of the core technologies of the exciting innovations we'll explore now, innovations that will in the future dramatically improve suicide prediction and reduction: the digitization of suicide prevention.

The Safety Plan Intervention and CAMS both address the gap between a crisis and therapy. But CAMS isn't available everywhere and both interventions are put in place *after* a suicide attempt or severe ideation occurs. Rutgers University's Evan Kleiman, PhD, backs up the focus of an intervention to the moments *before* a suicide attempt. As Dr. Kleiman frames it, a suicide is like a movie that contains a time bomb. It requires knowledge about when the bomb will go off and fast, decisive action to stop it. Defusing the bomb after it has exploded—not very effective.

"So the big problem is that we don't know enough about what happens right before someone kills themselves. And the bigger problem from that is for people who die by suicide, there is a buildup, right? Sometimes months or years. But the decision to act on the desire to die by suicide for many people can be a fast one. And so we need to know what happens in those hours and minutes so we can intervene. And that's probably the central challenge to suicide, just this time scale."

The time period can be so short from impulse to suicide, there's not enough time for actual human intervention—a real-time meeting with a therapist or a trip to the hospital. Take South Dakota farmer Chris Dykshorn for example. For months he displayed increasingly severe risk factors. He spoke about wanting to die and about feeling like a burden. He was briefly hospitalized. Then in the perilous window after discharge, he died by suicide. Obviously, there was no way to have a therapist on hand at that critical moment because no one could have precisely predicted it. But what if Chris Dykshorn had possessed the skills to recognize a crisis and get himself through it with behavioral health exercises, straight from an app on his smartphone? And what if that app had a record of his agitated episodes and was able to trigger an intervention by his therapist *before* the suicide occurred? That would be a game changer for reducing suicides.

Kleiman, working with his long-term collaborator Kate Bentley, PhD, of Massachusetts General Hospital, is developing a smartphone application that will deliver therapeutic help anytime and know in advance that a suicidal crisis is coming. It's being deployed to real patients as part of a suicide reduction trial at Rutgers University Behavioral Healthcare. Kleiman and Bentley's application is known as an ecological momentary intervention (EMI) for smartphones. There are many EMIs being developed by many researchers, so I'll refer to this specific smartphone app as Kleiman's EMI.

When I first learned about Kleiman's EMI, it made me wonder if the Safety Plan Intervention and other stabilization plans were not already designed for exactly this—filling in the dangerous gap between inpatient and outpatient care with distractions, activities, and contact information for friends and therapists. Stabilization plans have a long track record of putting a dent in suicide rates; in fact, in the six months following hospitalization, patients trained on the safety plan suffer half as many suicides as those not trained. But fortunately, Kleiman's EMI app contains the safety plan, complete with the data the patient entered in the hospital, as a component of its functionality. So Kleiman doesn't want to throw out the safety plan. But as a researcher, the fast-talking, mop-haired professor who could be mistaken for a graduate student thinks stabilization plans alone are not enough. He has a bone to pick with them, a few bones, in fact, which will make his technology a better choice in the long run.

Bone One: The Setting. What patients learn in calm they may not remember in crisis.

Kleiman told me, "Patients leave the hospital better, in theory, than when they came in. They learn skills there. Treatment that we call skills-based. They learn how to deal with negative emotions, negative social situations, and they learn to distract themselves. People in the inpatient unit or in an outpatient program are learning skills when they are calm. They're in a supportive environment. They're stable.

"But here's the problem. We throw them out in the real world and then they have to remember the stuff they learned when they were calm. They have to remember what to do, but now they're in a period of incredible distress. And this plays into the short time period, right?

"Because you can't really send people out in the real world and expect them to use these therapies they've only practiced when they're calm."

I could see Kleiman's point with complex therapies such as cognitive behavioral therapy, which trains you to change negative thinking patterns through repetition. You might learn CBT techniques during an extended hospital stay, though remembering them would be challenging during a suicidal crisis. But what about simple distraction techniques offered by stabilization plans? Watching an episode of *The Simpsons*? Playing with your dog? Not so challenging.

Sadly, many people who use the safety plan or other stabilization plans die by suicide anyway. A more robust treatment-based app might reduce more deaths than a stabilization plan alone. On average, patients engage with Kleiman's EMI for ninety minutes to three hours—a substantial amount of time, and much longer than any stabilization plan.

Bone Two: Continuity. Kleiman said, "If you meet with a therapist, after waiting days or weeks to get an appointment, you spend your first outpatient session telling the therapist about your background. Learning the background of your suicidal thoughts or suicide attempt will probably take your entire first appointment."

But you have already laid out your background to the therapist at the hospital. Now you're going through it all again? Wouldn't it be better if you could pick up where you left off with your inpatient provider?

This seems indisputable. A critical part of customizing Kleiman's EMI for the patient is connecting it to all the patient's data, which will simplify the handoff to an outpatient provider. Again, this is an aspiration for Kleiman's EMI, a feature that its co-creator, Dr. Kate Bentley, says will be online in about a year.

And Kleiman's Bone Three: Overkill. Not everyone having an emotional crisis is suicidal. Sometimes they're simply having an anxious afternoon and probably don't need to start working a plan aimed at preventing suicide. Wouldn't it be best if their plan could handle a range of psychological disturbances? This goes back to treating patients upstream, before they are suicidal. The app would be distributed to every patient in the medical system and be ready to address any level of mental health disorder.

Setting. Continuity. And no overkill.

Kleiman's technological solution to treatment has some unrealized capabilities, but cracking them is a perfect marriage of his lifelong nerdish obsession with computers and his professional focus on combating suicide. High on its plus side—almost everyone has a smartphone; 81 percent of adults have one with them at any given time. While they are hospital inpatients, individuals download the app to their phone and receive training about the exercises it offers. Thereafter, several times a day, the app contacts them. The patient responds to questions and performs activities that are intended to quickly evaluate their mental state. Then it guides them through calming and thought-restructuring techniques, should those be necessary.

Here's Kleiman's EMI in action, in an interface largely designed by his collaborator, Kate Bentley. When I activated the app, I was greeted by a cheerful blue screen. It presented me with three options: Anchor in the Present, Think Flexibly, and Change Emotional Behavior. Each addresses a different emotional need. I first chose Anchor in the Present. In the parlance of behavioral therapy, a lot of anxiety is caused by ruminating on events from the past and on future events that haven't happened yet. "Anchoring" encourages patients to focus on the present moment rather than the past or the future. It's a good idea for anyone.

The app offered some anchoring techniques—doing breath work and pressing my feet against the ground. Then it prompted me to identify my thoughts, feelings, and behaviors. I gave a one-word description of each, and it surprised me with an overarching question: "Are your thoughts, physical feelings, and behaviors in line with what is happening here and now in the present moment?" I found if I answered yes to the prompts, the session ended. On the other hand, if I indicated that my thoughts and feelings were focused on the past or future, I was given more anchoring exercises to do, including grounding myself with a physical activity, doing more breathing exercises, and focusing on spending time with someone I enjoyed being around.

Kleiman's EMI's other main options—Think Flexibly and Change Emotional Behavior—repeated this pattern. Think Flexibly is useful when you become fixated on unhelpful thoughts. When I indicated I had no negative thoughts, the session ended. But when I indicated a problem, a series of exercises followed.

Predictably, the Change Emotional Behavior option targeted feelings of distress, and there was no easy way to end the session. Instead, the app triggered exercises meant to help me soothe myself with more activities. This segment concluded with questions about the long- and short-term effects of my activities, and asked how I thought they would make me feel immediately after I'd finished the exercise and in the future.

I left my sessions with strong impressions. First, Kleiman's EMI worked as designed, as an enhanced stabilization program that has crossed over into behavioral therapy. And overall, working the app alone would be a valuable distraction from any negative thoughts I might have. The therapeutic exercises were engaging and scientific, derived from a form of cognitive behavioral therapy called the unified protocol, which was designed especially for those with anxiety, depression, and related disorders. This means it wasn't more than I needed. Someone having an anxious afternoon could benefit as well as someone having suicidal thoughts. And the instructions and exercises were simple and straightforward—probably not too taxing for someone in crisis.

I also felt that if my answers and activities went into my personal record, the Kleiman EMI's usefulness would multiply. It would prompt me to engage in activities that had in the past improved my condition. And building a record of my many daily responses would help its algorithm identify periods when I was at increased risk for an emotionally turbulent episode.

Kleiman's EMI is meant not to be used on its own but in conjunction with therapy. In its current deployment, however, it's trying to check one of the boxes identified in our discussion of the safety plan—to build resilience and self-sufficiency. That's because in times of crisis, help from others, from friends to experts, is not always available. However, if a suicidal urge is persistent and strong, Kleiman's EMI will alert medical personnel who will intervene.

Already the app has yielded important insights into the nature of suicidal thinking. Until now, suicidal ideation has been thought of as a homogenous phenomenon; individuals who were "actively" suicidal were thought to have the same intensity and quality of thoughts for about the same duration. These assumptions came about because in the past, individuals' suicidal thinking had been assessed irregularly over periods of weeks, months, or years. But getting information about suicidal thoughts that's updated multiple times a day, and recorded by the person suffering them, has changed everything.

In one study, Kleiman and his associates gathered two samples of eighty-four men and women of a variety of ages and races who had attempted suicide in the past year. Using smartphones, each reported on any suicidal thoughts they had four times a day for twenty-eight days. Analysis revealed something brand-new—patients suffered from five distinct types of suicidal thinking. Their differences were subtle but significant, with changes in duration—how long they lasted— and variability—how much they changed in strength. What's more, the thoughts rapidly moved from one type to another, sometimes within an hour. Participants who had more severe, unvarying suicidal thoughts were more likely to have attempted suicide recently. The study showed that suicidal thinking can speed up and shut back down over a four- to eight-hour period. What does that mean for therapists, and for Kleiman's goal of understanding precisely what happens right before a suicide attempt?

Kleiman said, "The first thing it tells us is that suicidal thinking can escalate very quickly and deescalate just as quickly. It tells us it's important to frequently monitor high-risk patients. Someone could say right now, 'I am not suicidal,' and then things rapidly change. But what causes that change? That's our challenge, to know what happens in the interim, what happens to put these people at high risk?"

Further study will determine how these types of suicidal thinking relate to *future* suicide attempts. Will severity and variability reveal that an attempt is imminent? Will therapists achieve the clinicians' Holy Grail: the ability to predict an attempt hours or days before it occurs?

Kleiman moves closer to answering these questions with the help of another technology currently expanding its role in suicide prevention—wearables. In health care, wearable technology includes a variety of gadgets that monitor a patient's health and point out anomalies. Rising demand for early diagnosis and preventive care is fueling growth in the wearables sector. A wearable vital signs monitor, a smartwatch glucose monitor, and wearable pain management devices are a few examples. Kleiman's wearable of choice is a smart-watch. He's used a bunch—Fitbits, Garmins, Ouras, and more. As suicide detection devices, they have issues.

Kleiman said, "Wearable devices are expensive, they are impre-cise, and they're sometimes annoying to wear. I say this knowing that my Apple Watch, which I in theory should wear, is currently in front of me because it was uncomfortable. And so if people are not wearing the devices, they're not really going to do much to predict any kind of state."

Kleiman has had luck with a device called the Empatica Embrace, which was developed to detect epileptic seizures and notify caregiv-ers, so it can't be blamed for not being a perfect suicide tracker. The Embrace does a fair job at obtaining real-time measurements of interest—movement, sweat, and skin temperature. When someone is in a state of agitation, their heart rate goes up, they perspire, and they move around more than usual. Excessive nighttime movement also characterizes poor sleep, which is correlated with suicide and other mental health issues.

First, the bad news. Wearables are not magic wands that help predict suicide in the short term or the next day. Kleiman told me, "Wearables alone have basically no predictive ability for suicidal thinking later on." That's because suicide has no signature measur-able by a wearable, no telltale combination of heart rate, perspiration, and movement that predicts a suicide attempt.

Now the good news. "Skin conductance response" is a fancy term for perspiration measured by a wearable. People perspire when they are surprised. When people are having a physiological response to distress—the fight-or-flight response—they have a skin conductance response that looks like surprise. As Kleiman explained, when you combine skin conductance responses with Kleiman's EMI's data about the strength and variation of suicidal thoughts, it improves the app's accuracy. The wearable verifies and augments what Kleiman's EMI tells you about some suicidal thoughts. That's a big deal. Real progress.

But ironically, if the Kleiman EMI's powers are all realized and it's able to anticipate a suicidal urge, its other capabilities almost make the point moot. That's because with behavioral therapy the app gives patients the ability to work through and minimize urges.

Kleiman said, "We don't really need to know if someone's going to attempt suicide. We're giving them the skills so if they feel like they're about to attempt, they can hopefully avert that attempt. And we don't have to do the hard work of figuring out when someone might do it. Recently I've become more aware of that. It's separating these two problems—anticipating a suicidal urge and treating one—because they are totally different."

Perhaps it's not as important to predict suicides as it is to treat suicidal thinking and help the vulnerable build resilience. Building resilience is a big theme in suicide prevention. Or as Kleiman says, "It's the 'teach a man to fish' parable that's going to cut down on suicides."

In the long term, the most promising development in suicide prediction may be the marriage of machine learning and health records. As we've noted, when you train a learning algorithm on large amounts of data, it develops powers of prediction. Train a neural net (simply put, a lot of learning algorithms) on the records of thousands of suicide victims and it should predict whether the person represented by a new record will attempt suicide. Incidentally, every time you buy something online, you trigger similar technology by adding data to your internet purchasing profile. This is why you may find yourself hounded everywhere you go online by promotions of things you've examined or purchased in the past. This technique is called affinity analysis and it's used by Amazon, Netflix, Meta, and innumerable online retailers and social networks.

Machine learning works best when algorithms are trained on structured data. Ideally all the medical records are formatted alike. In the United States the leader in electronic medical health records is a company called Epic Systems. It hosts a uniform electronic health record system for more than 250 health care organizations worldwide; 45 percent of the US population already have their medical records in an Epic system. In a smaller way, Kleiman's EMI has created its own database of many thousands of data points entered by patients several times a day. What's more, its data is highly pertinent for suicide prediction, detailing patients' emotional states, thoughts about suicide, and changes in suicidal thinking. In the future, Kleiman's EMI will work with Epic to possibly combine their data and increase their prognostication powers.

Kleiman's app should soon be able to help anticipate suicides. But what about Epic working on its own? Can it anticipate suicides?

The answer is a firm *maybe*. In 2018, researchers from Kaiser Permanente and other health care organizations trained an algorithm on data from almost 3 million patients who made a total of 20 million clinic visits. Epic's anonymized data included boilerplate information from primary care examinations but also from depression assessment questionnaires, prescriptions for psychiatric medications, and indications of substance abuse.

The algorithm correctly identified nearly half the patients who attempted or died by suicide within ninety days of a general care or mental health visit, according to a retrospective examination of patient data. Only 25 to 30 percent of subsequent suicide attempts or fatalities were previously detected by the suicide risk assessments used by some hospitals. Gregory E. Simon, MD, MPH, a psychiatrist and mental health researcher who coauthored the examination, concluded, "Risk predictions can supplement clinical judgment and direct clinicians' attention to where it's most needed. Predictions don't replace a clinical assessment, but they can help providers intervene with the right patients at the right time."

The study must be taken with a grain of salt. Note that half the cases of suicide attempts or deaths were identified after the fact. This suggests that half the time, using Epic's data, scientists should be able to anticipate which patients might try to kill themselves, and intervene. But clinical therapists have reported that they are able to anticipate which of their patients might attempt suicide no more than half the time. That's no better than flipping a coin, as Florida State University's Dr. Joseph Franklin pointed out.

Achieving nearly 50 percent using machine learning does not appear to constitute progress in forecasting. It could, however, provide support for an intervention once a patient's greater-than-average odds of suicide are detected.

I'm sorry, Daddy just can't be fixed. No matter how hard I try to be normal and levelheaded it always comes back and even worse. I wish I'd died in Afghanistan.

These desperate words came from Army National Guard veteran Anthony Morris. He developed post-traumatic stress disorder (PTSD) after serving two tours of duty in Afghanistan. This is part of a note he wrote to his four young children shortly before he killed himself near his home in Louisiana. Although veterans of the armed forces make up only 10 percent of the population, they account for nearly 25 percent of all suicides in the United States. According to 2021 research, 30,177 veterans and active duty service people who served in the military after 9/11 killed themselves. In contrast, during the same twenty-year period, 7,057 service members—or a quarter of that total—died in battle. This confounding statistic bears repeating: since 9/11, four times more service members killed themselves than died in combat.

While the United States Veterans Administration claims about twenty veterans kill themselves each day, a 2022 study from America's Warrior Partnership (AWP) claims that figure is shockingly low. According to the study, the VA failed to include overlooked deaths such as unexplained drug overdoses and the deaths of those whose families and home states did not identify them as veterans when they died and inform the Department of Defense. AWP claims as many as forty-four veterans die from suicide on average each day, more than twice the official estimate. The AWP report is contested by the nonprofit Veterans Healthcare Policy Institute, which cites flaws in the study and claims the VA's numbers are correct.

For veterans, suicide risk factors are legion. A sampling includes problems reentering civilian society, unemployment, prior suicide attempts, mood and anxiety disorders, alcohol and drug abuse, legal issues, financial troubles, firearms possession, and divorce. Physically, veterans contend with PTSD, traumatic brain injury (TBI), wound recovery and rehabilitation, and other injuries that are part and parcel of many military lives. Ironically, medical improvements that have allowed more troops to survive wounds have also let them repeatedly deploy and accumulate more physical and mental trauma.

Army clinical psychologist Sandra Pahl, PhD, spoke with me about a relatively new phenomenon—complex PTSD. "A lot of times there are multiple traumas that have been going on in your deployment, and then there's a TBI on top of that. And modern medicine is contributing to trauma because it used to be if somebody got a certain kind of wound, they'd go home or back to the States, but now they get fixed up and sent back into action. So they have an opportunity to get more traumatic injuries. And let's say both your legs get blown up. In the old days, that individual would have died in the field, but we've got so good in medicine that we can save that individual. So the problem becomes, how does that person manage this when they're coming home? When they have not only psychological trauma from being blown up and having seen friends and superiors being killed as well, now they're also dealing with losing both of their legs.

"There's a terrific cultural shock when you stop being deployed and you come home. You lose your identity, you stop being a soldier. On top of that, you're a paraplegic."

The rise of suicides among US veterans and active duty service members paralleled the country's participation in concurrent wars in Afghanistan and Iraq. But the connection of suicide to war turns out to be only half the story. The data about suicide during recent wars reveals a shocking fact: the majority of soldiers who kill themselves have never been deployed to a war zone, and the vast majority have never actually been in battle. Craig Bryan, PsyD, ABPP, formerly the executive director of the National Center for Veterans Studies at the University of Utah, is exasperated by the stereotype of the soldier who returns from war with PTSD and kills himself. "That's the storyline we've made up in our society because it's easy to understand and it makes sense," he says. "The problem is that the data doesn't support the notion that combat leads directly to suicide risk." For instance, 53 percent of service members who killed themselves in 2011 had never been deployed. Additionally, 85 percent of military personnel who died by suicide that year had no prior experience in direct combat, meaning they may have been deployed but did not take part in any actual conflict.

Dr. Bryan conducted a three-year investigation of the main factors that lead to military suicides. According to what he found, the suicide rate and stress levels in the military started to rise in 2004—even among those who hadn't been sent to Iraq or Afghanistan. As the "forever wars" on two battlefronts persisted, much was demanded of few. And there's another theory about noncombatant suicides that is underreported and underdiscussed. Because of the demand for personnel after 9/11, parts of the armed forces temporarily lowered their mental health requirements (interestingly, the same thing happened during World War II). More recruits with mental health disorders entered the military. That would partially account for a general rise in suicides. Furthermore, some inductees were deemed psychologically unfit to go overseas and instead served stateside in administrative and support roles. Financial, legal, and relationship problems—all stress factors for suicide—also kept many from being deployed. In this context it isn't so surprising that suicides among undeployed personnel are higher than deployed.

Dr. Pahl also connects veteran and active duty suicides to recruiting. She says, "I do think sometimes the people who choose to join the military, and we've known this for decades, are different than the ones in general who are going to college. If you're going to college, the idea is you probably come from a middle-class family or you have a family that is very determined that you need to go to college. This is important. Education matters.

"But when we're looking in the military, traditionally, some individuals join in order to get out of a bad situation. That means bad family circumstances, a bad life, and they're really trying to change their life. We would say there's probably some biological preloading for trauma. Some have parents who weren't quite stable and they have behavioral health issues or they were drinking or they were abusive or they abandoned their children. So once again, genetically, you load the gun, and the environment pulls the trigger. They're joining the military. They might struggle more because they might encounter something that reminds them of that abusive upbringing. I hate using the word 'trigger,' but it triggers them."

Too often the triggering event for women in the military is sexual assault. PTSD and traumatic events are predictors of suicide. It's commonly thought that battle experience is the only factor in military trauma. It isn't true. The trauma caused by sexual assault and harassment is more prevalent.

Nearly 25 percent of servicewomen report experiencing sexual assault in the service, and more than half report experiencing harassment. Sexual assault frequently serves as the first warning sign in a string of traumatic events that can lead to PTSD, depression, and suicide. In a 2019 study, researchers from three universities polled over 300 female service members and veterans who had been sexually assaulted. They discovered that 29 percent of them were actively thinking about suicide. From 2007 to 2017 age-adjusted suicide rates among female veterans increased by 73 percent. According to Department of Defense data, in 2019 female service members made up 31 percent of all active duty suicide attempts, despite women making up only 16.5 percent of the armed services.

Pahl attributes rising veteran suicides to a generational shift among military and civilian young adults alike, a lack of resilience that makes them more vulnerable to things not going their way. She feels they're more brittle than prior generations. Military officials I've spoken with claim that military suicides track civilian rates, in that they're both going up with no ceiling in sight. That part is painfully true. But in sheer numbers, military suicides have pulled well ahead. For 2021, the latest year on record, civilians died of suicide at a rate of about 13.5 people per 100,000 in the United States. Active-duty military suicides were almost twice that at 24.3 per 100,000. Veteran suicides were about 31.6 people per 100,000 in 2019, the latest year on record.

And then there are guns again. As we've discussed, just owning a gun triples the risk of suicide. A report by Thomas Suitt, PhD, of Brown University determined that a firearm is used in about 65 percent of active duty military suicides. Among veterans it's even higher—nearly 70 percent. The likelihood that a suicide attempt will result in death dramatically rises if a gun is used.

Officials who deal with veteran suicides hope a reduction is just around the corner, brought about by machine learning.

The US Department of Veterans Affairs (VA) has reached the same conclusion as suicide experts throughout the United States: clinical therapists are not very good at anticipating which patients will die from suicide. Traditionally, doctors have estimated a veteran's risk for suicide by drawing on past mental health diagnoses, substance abuse, various clinical assessment tools, and gut instinct. It didn't get them far. "The fact is we can't rely on trained medical experts to identify people who are truly at high risk," said Marianne Goodman, MD, a VA psychiatrist and clinical professor of medicine. "We're no good at it."

To complement clinical assessments, the VA created an algorithm that was trained on the records of thousands of people in the VA's database, including those who had died by suicide and those who had not. Reach Vet (Recovery Engagement and Coordination for Health—Veterans Enhanced Treatment) is a machine learning system that, starting in 2017, has been scrutinizing sixty-one variables from each patient's medical record, including physical ailments, prescription history, hospital visits, and marriage status.

Some variables, such as substance abuse, mental health admissions, and nonfatal suicide attempts, are on every list of suicide risk factors. Others, such as arthritis and the use of statins, are less intuitive. The algorithm then produces a score for each patient and flags the top 0.1 percent as "high risk." According to John McCarthy, PhD, the director of data and surveillance in the Suicide Prevention Program of the VA, "The risk concentration for people in the 0.1 percent on this score was about forty times. That is, they were forty times more likely to die of suicide" than the average person.

"The idea was that by developing these scores," Dr. McCarthy explained, "clinicians would have this additional information about the array of things that are in their electronic health record, such as prior diagnosis, prior encounters, prior suicide attempts, were they in the top 0.1 percent risk group or not? So, again, each month, we identify those individuals who are in the top predicted risk group.

And then we notify coordinators at their facility. They look at the patients who are identified and the individual providers working with those patients. For patients who are new to the list, the providers not only review the care and records for those patients, but also touch base with the patients and see how they're doing and try to address access barriers and just make sure that the patients are getting the best care that they can."

Veterans get on and fall off the regularly updated list, but at any given time, it consists of several hundred men and women who the program identifies as at elevated risk of suicide. In 2020, Vietnam veteran Barry, who didn't want his last name used, was notified that he was a 0.1 percenter. He was not a surprising pick—he'd been grievously wounded in the 1968 Tet offensive and had tried to take his own life twice before. He said, "I don't like this idea of a list, to tell you the truth, a computer telling me something like this. But I thought about it. I decided, you know, okay—if it's going to get me more support that I need, then I'm okay with it."

A recent study of Reach Vet performed by the US Government Accountability Office determined that veterans who were identified in the program scheduled and completed more outpatient appointments, received safety plans more often, and had fewer emergency department visits. More at-risk veterans were identified by Reach Vet than by any other means employed by the VA.

Reach Vet decreased documented suicide attempts by 5 percent. However, when compared with control groups, those notified had similar numbers of *deaths* resulting from suicide within six months of notification. Suicide deaths are recorded separately from suicide attempts. Reach Vet did not prevent any suicide deaths. John McCarthy, whose team's work on suicide predictive modeling prompted development of Reach Vet, noted, "It's discouraging. I mean, of course, we would love to say that by shining a spotlight on these patients, it's resulting in zero suicides for this very, very high-risk population or even that it's associated with fewer suicides. But we can't."

Furthermore, the 0.1 percent that the Reach Vet algorithm determined are most at risk turns out to be several hundred veterans among about 6 million tested. Even if Reach Vet prevented suicides among all identified veterans, it would have only a modest impact on the national suicide rate for veterans.

I asked SAVE's Dan Reidenberg for his take on the findings regarding the Reach Vet clinical program. He said, "What does the study say? It says veterans did more safety planning and more outpatient appointments, and that there were fewer inpatient admissions and fewer emergency department visits. That's all great news. But five years into the program they can't say it prevented a suicide and that is troubling to me. Should we toss it out and move on? Probably not. Maybe it will save some lives, and some lives is better than none."

Maybe part of the issue is how difficult it is to work with medical records in machine learning applications to begin with. Machine learning provides useful insights for some medical conditions, like cancer and heart disease, but it hasn't worked yet to prevent suicides. One problem is that the algorithms trained on medical records do not reveal anything about why some patients are designated as high risk while others are not. "Interpretability" is an issue with machine learning systems, and it's the main reason why their use is questioned in safety-sensitive processes, such as self-driving cars. The inputs are known—in this case, medical records—and the outputs are known—the roster of patients determined to be high risk. But computer scientists cannot know what's happening between the inputs and the outputs. The algorithm's decisions cannot be interpreted or explained, and so systems employing machine learning are often referred to as "black box" systems.

The problem with a black box system in suicide prevention is that while an algorithm may provide a general warning, it can yield no information about what triggered its conclusion and so no insight can be drawn about the proper treatment of the patient. What might work for one person on the 0.1 percent list may not work for another. But again, Reach Vet is intended to complement clinical assessment, not replace it. About Reach Vet and Department of Defense programs in general, Reidenberg concluded with a discouraging note. He had recently been on a call with someone on the DoD's suicide task force. They had discussed that in 2022 the military had just recorded the highest number of suicides ever. "This," he wrote to me, "despite the Reach Vet program being one among literally hundreds of programs being implemented throughout the branches of service."

John McCarthy takes the opposite view and cautions about the unrealistic expectations and subsequent disappointments. "Even small steps are good. Suicide is a really difficult thing to try to affect. It's encouraging that we're reducing suicide attempts. And now we're working to improve and update the algorithm. We're also considering other subgroups that might benefit from outreach, not in the highest tier but in a very high tier.

"People look at machine learning approaches as if they're a kind of magic bullet for suicide prevention and this is something we've been very clear on at the outset of the Reach Vet program. It's not the algorithm that would prevent suicide, it's the interaction with the patients that would prevent it."

If you are thinking about suicide or if you or someone you know is in emotional crisis, please call or text 988 at any time to reach the 988 Suicide and Crisis Lifeline for confidential, free crisis support.

CHAPTER TEN

SYSTEMS
APPROACHES:
THE UNITED STATES
AIR FORCE

"We're not going to cure our way out of this crisis."

Of all the words I've heard from suicide experts over the last five
years in the course of researching, writing, and producing the PBS
film *Facing Suicide* and writing this book, none have borne reexami-
nation more than these spoken to me by Eric Caine, MD, professor
emeritus of the University of Rochester Medical Center. Dr. Caine
spent years as a psychiatry department chair and clinical psychiatrist
and has helped countless patients climb out of the agony of a suicidal crisis. But at heart he's a public policy wonk, looking at the big
picture and asking, *How can we change our society to reduce suicide?
How can we change health care itself?* Sure, caregivers can help individuals with treatments such as CBT, DBT, CAMS, SSRIs, ketamine, and lithium, and often save their lives. Again and again
individual patients win this battle, and this is a source of hope. I've

presented some of these cases in this book, and there are tens of thousands more each year.

But we are indisputably losing the war. On average, despite suicide reduction measures, more people in America die by suicide each year than died the year before, and this has gone on since at least 1999. Suicide ravages the United States.

So far we've explored the power of important safety measures as simple as keeping an eye on those close to you, watching for suicide's signs, and connecting suicidal people with impactful care. We've seen how the Safety Plan Intervention can stabilize some patients and CAMS can reduce suicidal ideation. We've examined aspirational efforts in brain scans and digital technologies that show future promise for anticipating suicides. We've stepped inside the circles of danger described by Thomas Joiner's interpersonal theory and seen their expository and predictive power. For the most part, these measures have been individual-focused, aimed at helping one person at a time.

We're not going to cure our way out of this crisis.

For the remaining chapters of this book, we'll explore efforts that have made meaningful reductions in suicide across whole populations. This, many experts claim, is the natural and desirable evolution of suicide reduction. It's where the field of suicidology appears to be headed. Population-based strategies are sometimes called *systems approaches*. There aren't very many, and the most prominent in the United States was relatively short-lived. But according to Caine and many other suicidologists, they represent the ultimate hope, a big net that doesn't rely on treating suicidal individuals one at a time and curing our way out of this crisis. Instead, systems approaches protect populations by trying to alter suicide outcomes upstream of suicidal events, well before they occur, and then using proven therapies and medicines to stop suicidal behavior in those who slip through the dragnet. But the effect is the same: substantial suicide reduction.

The following is the first paragraph of a 2001 US Air Force report on suicide reduction. It comes with a plot twist worthy of a horror film.

> In the spring of 1996, the Air Force's most senior leaders sensed that the details of far too many suicides were crossing their desks in daily reports of major events. In May of that year, the suicide of Admiral Jeremy Boorda, the top-ranking officer in the US Navy, caused them to take an even closer look. It was time to take more aggressive action against the problem of suicide among Air Force members.

Like teenagers in a cabin in the woods, the Air Force's upper command felt foreboding. But they were convinced to take action when one from their own echelon tragically took his life. When the Air Force Suicide Prevention Program began in 1996 the situation was critical and getting worse. Suicide had recently become the second-biggest killer of Air Force service members after accidents, responsible for almost one-quarter of all active duty deaths. Fewer than a third of those who killed themselves had contacted Air Force mental health services. At the time, suicide rates in the Air Force were about 40 percent less than those in the United States population at large, but growing fast. I found this stunning. I had become so accustomed to astronomical active duty and veteran suicide numbers—up to forty-four veteran suicides per day according to a recent but contested account—that it seems remarkable that just thirty years ago the Air Force suicide rate was only a little more than half the civilian rate. Still, by the standards of 1996, when the Air Force Suicide Prevention Program was introduced, suicide among airmen had become rampant.

David Litts, MD, now a retired colonel, functioned as the "chief of staff" in the development effort and cultivated the key insight that suicides should be viewed as community problems rather than individual ones. As it turns out, the biggest risk factors among members of the Air Force aren't very different from civilian risk factors. The majority of suicides involved problems with relationships, the law, and finances. What mainly prevented help-seeking was stigma, the shame and disgrace associated with mental health conditions. The facets of stigma paralleled those we explored in Chapter Five. People with suicidal ideation fear their own minds' destructive drives, and they fear what others think of them. They worry about social and religious condemnation, which has pushed suicide into a claustrophobic dungeon for centuries. Self-reliance, highly valued in military personnel, made Air Force members embrace a stoic, go-it-alone mindset and reject help-seeking. Alien to their thinking was Christine Moutier's maxim that mental health problems are *health* problems, no different from heart disease or broken bones.

The experts found that airmen were wary of repercussions for seeking professional help, such as losing their jobs and getting drummed out of the Air Force. They believed their managers and commanders inspected their mental health records, an absolute barrier for some to seeking help. Overall, the Air Force seemed to have lost one of its distinguishing characteristics, a supporting interconnection among personnel of all ranks best summed up by an old but frequently used adage, "The Air Force looks out for its own."

But that all changed. Working with experts, Air Force brass

assembled a suicide prevention program that wasn't one program but many overlapping programs. Their shared theme was community cohesion. Reducing suicide became everyone's responsibility. According to Eric Caine, who was instrumental in evaluating the program as it developed, it started at the top. "It began with leadership, it was a top-down effort, there's no question. The vice chief of staff and surgeon general of the Air Force at the time saw suicide as one of the biggest problems that the Air Force family faced, and they really viewed it as a family. They looked at what the World Health Organization had recommended and they put together a sort of throw-everything-including-the-kitchen-sink plan. It's hard to know what element worked the most, but they threw in all the elements."

Eleven elements defined the plan, and they systematically attacked risk factors among Air Force members. To point out a few, when examined by mental health professionals, patients at risk for suicide were given greater confidentiality; their mental health issues around suicide would not impact their Air Force careers. Suicide prevention was included in all military training for all ranks and all civilian employees in the Air Force. All were taught warning signs for suicide, how to care for fellow members they deemed at risk, and how to encourage early help-seeking.

Right after an arrest or criminal investigation is a high-risk time for suicides, and so is immediately after traumatic events like terrorist attacks and suicides themselves. Planners focused extra resources and procedures on these moments to deal with destructive emotions.

The scale of the suicide reduction plan becomes clear if you witness the small town that is an Air Force base, with a town's commensurate sprawl and population. There are about 800 active US Air Force bases around the world, with a total population of about 330,000. Travis Air Force Base in California (2023 population about

8,020) is a living township, with innumerable airplanes, trucks, and other vehicles and vast numbers of people whose job it is to fly them, drive them, and keep them all running. These Air Force officers, enlisted personnel, and civilians have to be fed, housed, clothed, and entertained, and many go to church. Many are retirees. Caine said, "So there's housing, there's health care, there's legal, there's judge advocacy, there's chaplaincy, you can go on and on and on about the elements. And they pulled all those together, along with medical and the investigation services, and educated them about suicide. They created a culture of caring. They had a phrase that attacked stigma. 'Strong men—and women—can ask for help.'"

The program was an immediate success. In a few years, suicides in the Air Force were cut in half. The year 1994 saw sixty-eight suicides; 1999 had just thirty-four. In 1999, the Air Force suicide rate was 9 per 100,000, lower than the national rate of 11 per 100,000. For eleven years after launch, the reduction was sustained, resulting in an overall 33 percent reduction in suicides from the years preceding the intervention. Through 2008, with the exception of 2004, the Air Force Suicide Prevention Program also significantly decreased the risk of other violence-related outcomes, such as accidental death and domestic violence. But 2004 was important. It displayed stress fractures that would ultimately threaten the program.

In the program's heyday, however, the Air Force had achieved an amazing milestone—it had reduced suicide rates while there had been no reduction in suicide rates in the civilian population of the United States since the 1940s. The Air Force Suicide Prevention Program has been copied by institutions, and even nations, around the world.

There was just one problem. All the Air Force's success took place in peacetime. How would it hold up in the crucible of war? In 2001 the United States invaded Afghanistan. In 2003 it invaded Iraq. By 2004 the stress fractures opened. Caine was there. "We saw the first cracks in the Air Force Suicide Prevention Program in late 2003, 2004. And at the time we had a discussion [about] what was causing it. Now the three colonels who had overseen the program basically said we think everybody is still doing it because the command structure said it's important. And some of us said, well, you know we're at war now and it's very hard to do this even if the command structure says do it.

"And my colleagues and some of the people in the Air Force did some surveys and published them and the thing that was really clear was that a lot of the program implementation was falling off the screen because it was wartime."

The study got midlevel leaders back on track and energetically reimplementing the program. For a while, that worked. But after 2007, the fissures reappeared, and this time they didn't heal. Caine identified one prominent reason: a massive downsizing in the '80s and '90s as the Cold War ended, the Berlin Wall came down, and the Soviet Union dissolved.

Caine said, "In 1985 the Air Force had about 650,000 service members. In 1995 it had about 350,000." Later, at war in both Afghanistan and Iraq, the Air Force was stretched too thin. "It was 24-7 for everyone," said Caine. "When the Army and the Marines withdrew from Iraq, the Air Force didn't withdraw. The Air Force didn't withdraw from Afghanistan or Europe or the borders with Russia. The Air Force has been on overtime."

Control of the skies has become a mainstay of modern warfare, so the Air Force wasn't able to let up. This took a toll on every service member. Caine said, "If you're working multiple shifts or twelve- or fourteen-hour shifts, or even if it's eight hours a day but it's six or seven days a week, you're on edge and it's hard to keep going. It's hard to develop community. It's hard to maintain family relationships."

And it was hard to rigorously implement the Air Force Suicide Prevention Program. After 2008, suicide rates returned to preprogram levels and continued to rise. Now, by 1990s standards, suicide is out of control in the Air Force. The year 2020 saw 582 Air Force service members die by suicide, and the next year 519. No one can explain the 2021 dip, and no one expects the downward trend to continue. No one knows the genesis of suicide's dramatic upward curve among the armed forces except to suggest it is a consequence of America's "forever wars."

Nevertheless, the USAF's achievement can't be overstated. It has demonstrated that a multifaceted, overlapping, community-based approach can reduce the rate of suicide over a number of years. Its enduring public health message is that suicide rates in large institutions may be decreased and that, for programs to be successful, interventions must be regularly supported and checked for compliance. Reductions in suicide rates cannot simply be maintained by a program's momentum. The USAF's strategy for preventing suicide should be tried out in other job-related communities, such as law enforcement and corporations, to see if the programs can work with other groups.

Meanwhile, the Air Force isn't accepting its setback in suicide rates. Instead, the USAF is developing exciting high-tech tools to tackle suicide reduction.

The light comes up. You are in in a dimly lit apartment with empty beer bottles on the floor. Takeout containers litter the tables, and the shades are down, increasing the gloom. The place could use a power wash. And so could the airman in it. He's a slight man in a wrinkled T-shirt, downing a beer, when you startle him. He looks to be in his early thirties.

"Jesus, you scared me," he says. "Just because a guy leaves his door open doesn't mean he wants visitors. What's up?"

Two phrases float in white letters in the foreground. You choose one and say out loud, "I saw the Instagram post. Wanted to check in on you."

He's suspicious. "Only checking in. I'm fine. It's just some stupid drunk post, all right? You know how girls are."

"It doesn't seem like nothing, Mike. Can we sit down and talk about it?"

He gives you a hostile glare.

Meet Airman Mike. He's the star of a virtual reality module expertly designed by a provider of immersive training experiences called Moth+Flame. Created for the USAF, the module's goal is to plunge service members into Mike's suicidal crisis and teach them the skills to get him to safety. Once you don the Oculus virtual reality headset, you're immersed in Mike's apartment, and pretty soon in Mike's problems.

"What do you know about my problems?" Mike snarls. "You don't know me."

At regular junctures in your conversation, options for what you can say appear on the screen. For the experience to work, you must choose one option and say it out loud. The backstory, which you uncover, is that Mike's wife, Nicole, found pictures of Mike and another woman on his phone. Nicole's tearful outburst went straight to divorce and who will get the children. Mike tried to grab her. She fell and hit her head.

"I did not try to hurt her, okay?" Mike insists. "But if she tells them that I did, come on, you know what that means. That's Article Fifteen. My life's over. There's no Nicole. I don't know where she's going to take the kids. There's no Air Force. I'm done."

Article Fifteen means Mike could get kicked out of the Air Force on charges of domestic violence. And there's one more thing. Mike's been making Instagram posts. They contain veiled threats about killing himself. What do you do now?

Air Force colonel Matthew Sandelier works at the Pentagon's Office of Force Resiliency (OFR), which was developed to prevent violence and promote resilience of personnel across the Air Force and the Space Force. At Travis Air Force Base he told me, "The virtual reality research program happening here at Travis is a new and interesting method of delivering the kind of bystander intervention training that we've been providing for quite some time. When it comes to content delivery, virtual reality has got great benefits."

Chiefly, it bypasses time-consuming and costly lectures and role-playing, which was how the Air Force trained for interventions in the past. Now the VR program shoulders the load by training airmen how to apply the ACE concept, which has been used in the USAF for decades. ACE—which stands for Ask, Care, and Escort—is the essence of how to care for an individual in a suicidal crisis. As we've discussed, one should ASK the question "Are you thinking about killing yourself?" CARE is a broad term for ridding the environment of deadly means of suicide, mainly firearms, medicines, and poisons. Then ESCORT the individual to safety, which in the Air Force comes with specific guidelines. Get the service member into the hands of his superior or a therapist or faith leader such as a chaplain or rabbi, or take him or her to a hospital emergency department.

Colonel Sandelier said, "It allows our airmen to not only hear and understand what a bystander event may look like and how to apply the ACE training in a situation, but actually do that in an interactive manner, get that kind of immersion in the situation and not just hear about it in a classroom with ten or twenty of their peers. With VR they can receive that training individually, and get feedback. Does Mike survive that situation, and has the airman executed his duty in the way he should?"

Well, does Mike survive?

Now you are back in Mike's apartment, and he's even more agitated. He says, "There is no helping, man. This has been going on for way too long. All right? Because I see what I see when I look in the mirror. My whole life has been leading to this. *This.* And it just keeps repeating, just keeps going over and over again. Why? Why? Hell, I can't even be here. I cannot be here. I'm sorry."

"Mike, I got to ask. Have you thought about taking your own life?"

Mike is tearful. "Sometimes I think that I'm not good for people. It's not good for people to be around me. So, do I think that people would be better off if I wasn't a burden to them? Yes. Yes, I have."

"I don't mean to overstep, but I think you need help."

So far, you're doing well. You're listening. Closing down the conversation by saying something like "Man up and get your act together" will get you kicked out of the apartment. You can assume Airman Mike then kills himself.

However, keep the conversation open, offer options and an understanding shoulder, and Mike won't kill himself. He'll repeatedly ask you to leave but you won't. Why not? Because you never, ever leave someone in a suicidal crisis alone.

You say, "I'm not going to leave you here alone. We'll get through this together."

And you will. If you absorb the coaching provided by the training module, you will get through the crisis together with Airman Mike. You'll escort him to his first sergeant's home and pass him into caring hands. And even though it's just virtual reality, it will feel good.

Obviously, this is a very specific scenario. Other modules were created for different individuals in different situations, including one for a woman on the brink of suicide and another that addresses sexual assault.

Air Force officials have more reasons besides efficiency for adopting immersive VR modules aimed at reducing suicide. They hope a VR experience will succeed where years of traditional instruction have failed. The year 2021, the last for which records are available, was a good one for the Air Force. While the Army's suicide rate increased, the Marine Corps, Navy, and Air Force (including Space Force guardians) all had declines. Only the Air Force's decline was substantial, with a reduction to about 2011 levels. But 2021 was an outlier; on average, USAF suicides are climbing. The year 2015 had been the highest number of suicides, sixty-four, in the Air Force in the twenty-first century, but was surpassed in 2019 when eighty-four active duty Air Force members took their lives.

The Air Force, however, isn't about to throw in the towel. The VR prevention module isn't the only innovative tool up their sleeve. Colonel Sandelier told me, "Another is a program called Wingman Connect. Our new airmen are being immersed in a new type of resilience training, where they are put in a group environment and really taught how to develop appropriate supportive group dynamics. Wingman Connect teaches each airman to build the kind of social network needed to detect when airmen are under distress, when they're self-isolating. The group can sense that self-isolation and immediately bring that person back in. They can elevate each other based on their strengths to the point where the entire group is stronger than any of the individuals is."

Wingman Connect is an "upstream" intervention because from day one on the job, airmen are trained in small groups. If suicide is a "disease of isolation," as it's often called, then small groups trained to manage career and personal challenges together, and to sense when any airman pulls away, may provide a cure. And it may short-circuit mental health issues that could later result in self-harm. Studies have shown that Wingman Connect is the first preventive program to lessen suicidal ideation, depressive symptoms, and occupational conflicts in the Air Force community. I think it's tempting but a mistake to view military suicides as separate from suicides among civilians in the United States. Instead, it's another facet of our nation's suicide crisis, and like that crisis, it defies easy explanation. Yes, individuals who choose military careers may come with risk factors that aren't evenly distributed in the general population. Recruitment policies may draw more people with risk factors into some parts of the military. Military careers expose individuals to danger and strong emotions. But to ask why suicide steadily increases in the armed forces is to ask why, since 1999, suicide rates in the US have been on the rise; between 2007 and 2018, overall suicide rates have increased by a third; and suicide among ten- to twenty-four-year-olds has increased by nearly 60 percent. It's not a coincidence that

the Air Force suicide rates also increased; it should have been ex-
pected. So the mystery of Air Force and other military suicides folds
into the larger, confounding mystery that should haunt us all.

Lieutenant General Brian Kelly, formerly the Air Force's deputy
chief of staff for manpower, personnel, and services, said, "Suicide
is a difficult national problem without easily identifiable solutions
that has the full attention of leadership." He said the Air Force seeks
immediate, midterm, and long-range answers to a military and nationwide problem. It is encouraging to know the Air Force has
achieved this seemingly impossible goal before.

CHAPTER ELEVEN

SYSTEMS APPROACHES: DENMARK

In some ways the United States as a whole is in the same dilemma as the US Air Force but with one important caveat. As a nation, we have never reduced suicide rates by design, as the Air Force has. And since 2007, with suicide rates up by 35 percent overall and by more than 57 percent in some groups, any illusion of control or impact on suicide rates we might have had is surely gone. You probably don't know that the United States has a national suicide policy created by a distinguished organization called the National Action Alliance for Suicide Prevention. The policy came out in 2012. But no expert I spoke with even mentioned it, and until I looked it up, I'd never read a word of it. A recent report by SAMHSA about the national policy contained these words:

> This report concludes that despite this increasing level of activity, efforts to implement all that we know about suicide prevention as part of a comprehensive approach that seeks to prevent suicide across the lifespan (including adults as well as youth) have been rare.

"Rare" is putting it mildly. The truth is our government has not attempted a systemwide approach to suicide prevention. There have never been more federal, state, and local initiatives to stop suicide, at great cost, but they've operated outside any unified national plan. And remarkably, virtually no data is available about the success or failure of most of these efforts. Meanwhile, suicides have only risen. What are we to conclude except that these efforts are failing? Ten years later, one is right to wonder if there is any difference between a national policy and none at all. About the Action Alliance strategy, Eric Caine wrote, "The National Strategy is not a true strategy that is implemented nationally. It is an encouraging document, meant to provide grist for states and to use in some fashion with Congress. But the bits and pieces that have been created in no way constitute the implementation of an integrated 'strategy.'"

SAMHSA's 988 Suicide and Crisis Lifeline is an example of an important part of the plan that came into existence and has already created positive change. Certified Community Behavioral Health Clinics are another encouraging part, but there are presently too few of them to make a substantial difference in suicide rates.

It's not as if the United States doesn't know how to create a systems approach to suicide prevention. The USAF provided a blueprint of a community-based network of overlapping systems of care. Another US-based initiative bears exploring even though its benefits apply only to members of private health care organizations, not the general public. The Zero Suicide program, developed by the Henry Ford Health System in Michigan, aims to prevent *all* suicides among its patients. The program was created almost twenty years ago by a group of Henry Ford mental health practitioners who wanted to improve support for patients suffering from depression. Under the

Zero Suicide program, patients are assessed for suicide risk at every visit and assigned to one of four risk categories. Each risk level comes with a specific treatment plan and timeline for care, ranging from immediate inpatient treatment for those at high risk to referrals for outpatient therapy for those at moderate risk. The program also includes the development of a safety plan for at-risk patients, which can include removing access to firearms or other lethal means from the home. Staff members also follow up with patients during transitions in care, particularly after psychiatric hospitalization, when the risk of suicide is highest.

The impact of the Zero Suicide program has been impressive. Before its implementation, the suicide rate among Henry Ford's mental health patients was approximately 100 per 100,000, similar to rates in other mental health populations. However, in the program's first nine years, the rate dropped to an average of 22 per 100,000, according to a 2015 report published in *JAMA Psychiatry.* That's a huge success. The program will be expanded to primary care, since 83 percent of those who attempt suicide visit a doctor in the year preceding their death. Henry Ford aims to provide all its one million patients with at least one annual suicide evaluation during a visit to their general practitioner.

The success of the Zero Suicide program, combined with its relatively low cost for training staff and updating electronic health records, has led to its adoption by at least 500 other US health care systems, as well as hospitals in the United Kingdom, Australia, and other countries. The Zero Suicide Institute provides guidelines for implementing the program. The director of the institute, Julie Goldstein Grumet, PhD, is optimistic about the program's potential to be successful in a variety of settings. "It just makes sense," she said. "And that's what's inspiring people to try it."

Its downside? It's available only to members of participating health care networks.

Applying a systems approach to an entire nation is far from impossible. Some nations have faced a suicide crisis as harrowing as the United States' and enacted public policies that reduced suicides in the entire country—broad, community-based approaches that catch a great number of suicidal individuals in a big net. Denmark, once plagued by an astronomical number of suicides, is one such place.

"My name is Troels Torp. Most mornings I get up and turn on the TV, put on the news. Then I make a pot of coffee and just open my work PC to start working."

Troels Torp, over six feet tall, is a boyish, red-haired man of thirty-four. And since his condominium is at the top of his building and the roof intrudes with oblique angles and windows, he frequently ducks and minds his head. Yet his apartment is spacious for one occupant, with a quirky, cozy feeling in the bedroom, kitchen, living room, and music room, where he plays guitar. He goes to work at the kitchen table, which he keeps spotless like the rest of his quarters. The space is airy and spare, which seems to be the Scandinavian way.

Troels says, "I write a lot of articles so there is a lot of research and I do that in the morning. I enjoy it because I am a very curious person, and I love to embrace new knowledge. I love to study different things and kind of be a nerd about it. I'm never satisfied, I want to know it all." Troels's smile contains a hint of frustration, as if I'm standing between him and his research, which I am. "In the afternoons I write."

Research, writing, then well before sunset each day Troels shuts down his computer and goes for a walk in the parks of Aarhus, Denmark's second-largest city. It's located on the eastern coast of the Jutland peninsula, which borders the Kattegat Sea, gateway to the North Sea. Aarhus has a rich history dating back to the Vikings. Several universities call it home and it enjoys waves of invasions by students from all around Denmark and the world.

Troels walks on beaches and in the woods to escape the crowds. "What nature does for me is give me tranquility." Troels laughs ironically as he claims, "It's my safe place. It's where I can clear my head and put on music and walk and I don't have a direction or a goal in mind. I just follow the path wherever it takes me.

"I have a rule to walk at least once every day, and not just for ten minutes. It has to be thirty or forty minutes but usually an hour. That way when I come home, my head is clear and I'm feeling calm, and not feeling stressed about the workday. And that gives me time to prepare for the day tomorrow."

In short pants over long legs, Troels strides across black coral rocks on a white sand beach. In dark woods he feeds apples to fearless deer. His life was not always so orderly.

"I had always been this very easy to talk to, happy-go-lucky guy, never having a bad day. But when I was in my last year of high school I was a runner on an elite track and cross-country team. And I got a lot of back injuries. The doctor took an MRI and they told me I have to stop running; otherwise I will have three disks extrude in my back.

"So I just lost my entire identity at that point. I was an elite run-ner, then suddenly I wasn't. At the same time, my best friend stopped talking to me. I never knew why but he just stopped."

His best friend turned his back on Troels and, worse, encour-aged others to do so too. Fifteen years later the memory still creases Troels's brow. But his high school growing pains were just a warm-up for the calamities of college. Troels studied medicine, intending to become a physician. His fellow students seemed overly competi-tive and harsh. In the words of neuroscientist John Mann, the world seemed excessively cruel.

Troels said, "The students were very hard on each other. Always trying to put each other down, always trying to be the best. I got trampled on a lot. Not physically but mentally."

The academics and hostile atmosphere stressed Troels so much he began drinking alcohol to get to sleep. Soon he drank alcohol to get himself up. He stumbled through two semesters but had to re-peat one. An accidental injury introduced Troels to self-cutting. Cutting provides short-term relief to some people in deep psycho-logical pain, but it's a losing proposition. The relief quickly dimin-ishes, and the self-harm can lead to suicide. Anyone self-cutting should immediately seek care.

Troels spent a few weeks in a psychiatric hospital. Then, instead of relief, visions and voices haunted him. He said, "I suddenly started to hear voices, and I started having visions. The scariest one was when I was watching television. One of the actors' shadows went out of the screen and into the room and just ran around me and out the door. I knew it wasn't real. But I still saw it."

The voices were persistent and cruel. "I had two different voices, a woman's voice on my left side, and a man's voice on my right. And both of them were just talking negatively about me and saying,

'You're no good. You can't do anything right. You should just kill yourself. You should cut yourself. Nobody loves you. You don't even love yourself.'"

Troels took a leave of absence from college. The voices pushed him to the edge. To keep them at bay, he spent days drinking and cutting. Finally he'd had enough. He attempted to kill himself three times.

"I don't think that I actually wanted to die," Troels told me in a quiet voice. "It was more a feeling of just getting relief. Kind of just, make it all stop. Just stop."

Troels failed his first two suicide attempts, and his father interrupted the third. Troels grabbed the lifeline he extended. He let his father take him to a psychiatric hospital. There, psychiatrists added personality disorders to his prior diagnoses of depression and anxiety.

There is a cultural perception that college provides some of the most memorably upbeat years of the lives of those lucky enough to attend. It's a period of physical and intellectual maturing, a time to learn exuberantly, to gain freedom from parental supervision and family dynamics. Many students get their first thrilling glimpse of their careers. Many make lifelong friends. Some meet their husbands or wives. College is transformative. It expands the world a hundredfold.

But college and university students have the deck stacked against them. Suicide is the second-biggest killer in their age group, from ten to thirty-five, and suicide is one of the most common causes of student deaths. Each year, some 24,000 college students attempt suicide, while about 1,100 die trying. About 12 percent of students report suicidal ideation during their college years. In 2019, according to reports, 36 percent of undergraduate college students tested positive for depression, and 31 percent for anxiety. The majority of students are exposed to the suicide or suicidal attempt of someone they know.

There are reasons for these suicides. Young adulthood, the college years, are when serious mental health issues, such as schizophrenia and bipolar disorder, typically first appear. College years come with a raft of risk factors. It is many students' first time away from home; many face stiff competition for grades, and students worry about their academic performance in a way they never did before. Drugs and alcohol are easy to obtain and abuse. Students have to build a new support network and come to rely on their families less and less. Many face financial strain. Some become homeless.

In the United States, there are about 1.3 million homeless students enrolled in college. About one-fifth of them have disabilities. Imagine the academic and social challenges of college while you're sleeping in a shelter, in a tent under a bridge, or in a car, or are perpetually couch surfing at the homes of friends.

Men in their college years are four to six times more likely than college women to kill themselves. Women in college are two to three times more likely to attempt suicide. For students of color and LGBTQIA+ students, overall mental health impacts are even more severe. Fortunately, there are organizations that can prevent higher education from becoming a mental health minefield. Interestingly, some of them, such as the Jed Foundation (JED), were influenced by the Air Force's successful eleven-year suicide prevention campaign.

In 2000, Donna and Phil Satow founded JED, naming it for their youngest son, who died by suicide. Today the foundation is a leading nonprofit dedicated to promoting emotional health and preventing suicide among young adults. One of the key resources JED offers is its educational program for schools and colleges. The foundation provides training and support for school administrators and educators to help them create safe and supportive environments for students and catch mental health issues upstream of crisis events. This includes training on how to recognize signs of mental distress, how to provide appropriate support, and how to connect students to mental health resources. JED's efforts don't end on campus; the foundation provides resources for families and individuals not affiliated with a school. Its website offers a range of resources on topics related to common mental health conditions, self-care strategies, and ways to support someone in need.

Effective campus programs including JED emphasize social connectedness and life skills. To stay mentally healthy, students must pursue a healthy lifestyle, which incorporates nutrition, exercise, sleep, and general work-life balance. And many enter college without must-have practical knowledge, such as how to balance a budget and pay bills on time. Staying organized and protected from many sources of stress is a big part of college success.

Some students enter college with long-standing mental health disorders; caregivers must be alerted to their needs, and their treatment must continue through their transition. Some centers of higher learning train staff members and students to be "gatekeepers." They learn the warning signs of people at risk of suicide, and how to assist them in getting care. Professional services such as crisis management, substance abuse therapy, and mental health assistance are crucial components of on-campus treatment. Campuses must fight the stigma attached to mental health conditions and normalize help-seeking.

And finally, campuses must attend to means restriction. As way too many school shootings have shown us, student gatherings are no

place for firearms. Restricting the availability of poisons and dangerous lab chemicals, and erecting barriers on bridges, parking garages,
and residence towers are all proven means of reducing suicides at
school.

The suicide rate in Troels Torp's native Denmark has historically
been among the world's highest. In 1980 it was 38 per 100,000
people over the age of fifteen. By comparison, that same year the
United States' suicide rate was 12.3 per 100,000 people of all ages.
By 2007, however, the Danish rate dropped to 11.4 per 100,000, or
approximately where it is right now. That's more than a 30 percent
drop in suicides, and among high-income countries, Denmark has
one of the lowest rates.

In 2007 the US suicide rate was just 11.4 per 100,000; today it's
about 13.9. Between 1999 and 2006, the US rate increased by less
than 2 percent per year; however, after that, it increased at twice
that rate.

How did Demark achieve a 30 percent reduction? Over decades
the country took action against their suicide emergency with a multi-
pronged systems approach. Like the US Air Force program and
Zero Suicide, Denmark did not implement one approach but many
overlapping approaches, and this seems to be key to the success of
any systems approach. One substantial prong is that Denmark provides all its citizens with free health care, including mental health
care. This includes access to psychiatric emergency rooms, early intervention services for young individuals experiencing psychosis,
and specialized treatment for anxiety and depression.

The jewels in the crown of the Danish approach to suicide reduction are nineteen specialized medical centers dedicated to

treating suicidal patients. These clinics, called suicide prevention clinics, are open twenty-four hours a day, seven days a week, and are available to provide vital support and treatment to individuals who have attempted suicide or are struggling with thoughts of suicide, including young people and children. They offer counseling, therapy, and medication, and long- and short-term treatment as needed.

I can't help but contrast this immediate access to care with stories I've repeatedly heard across America of individuals, especially the young, who are in suicidal crisis but do not receive meaningful treatment for days or weeks after seeking it. From 2007 to 2016, emergency department visits for pediatric mental health conditions increased by 70 percent, but hospitals and state and local governments have done little to address this sea change. A shortage of beds in psychiatric units results in "boarding" the patient in featureless rooms with no phone or television for days, even weeks at a time. Often the doors to the rooms are left open day and night so staff can keep an eye on the patients. Anyone who's tried to sleep in a busy, noisy hospital understands that this can be torture. And as we know, adequate sleep is fundamental to mental health.

In the worst cases, these environments exacerbate the young patient's condition, and the long-term impacts can be catastrophic. "We have a national crisis," says JoAnna Leyenaar, MD, PhD, MPH, a pediatrician at Dartmouth-Hitchcock Medical Center who led a study on pediatric boarding in emergency departments. Dr. Leyenaar estimates that between one thousand and five thousand young people board each night in the some four thousand US emergency departments.

It is excruciating to imagine as many as five thousand young people in crisis each night boarded in noisy, prison-like holding rooms until psychiatric beds and basic psychiatric care become available. But that's the disgraceful reality in one of the world's wealthiest nations.

Denmark has a population of about 5.9 million, about the same as the state of Minnesota. While the United States, with a population of about 331 million, has no suicide-specific hospitals or clinics, Denmark has nineteen. One of them, Amager Psychiatric Center in Copenhagen, is an elegant, modern building composed of stainless steel, floor-to-ceiling windows, and bright, welcoming interiors. It breathes a mood of calm. Troels Torp spent seven weeks in a hospital much like this one near his home in Aarhus. He underwent intensive psychoanalysis and was painfully weaned off psychotropic medications and alcohol. He credits the hospital with saving his life.

At Amager Psychiatric Center, therapists like psychologist Titia Lahoz explore patients' dangerous thoughts. Lahoz, originally from Spain, told me how it felt to lose a patient to those thoughts.

"When a patient dies in our center, of course it affects us very much. I have colleagues who stopped working in the field afterwards. It takes time to recover. We have an expression in Denmark, 'to have ice in the stomach.' It means that you keep cool or calm in crisis situations. You lose the ice in your stomach when a patient dies, but it's good to know that after a while it returns. And then you evaluate what you might have done differently with that patient."

The core of Lahoz's approach, which combines elements of different therapeutic styles, is to establish a strong personal connection with her patients. David Jobes, whose Collaborative Assessment and Management of Suicidality (CAMS) approach is widely used in suicide prevention clinics throughout Denmark, would simply call this empathy. Lahoz says, "When you are suicidal, it's difficult to find solutions by yourself. I think you need to talk to other people to get some other perspectives and to share your emotional pain. It gives some relief."

In fact, it gives proven relief. According to research led by the Johns Hopkins Bloomberg School of Public Health, a group of Danish men and women who underwent voluntary short-term psychosocial counseling after a suicide attempt experienced a 25 percent reduced rate of subsequent suicide attempts and suicide deaths.

Lahoz proposes ten therapeutic sessions for each patient. "While they are having those ten sessions, we find out if they have any psychiatric disease that needs to be treated. Because people can come in from the street to the suicide prevention clinics and have no prior psychiatric record. We can diagnose them."

Patient Thea Pedersen is twenty years old and dropped out of university because of her suicidal ideation. Lahoz and Thea are both petite women with brown hair; they could be mistaken for mother and daughter. The two sit facing each other in a bright wood-paneled space lit by ceiling-high windows. It looks more like an upscale boardroom than a room for therapy. At first, Thea rarely makes eye contact. Lahoz slowly gets her to open up as she learns the broad strokes of her circumstances.

"When you have suicidal thoughts, what are they really about? If you weren't here anymore, what would you really like to get rid of?"

Thea gently cries. One of her thumbs vigorously rubs the top of the other. "The thoughts that are going on in my head. All the time."

"What kind of thoughts?"

"I do not know what I am going to do with my life. My mother wants me to settle down and give her grandchildren. And my boyfriend just broke up with me because I'm so sad."

"Wow, that's a lot. You feel your mother's expectations. And you just had a breakup. How long have you had thoughts about killing yourself?"

Thea considers. "Six months. I was still in college and I couldn't focus on my work. We studied in groups. The others got mad at me because I was always distracted."

"School too. What else sets off these thoughts about ending your life?"

"Many of my friends got married and have children and things like that. And careers. I can't see any of it. I want it all to stop. I want it to just be over."

I want it all to stop. Thea's words echo Troels Torp's. Generally speaking, suicidal people aren't planning to go to a better world but to escape the pain of this one. Put another way, they're ambivalent about dying, but they will often do what it takes to stop immeasurable pain.

Lahoz says to Thea, "So there's your mother's expectations, your studies, your boyfriend breaking up with you. And life seems to be passing you by while your friends get on with theirs. All together in your head and you want it to stop. It's quite heavy to think such thoughts, Thea. I am so glad you made the decision to come here. That is a great first step."

From the Safety Plan Intervention to CAMS to Titia Lahoz's hybrid approach, therapists quickly cover the basics with people in crisis. It gives them an understanding of the source and severity of their suicidal ideas and tells them if the patient needs inpatient care and supervision. Often the therapist moves on to the safety plan, created by Drs. Barbara Stanley and Gregory Brown, in use in Denmark and around the world. They help the patient create a list of distracting activities that can hold off a suicidal impulse. To that they add people who can help the patient, friends first and then professionals. They urge limiting dangerous means, such as medications, the use of trains, crossing bridges and highways, and other activities that could inspire an impulsive act. And invariably the therapist assures the person in crisis that her condition is temporary, and with sessions of therapy and perhaps medication, the persistent thoughts assailing her can be tamed, perhaps even eliminated.

In 2016, the Johns Hopkins Bloomberg School of Public Health examined the long-term impact of Danish suicide clinics. The researchers scrutinized health data from over 65,000 Danish people who attempted suicide between 1992 and 2010. Of those people, 5,678 received psychosocial therapy at one of Denmark's suicide crisis centers. Their outcomes were compared with 17,304 people who had attempted suicide but hadn't sought treatment afterward. Both groups were followed for about twenty years. According to the study, individuals who got therapy had a 38 percent lower risk of dying from any cause and a 27 percent lower risk of making another suicide attempt over the first year. After five years, the number of suicides in the group that had received treatment after an attempt was 26 percent lower. In the group receiving therapy, the ten-year suicide rate was 229 per 100,000, compared to 314 per 100,000 in the group not receiving therapy.

Lahoz knows the treatment isn't wholly effective for every patient for the rest of their lives. No inpatient or outpatient treatment appears to be. "It seems like the effect is tapering off after three, four years," she told me. "But of course, when we finish with people here, we always tell them that now we know you. So you're very welcome at another time. If you need to, you just call us again and we can start a new session."

Thea Pedersen is just starting out. A veteran of intensive suicide therapy, Troels Torp is doing exceptionally well. It's been six years since he left a hospital and he no longer feels the need for medicine or talk therapy.

But the fact that Troels wound up in a hospital is not what the Danish systems approach to suicide prevention intends at all. It is designed to keep as few people as possible from ever having to go into inpatient care. Denmark's suicide reduction system begins well upstream of suicidal ideation to nip mental health issues in the bud.

Rows of colorful children's bikes line the front entrance to Ny Hollænderskolen, a Danish elementary school in Frederiksberg Municipality, Copenhagen. Inside, student artwork papers the walls, and the familiar scent of industrial cleaner, which must have been agreed upon by an international treaty of school janitors, gently accosts your nose. Ann Eskildsen's third-grade class of twenty students is, with a couple of exceptions, a sea of blond hair, blue eyes, and pale skin. Like third graders everywhere, her kids are allergic to calm and addicted to bouncing out of their seats. But while they bubble with intelligence and mischief, they closely listen to their teacher and rarely misbehave. Her secret? A classroom contest called the Good Behavior Game.

First, Ms. Eskildsen divides the class into two teams and writes *I* and *II* on the chalkboard. Throughout the morning lessons, whenever a student speaks out of turn, leaves their seat, or causes any kind of disruption, Ms. Eskildsen rewards the *other* team with a point. By recess time two hours later, Team I has won 3–2. Victorious, and with whoops and high fives, Team I celebrates. Then both teams pile into coats and head outside.

In Kansas in 1969, a group of teachers and academics created the Good Behavior Game to help teachers keep control of classrooms without having to correct every little instance of disruptive or aggressive behavior. At the same time, the intervention promotes self-regulation, group regulation, and social behavior. The game treats the classroom as a community. To get along in the community, students must identify their desire to act up, and curb it. Behaving earns your team a victory shared by every member. Misbehaving, and earning points for the other team, earns derision and self-reproach. But these effects are short-lived; the game is played many times a week, and everyone gets a chance to shine.

For such a mild intervention, the Good Behavior Game is disproportionately impactful. Annette Erlangsen, PhD, the head of program at the Danish Research Institute for Suicide Prevention, is a big fan of the Good Behavior Game. She told me, "The Good Behavior Game is a way of trying to make young people have a more reflective knowledge of their own emotions and how they deal with extreme emotions. One can see it as a kind of suicide prevention initiative in the sense that it helps young people get onto a healthy pathway for mental health."

One study of the Good Behavior Game in first- and second-grade classrooms in the 1985–86 academic year yielded remarkable long-term results. The study followed up with students at the ages of nineteen and twenty-one. Researchers discovered that relative to a control group, they had significantly lower rates of antisocial personality disorder, drug and alcohol use disorders, regular smoking, delinquency and incarceration for violent crimes, *and* suicidal ideation. Earlier studies with shorter follow-up times showed similar results.

Dr. Erlangsen reports that Denmark's suicide reduction program has a host of additional components, some of them carefully planned and others that arose from social norms. They fall into

three categories. *Universal* interventions impact the entire population; *selective* interventions are aimed at those who are at greater risk
for suicidal behavior; and *indicated* preventions focus on individuals
who have already engaged in harming themselves. Patients like
Troels Torp, hospitalized for suicide attempts, come under the third
category. Thea Pedersen, who had not yet attempted suicide, belongs
in the second.

Erlangsen acknowledges the huge role of universal health care,
including free mental health care, but she says restriction of means—
a universal intervention—has had the biggest impact.

"Medical doctors became much more aware of prescribing medications in smaller amounts to make sure people with severe mental
disorders didn't have large quantities of dangerous medications at
home. Other means restriction were weapons. We have an abun-
dance of international evidence that shows if one makes restrictions
on the number of firearms, then the suicide rate goes down. So it's
very evident that this is really a low-hanging fruit in terms of suicide
prevention. In a Danish context, weapons are for hunting. Handguns
are practically absent in Denmark.

"Catalytic converters on cars were introduced in the 1980s and
'90s. So carbon monoxide poisoning from car exhaust became practically nonexistent."

Restricting household gases that contained carbon monoxide was
another universal component of means restriction, a strategy that
had stunning success in reducing suicides in Great Britain beginning in the 1950s. Others included restricting barbiturates and opioid painkillers. Ibuprofen and acetaminophen come in blister packs
of just ten pills. Train stations and platforms throughout Denmark
use barriers to prevent pedestrians from stepping onto train tracks
and jumping from bridges onto tracks.

At the selective level, there are many significant risk groups who are in danger of suicide, including those who are addicted to alcohol or drugs, have recently been diagnosed with a serious physical illness, have previously attempted suicide, and people who are homeless, institutionalized, or imprisoned. A psychiatrist and an ambulance are always available as part of a psychiatric emergency outreach team to help patients who are experiencing a serious crisis. Home visits and family assistance are provided to patients who have been released from a mental hospital. Additionally, the Danish charitable group Lifeline has a suicide hotline that provides trained volunteers to those in need.

Hospitals and clinics in Denmark aim to bridge the gap between treatment and social support services, such as housing assistance and vocational training. In the United States, psychiatric care and social services are often strangers. When individuals are released from inpatient psychiatric care in the US, many fall back into the conditions of unemployment, homelessness, and substance abuse that added to their suicidal inclinations to begin with. This partly accounts for why US patients' chances of killing themselves are highest in the first few weeks after discharge, and remain elevated for several months afterward (though, to be fair, to some degree this is true almost everywhere). When Troels Torp was discharged after seven weeks in a hospital, he was provided with a place to live. Like every Dane, he received funds to finish college. He graduated and soon became financially independent, as he is today. Troels's story is one of hope.

In the music room of his condo, Troels skillfully picks at his Washburn acoustic guitar. The room's bare wooden walls make a

natural amplifier—the tuneful melody carries through the apartment. Troels schedules his music too. For him it doesn't pay to be
too busy, but neither is it good to have too much unstructured time.

He says, "Today I live a modest life, I will say, a simple life. And
that's how it should be for me. I always say to myself that I have to
be as content when I go to bed in the evening as I am when I get up
in the morning. I have my strategies for when I'm kind of starting
to feel bad, kind of feeling stressed out or feeling the need to do self-
harm. I have my different strategies. And I'm sticking to 'em." Troels
smiles bashfully.

Two hours later, something completely unexpected is happening. Applause breaks out as Troels Torp confidently strides onto
a stage in an auditorium at Odder Højskole, a Danish Folk High
School. Folk high schools in Scandinavian countries are boarding
schools where mostly young people can study whatever they like before embarking on college or careers. There are no grades, no pressure. A faculty member has introduced Troels and the subject of his
talk—surviving suicide—to about a hundred young adults in folding
chairs. Commenting on his introduction, Troels jokes, "That was a
little depressing, wasn't it? How 'bout we change gears?"

Gone is the modest, simple-living Troels, and in his place a char-
ismatic orator in a flowered T-shirt. He has a harrowing but hopeful
story to tell. With humor he disarms the students, hooking them
from the start. I learn this is Troels's 150th talk for an organization
called One of Us. Since 2017 he's given talks, sat on roundtables,
even met with the United Kingdom's Prince Harry to discuss mental health issues among young Britons.

In the back of the auditorium, a blond woman whose black-
framed glasses make her look teacherly is here to support Troels.
Anja Kare Vedelsby is a One of Us program manager and soldier in

the battle against mental health stigma. She tells me about One of Us. "We fight stigma by promoting inclusion and combating discrimination related to mental illness. We do that with a big core of ambassadors. And ambassadors in One of Us are all people with lived experience of mental illness. Like Troels." One of Us is one more tool in Denmark's systems approach to suicide prevention. After the initiative achieved impressive results in the nonprofit sector, the Danish government decided to fund it indefinitely. Vedelsby says, "People with mental illness risk being excluded from many different areas of life, from society in general, from social life and even within the family. And in the labor market you risk not getting a job, or being excluded from the labor market once you get ill. We're trying to change all that."

They change that by putting people with behavioral health issues, and sometimes their relatives, in the public eye, in talks, media interviews, and on television. They promote the idea that you can recover from mental health problems, or you can struggle with them your whole life. Either way, you are still a valuable human, still "one of us." The organization's motto: *No more silence, doubt and taboo about mental illness!*

At the front of the room, Troels talks about social exclusion, being ostracized by friends, and badly fumbling college his first time out. He has set the stage for his years of struggle and wants to brace the young audience for it. "So, are you ready for a heavy load?" he asks. "Because here comes my diagnosis." As he starts describing his horrifying visions and voices, you want to reach out and tell this earnest young man it's okay now, but of course he knows it. It's okay *now*. The Troels you really want to comfort is eighteen years old, and lost.

Vedelsby continues, "Troels is a really excellent ambassador in

One of Us, because he worked through so many of his very serious mental health problems in a way that he is able to share today.
And he shares them in a very reflective, engaging manner."

Troels concludes his talk under a rain of applause. He blinks in
the spotlight, returning to his humble core, a modest man bewil-
dered by resounding approval. It's like payback for many years in the
wilderness. You find yourself cheering too.

CHAPTER TWELVE

FACING SUICIDE

In a country as vast and diverse as the United States, creating a national suicide prevention system like Denmark's would pose significant challenges. In its absence, it's worthwhile to explore causes for America's ever-increasing suicide rate and seek solutions there. In this book we've looked at common risk factors for individuals and some groups, including Natives, agricultural workers and rural people, Black Americans, and military personnel. Many of the risk factors and social causes contributing to suicide in these groups can be generalized to our entire population.

Poverty and unemployment are recurring themes, as rising suicide rates since around 1999 and accelerated rates since 2007 are linked to periods of increasing unemployment and economic instability. And as we know, people without jobs, benefits, and resources have the most challenging time getting mental health support in America. Here is a chilling example of just one cohort. In the late 1960s, according to Anne Case and Angus Deaton, authors of the excellent book *Deaths of Despair and the Future of Capitalism*, 95 percent of white men from ages twenty-five to fifty-four had jobs. By 2010, 80 percent had jobs. By 2018, recovering from the 2008 recession, 86 percent had jobs. Of the jobless in 2018, only 20 percent were looking for work and were designated unemployed. The rest were considered absent from the labor force. Case and Deaton determined that places where fewer members of the working-age population were employed had higher rates of suicide, drug overdoses, and alcohol-related liver diseases. Other studies indicate that unemployment adds to suicide risk in both men and women, and that job loss is a stronger predictor of suicide than other economic factors, such as income or education level.

Unemployment can rob individuals of self-esteem, status, job satisfaction, and financial stability. Unemployed people may feel like a burden to their families and develop the idea that friends and family would be better off without them. They may have feet firmly planted in the circles of danger described by Thomas Joiner's interpersonal theory of suicide. For those with mental health issues, joblessness and its resulting poverty make it even harder to benefit from mental health care. At least with jobs, they had a chance to purchase therapy if they could find it.

In the ever-evolving science of suicide, new and unexpected causes percolate to the surface. For example, climate change. Climate change can contribute to extreme weather events and natural disasters such as floods, hurricanes, and wildfires. Resulting social disruption, including crop failures, loss of livelihood, and displacement, add to mental health stressors and increase the risk of self-harm. Complicating all this is the general anxiety of knowing that we're methodically destroying our planet, which seems to be most acutely felt by the young.

Interestingly, in the last two decades, researchers have noted that living at higher altitudes lowers mortality from all causes . . . except suicide. Suicide rates increase by 0.4 per 100,000 individuals for every 100 meters gained. One likely reason is that decreased atmospheric oxygen interferes with brain function. However, the declines in cancer and cardiovascular disease found at altitude surpass the rise in suicide rates.

Further research will determine if higher altitudes in the western and mountain regions of the United States contribute to higher suicide rates. Montana, Wyoming, Colorado, Utah, Nevada, and New Mexico suffer about 30 percent more suicides than the national average, earning this collection of states the nickname the "suicide belt." More accepted causes include the rural nature of many of these states, their corresponding lack of mental health resources, the high rate of gun ownership, and high rates of population shift. These states have more transient people, which results in weakened social bonds and social institutions like marriage and religion. Decreased social integration raises the suicide rate. Add to that a high population of older single white men, many of whom are unemployed. While 80 percent of suicide deaths in America are among men and women ages forty-five to fifty-four, men age eighty-five and older have the highest rate of any group in the country.

Early puberty, defined as the onset of secondary sexual characteristics before the age of eight in girls and nine in boys, has been linked to an increased suicide risk. The exact causes of early puberty are not fully understood, but factors include genetics, environmental toxins, and obesity. One potential link between early puberty and suicide is through the psychological and social stressors that often accompany this developmental stage. With the onset of puberty comes a significant increase in the levels of the hormones estrogen and testosterone, which can affect brain development and lead to changes in mood and behavior. Adolescence is a time of important social and emotional development, and an early puberty can lead to a mismatch between physical and emotional maturity, causing feelings of discomfort and confusion. Put another way, the brains of adolescents are not developed enough to maturely deal with the flood of emotions brought on by puberty. These emotions can lead to an increased risk of depression, anxiety, and other mental health problems that are known risk factors for suicide.

According to the CDC (Centers for Disease Control and Prevention) the suicide rate among young people ages ten to twenty-four increased by 57 percent between 2007 and 2018. Around 2000, scientists first noticed that puberty had been coming earlier for American children, a trend that continues today. It is plausible that the early onset of puberty and the increase in adolescent suicide rates are connected.

The biggest, most obvious roadblock to reducing suicide in the United States is our profit-driven, deeply inequitable health care system. Rising costs of medical care result in many Americans delaying or skipping checkups and procedures. Individuals are being diagnosed with cancer at later stages than necessary and are rationing or forgoing critical medicines such as insulin. Almost 50 percent of Americans have delayed or skipped medical care because of its steep price tag. Short of making medical care available to everyone, as Denmark has, there are many improvements we can make.

About a third of health care dollars spent in the US go toward administration, which is significantly higher than in other countries. Experts attribute its high cost to lack of standardization in health care systems, which leads to great discretion and variance in billing from one hospital to the next and from one provider's office to the next. The federal government could enforce standardization. It has chosen not to in large part because of the powerful lobbies of health services and drug and device manufacturers. These lobbies aggressively fight such progressive, lifesaving ideas. Instead, the government has chosen to provide insurance, a job for which it's uniquely unsuited, rather than reforming health care as a whole.

Insulin in the United States costs ten times more than in Canada, and simple procedures at monopoly hospitals are 12 percent higher than those in markets with four or more competitors. This tells us that unvarnished greed plays a role in our medical system's dysfunction. The US has more advanced technology and sophisticated medical systems than any other country, leading, for instance, to a greater number of MRIs and cardiac surgeons per capita. But this does not result in better outcomes. Survival rates for heart disease have risen relative to other developed countries, but there's been underprovision of routine care for conditions such as high blood pressure and mental illness. Treating mental illness and particularly suicidal ideation is not as lucrative or prestigious as other medical services. As we've seen again and again, finding affordable, good-quality mental health care is ludicrously challenging and doubtless adds to our epidemic suicide rate. One recent study of young people concluded that living in a county with a shortage of mental health providers was connected to a 16 percent higher suicide rate. About 20 percent of children in the US have a mental health condition, but only about half of those who need mental health care are currently receiving it. This is as stark a rebuke as any I've seen of the way our nation faces mental health and suicide.

Experts argue a coordinated national plan is a must to make a real dent in America's suicide crisis—along with much more funding. In some places, private health care systems and other organizations are making headway in creating comprehensive suicide reduction plans. In particular, the Zero Suicide initiative and CCBHCs (Certified Community Behavioral Health Centers) show promise. But the impact of both is far too small to be felt nationally, and will be so for the foreseeable future.

It may be impossible in a book about suicide to explore every demographic and marginalized group who battle with self-harm. I have failed to address groups whose challenges are deserving of books of their own. Two immediately come to mind.

Studies indicate LGBTQIA+ youth are more vulnerable to suicidal ideation and attempts; they are more than four times as likely to attempt suicide as their peers. This is due to their experiences of prejudice, discrimination, and societal rejection. LGBTQIA+ youth may also deal with other stressors like coming out, the worry of being rejected by their loved ones and friends, and a lack of access to the right mental health supports. To lower the risk of suicide and to advance mental health, it is crucial for our country to adopt proactive measures to assist and welcome LGBTQIA+ people.

The suicide rate for persons seventy-five and older is currently 19.1 per 100,000 people, higher than the general suicide rate of 14.5 per 100,000 people, according to the CDC. Several factors can raise an older person's risk of suicide. Physical and mental health issues are the primary cause. As people age, they are more prone to develop chronic illnesses such as cancer and heart disease, which can cause discomfort and impairment. Cognitive decline, depression, and other mental health issues may be more prevalent in older persons, and they contribute to social isolation and loneliness. As friends and family members die, many older people face a loss of social connections and may become less engaged in social activities. After retiring, many older persons can feel as though their lives no longer have any purpose. They may not know what their place in society is.

Support and services for older persons are essential, especially for those who might be in danger. This includes having access to programs that encourage social involvement and relationships, support groups, and mental health services. By addressing these problems, we can lower the suicide rate among senior citizens and raise their standard of living in general.

Until our government does what needs to be done and enacts the measures that experts say are necessary to bring our suicide emergency under control, the battle against self-killing will be fought town by town and family by family. Friends and loved ones just like you and me must take on the formidable challenge of facing suicide. Fortunately, as we've seen in communities across the country, hope emerges from unexpected places.

Butte Civic Center, Montana, Winter 2018. Outside the gym it's just 26° Fahrenheit and snowing. Inside it's deafening with drumbeats, foot stomps, handclaps, and the nonstop roar of two teams' fans trying to out-stomp and out-roar each other. And the game hasn't even begun. More than two thousand people pack the stadium, and maybe half have made the 145-mile trip from Arlee to watch the Warriors as they prepare to defend their Title C Division Championship against Manhattan Christian, a private school. They don't care that they'll drive more than two hours back home through snow. The Warriors warm up with conspicuously fast displays of three-pointers, behind-the-back passes, wraparounds, layups, and fakes. The Warriors are favored to win—they won the division last year. But can they do it again, subjecting Manhattan Christian to their own personal Groundhog Day by making them relive last year's defeat? And can the Warriors do it in the middle of a suicide cluster that's taken twenty lives and is ripping the soul out of the Flathead Indian Reservation?

In the midst of unthinkable pressure, the team takes a time-out in the locker room. They feel a burning desire to do something to address the suicide crisis, to punch a hole in the stigma surrounding the disease that's been killing their community. Urged on by Coach Zanen Pitts, they decide to make a video for social media. Crowded into a drab cinder-block hallway as hundreds clamor for them mere feet away, the Warriors take a stab at words they've committed to memory, each taking a sentence and delivering lines with halting sincerity. Phillip Malatare, Greg Whitesell, Lane Johnson, Darshan Bolen, Will Mesteth, Isaac Fisher.

> We the Arlee Warriors are dedicating this divisional tournament to all the families that have lost a loved one due to the pressures of life. We want you to know that you will be in our hearts and in our prayers as we step onto the floor to represent our school, community and our reservation. As a team, we rely on each other to get through the challenges on the court or in life. To all the youth on the Flathead reservation, we want you to know that we stand together with you. Remember, you are the future. Please help us share this message and join our team as we battle against suicide.

The Warriors shoot their video off to social media and take to the court. Coach Pitts takes up the tale. "And then right after that, they ran out and played an epic game and we won. And, you know, the fairy tale continued. So we get on the bus that night and we're going home and my wife says, look how many views this has. So I look at it. It's got like a hundred thousand views. I'm like, whoa, it wasn't even that good."

That homemade video spawned more videos professionally shot by team videographer Jordan Lefler. Emails, snail mail, and phone calls poured in. The media wanted a piece of the Warriors, but what touched the team the most were young people who wrote to praise, commiserate, and even confess their own suicidal thoughts. Their overwhelming response gave birth to a suicide prevention campaign called the Warrior Movement. Their motto: *Together We Rise.* Their videos live online at jointhewarriormovement.com. Greg Whitesell and his fellow athletes, young men and women alike, began visiting schools around the state to spread powerful messages of hope and unity in the face of suicide. Greg admits he is by no means a natural speaker, but before crowds of strangers, he tells his tale while revealing the joyful charisma he exudes on the court. He feels compelled to spread the idea without which he probably wouldn't have survived until the critical night his friends rescued him.

He says, "It's all about getting to the next minute. I remember Coach Zanen told me that one time, and it wasn't even about suicide. We were just working out and that really resonated with me. Just get to the next minute, you know. Sure this minute's hard but the next minute, something new could happen. So if you're going through a hard time, try to stay positive. It's hard I know, but there are good things to come."

"All right. If you have a friend, a family member, a coworker, check on 'em. Check on 'em. It's the best deterrent—'how are you doing today?' Suicide is the most preventable kind of death and almost any positive action may save a life."

At a packed Charlotte music venue, Fonda Bryant's hour-long presentation about getting in suicide's face is part confessional and part revival meeting. Her big personality is set to stun; she holds nothing back. After her near-miss with suicide in 1995, she founded a nonprofit called Wellness Action Recovery, which is her springboard for public talks, podcasts, television appearances, and a whirlwind of suicide-prevention activities. She's won too many prizes and accolades to list, but they include the 2021 Nexstar Remarkable Woman of the Year award, the 2021 Black Mental Health Symposium Mental Health Advocate of the Year award, and many others.

Fonda thought the high-rise parking garages in Charlotte, some up to nine stories tall, attracted too many people who jumped to their deaths. She wrote letters to garage managers and has so far succeeded in placing signs at strategic points in five garages and counting. They read YOU'RE NOT ALONE. NEED HELP? along with the National Suicide Prevention hotline number. Fonda's lifesaving efforts are achieving results. Garage suicides are trailing off.

On countless afternoons like this one before a crowd in Charlotte, Fonda speaks in her role as a Gatekeeper Trainer for QPR Institute, a national suicide prevention organization. People trained in the methods of QPR—which stands for Question, Persuade, Refer—learn to see the warning signs of a suicidal crisis and how to question, persuade, and refer someone to assistance. Fonda draws from her 1995 near-tragedy and recounts her aunt Spankie's speedy intervention after Fonda told Spankie she could have her shoes.

"Watch behavior clues," Fonda tells her Charlotte audience. "Talking about wanting to die. Being a burden to everybody. Giving away prized possessions. You all heard what I said; I called my aunt Spankie, my shoes were my prized possession and I told her she could have them."

Prized possessions might not seem like a big factor in suicide prevention, but they stand for so much more. They embody the web of interpersonal connections most of us inhabit, intimate bonds that help keep us alive or torment us with their absence. So it stands to reason that after her talk in Charlotte, when Fonda paid a visit to Spankie's house in Gastonia, her aunt would disappear for a few moments, then return with a half-dozen boxes of her own shoes to show off.

"Oh my goodness, look at your shoes!" Fonda's hands nearly shook with anticipation. Spankie's collection had a more practical bent than hers, so rather than flowered pumps and elaborate heels, Spankie modeled hiking shoes, equestrian boots, and whimsical sneakers embroidered with images of Bart Simpson. Fonda had something nice to say about each pair.

Spankie said, "I'm renovating my house, so keep in mind some of my shoes I cannot get to right now." She gave me a conspiratorial look. "And I don't think I should say out loud how many pairs of shoes I actually have."

Amber Dykshorn has been a farmer, a farmer's wife, a widow, and now an insurance agent. But mainly she's the proud mom of Kalee, Kahne, and Kolbe. If she talks about her late husband, Chris, for more than a few seconds, her voice catches and her eyes fill, but she's got way too much can-do to let Chris's suicide define the future for her family or herself. Being a professional widow isn't in her DNA. On this bright August morning, there's a family meetup at Lake Francis Case, a reservoir on the Missouri River in South Dakota. Amber's parents are taking the family boating, which means float-towing and waterskiing. Strapped into flotation devices, the kids grin with anticipation. Standoffish Kahne removes his sunglasses long enough to show me eyes shining with mirth. Kahne, Kolbe, and Amber go first in the big float.

"Here we go, here we go!" Amber wraps her arms around her boys and holds them tight. Kalee, tall and bronzed, is the only real water-skier in the bunch, so she's up next. Later, Amber tells me, "Chris is still with us in a very big sense. I never want my kids to forget their dad. I am looking forward to seeing my kids grow up. And I don't want to miss out in any part of their life. Seeing my kids grow up is what gives me hope. Hope of a bright future for each one of them."

On the subject of hope, SAVE's Dan Reidenberg draws from his years of guiding suicidal people out of darkness and toward lives worth living. He says, "Ultimately, I really get hope from those that are really close to death that we can keep alive. That we can see that finding a way to connect with them keeps them alive. And sometimes that is through therapy and sometimes it is just through a good listening ear. Sometimes it is by checking in with them when they most need it and being there for them."

CAMS developer David Jobes finds hope by looking into the future. "What gives me hope in the field of suicide prevention are the young people. You know, I've got a lab of twenty to thirty students who are on fire! They are so excited to be part of the solution, to be doing research and learning about this and going on to academic careers or going on as clinicians or working in the field. That's what gives me hope."

Anna Whiting Sorrell, in charge of responding to the firestorm of suicides that tore through the Flathead Indian Reservation, and her family long before that, hasn't been touched by hope yet, but she's homing in on it. When I interviewed her for the camera, she said, "I am really, really proud to be a Salish woman sitting in this chair today. That, somehow, I can help communicate to a broader world, to understand how this epidemic of suicide has impacted my own family, certainly my community, my tribe overall. And I am so indebted that people are willing to hear our story and help us get to a place of hope."

Columbia University epidemiologist Madelyn Gould has made a close study of hope in the face of suicide. She's found hope in the most hopeless and has put her finger on how to cultivate it. Her perspective deeply influenced the creation of this book.

"Rather than the social transmission of suicide, what we're trying to do is to turn it on its head and start the social transmission of suicide prevention. The way you start a contagion of hope is to start spreading stories of recovery, spreading stories of resilience, spreading stories of hope. Because people don't think that you can recover from many different types of mental illnesses. But you can."

If you are thinking about suicide or if you or someone you know is in emotional crisis, please call or text 988 at any time to reach the 988 Suicide and Crisis Lifeline for confidential, free crisis support.

ACKNOWLEDGMENTS

I'm indebted to all the people who shared their most personal stories about life and death with me. It was a privilege to spend time with you and I hope you see much of your most hopeful selves in these pages. I'm grateful to the suicide specialists interviewed for this book and for the PBS film *Facing Suicide.* Our energetic corps of suicidologists put in yeoman's service discussing ideas, reviewing chapters, and sharing the wisdom they've acquired saving lives over many years. I especially want to thank Dr. Eric Caine, who never failed to return my emails and calls and steer me back from errant paths onto which I'd wandered. And there's no part of suicide studies and treatment that doesn't have Dr. Caine's imprint on it. Similarly, Dr. Dan Reidenberg of SAVE fielded my queries with boundless energy for the subject and refreshing bluntness about the state of suicide prevention and health care in the US. Dr. Jill Harkavy-Friedman of the American Foundation for Suicide Prevention tirelessly answered queries and recommended experts and those with lived experience for me to speak with. AFSP was a gracious and generous partner throughout the film process. Early on, Dr. Thomas Joiner did me a great favor by insisting I read a collection of over a hundred psychological autopsies before I'd gone very far into suicide research. It made me take a hard look at the road ahead, and I think that's what he intended.

Michael Rosenfeld at Twin Cities Public Television was an exemplary executive producer of the film and a wonderful partner throughout the whole creative endeavor. He and the gifted crew at TPT embraced *Facing Suicide* with courage and grace from the start. Thanks to my agent, William Clark, for having the heart and vision to energetically promote a book on such a difficult, important subject. I'm grateful for the team at Avery Publishing and for editor Caroline Sutton's expert hand at helping bring these words to the page. Finally, I want to thank my wife, Alison, who is always the first to read and trade ideas about anything I write.

CRISIS RESOURCES

Please contact these resources 24-7 to reach trained counselors for confidential, free crisis support

988 Suicide & Crisis Lifeline. Call or text 988, or chat
   988lifeline.org. Spanish language available.
Veterans Crisis Line. Dial 988, then press 1.
LGBTQ Youth, The Trevor Project. Call (866) 488-7386; text
   "START" to 678678; or chat thetrevorproject.org/get-help

For additional information and resources, please see

American Foundation for Suicide Prevention (AFSP):
   https://afsp.org
Centers for Disease Control and Prevention (CDC):
   https://www.cdc.gov/suicide/index.html
National Action Alliance for Suicide Prevention:
   http://theactionalliance.org/resource-library
National Institute of Mental Health (NIMH): https://www
   .nimh.nih.gov/health/topics/suicide-prevention/index.shtml

Substance Abuse and Mental Health Services Administration
    (SAMSHA): https://www.samhsa.gov
Suicide Awareness Voices of Education (SAVE):
    https://save.org/who-we-are
Suicide Prevention Resource Center (SPRC): http://www.sprc.org
The Trevor Project: https://www.thetrevorproject.org

NOTES

Chapter One: What's Suicide Got to Do with Me?

1 **the act of taking one's own life:** "Suicide Definition & Meaning." (n.d.) Merriam-Webster. Accessed August 30, 2023. https://www.merriam -webster.com/dictionary/suicide.

2 **"a sudden, widespread occurrence":** "Epidemics & Empires: An Optimistic Game about the Human Species." (2021, June 24). UChicago.edu. https://voices.uchicago.edu/202102bpro25800/2021/06 /04/epidemics-empires-an-optimistic-game-about-the-human-species/.

2 **Just since 2007 the suicide rate:** Hedegaard, Holly, Sally C. Curtin, and Margaret Warner. (2018, June). "Suicide Rates in the United States Continue to Increase." NCHS Data Brief No. 309. https://www.cdc .gov/nchs/products/databriefs/db309.htm.

3 **And every day some 15 million:** Richesson, Douglas, Iva Magas, Samantha Brown, et al. (2022). *Key Substance Use and Mental Health Indicators in the United States: Results from the 2021 National Survey on Drug Use and Health.* (HHS Publication No. PEP22-07-01-005, NSDUH Series H-57). Center for Behavioral Health Statistics and Quality, Substance Abuse and Mental Health Services Administration. https://www.samhsa.gov/data/sites/default/files/reports/rpt39443 /2021NSDUHNNR122322/2021NSDUHNNR122322.htm.

Chapter Two: The Ballad of Greg Whitesell, Part One

11 **They were white, taller:** Streep, Abe. (2021). *Brothers on Three: A True Story of Family, Resistance, and Hope on a Reservation in Montana* (New York: Celadon Books), 16.

13 **The closeness to family:** *The ASAM National Practice Guideline for the Treatment of Opioid Use Disorder: 2020 Focused Update.* (2020). SAMHSA. https://www.asam.org/Quality-Science/quality/2020 -national-practice-guideline.

14 **After the cluster:** Flathead City-County Health Department. *Suicide Data Report 2018–2020.* (2021). https://www.flatheadhealth.org/wp -content/uploads/2021/03/Flathead-County-2018-2020-Suicide-Data -Report-2.pdf.

15 **In 2014, after beloved:** Fink, David S., Julian Santaella-Tenorio, and Katherine M. Keyes. (2018). "Increase in Suicides the Months after the Death of Robin Williams in the US." *PLOS ONE* 13(2): e0191405. https://doi.org/10.1371/journal.pone.0191405.

15 **Many copied:** Fink et al., "Increase in Suicides."

15 **The deaths following Robin:** Whitley, Rob. (2019, August 6). "Robin Williams' Death and Subsequent Suicide Contagion." *Psychology Today.* https://www.psychologytoday.com/us/blog/talking-about-men /201908/robin-williams-death-and-subsequent-suicide-contagion.

15 **One of the best information:** "Best Practices and Recommendations for Reporting on Suicide." (n.d.). Reporting on Suicide. https:// reportingonsuicide.org/wp-content/uploads/2022/05/ROS-001-One -Pager-1.13.pdf.

15 **Some of these include:** "The Lifeline and 988." (n.d.). 988 Suicide & Crisis Lifeline. Accessed August 30, 2023. https://988lifeline.org /current-events/the-lifeline-and-988.

16 **According to a study published in the *Journal*:** "Release of '13 Reasons Why' Associated with Increase in Youth Suicide Rates." (2019, April 29). National Institute of Mental Health (NIMH). https://www .nimh.nih.gov/news/science-news/2019/release-of-13-reasons-why -associated-with-increase-in-youth-suicide-rates.

17 **The National Indian Health:** Rose Bear Don't Walk. (n.d.). "Suicide Clusters in Montana Native American Youth: Policy Recommendations for Prevention and Services on the Flathead Indian Reservation." National Indian Health Board (NIHB). https://www.nihb.org /docs/03092020/Rose%20BDW_Suicide%20Prevention_PAPER.pdf.

17 **During the 2009–10 school year:** "Fort Belknap and Fort Peck Indian Reservation Suicide Crises." (2020, April 1). Project Censored (blog). https://www.projectcensored.org/fort-belknap-and-fort-peck-indian -reservation-suicide-crises.

17 **In 2019, officials:** Project Censored, "Fort Belknap."

17 **Between 2009 and 2011:** SAMHSA. (2014). *Preventing and Responding to Suicide Clusters in American Indian and Alaska Native Communities.* Department of Health and Human Services Publication No. SMA16-4969. Rockville, MD: Substance Abuse and Mental Health Services Administration. https://store.samhsa.gov/sites/default /files/d7/priv/sma16-4969.pdf.

17 **From 2006 to 2012:** ASPPH Member Research and Reports. (2016, December 15). "Johns Hopkins: Suicide Rates Drop among Members of White Mountain Apache Tribe." Association of Schools and Programs of Public Health. https://aspphbeta.org/johns-hopkins-suicide-rates -drop-among-members-of-white-mountain-apache-tribe-2.

17 **Between 1966 and 1988:** Stack, Steven. (2000). "Media Impacts on Suicide: A Quantitative Review of 293 Findings." *Social Science Quarterly* 81(4): 957–71. http://www.jstor.org/stable/42864031.

18 **Some consider owls:** Clifford, Garth C. (2022, November 19). "Owl Symbolism & Meaning (+Totem, Spirit & Omens)." World Birds. https://worldbirds.com/owl-symbolism.

20 **However, it is important:** Harkavy-Friedman, Jill. (2020, February 7). "Ask Dr. Jill: Does Mental Illness Play a Role in Suicide?" American Foundation for Suicide Prevention. https://afsp.org/story/ask-dr-jill-does -mental-illness-play-a-role-in-suicide.

24 **Those closest to the victim:** Aten, Jamie D. (2020, June 16). "Grasping the Complicated Grief of a Suicide." *Psychology Today.* https://www .psychologytoday.com/us/blog/hope-resilience/202006/grasping -the-complicated-grief-suicide.

24 **Accompanying the torment:** Tal Young, Ilanit, et al. (2012). "Suicide Bereavement and Complicated Grief." *Dialogues in Clinical Neuroscience* 14(2): 177–86. https://doi.org/10.31887/DCNS.2012.14.2/iyoung.

25 **And with this endurance:** Tal Young et al., "Suicide Bereavement."

25 **Their own death:** Tal Young et al., "Suicide Bereavement."

25 **People who were close:** Tal Young et al., "Suicide Bereavement."

25 **They're also 1.6 times more likely:** Tal Young et al., "Suicide Bereavement."

30 **Experts claim that while:** Spyker, Marisa. (2017, June 19). "In Giftedness, Is There More Darkness?" William & Mary News Archive. https://www.wm.edu/news/stories/2017/in-giftedness,-is-there-more -darkness.php.

30 **The grieving community:** Jouvenal, Justin, and T. Rees Shapiro. (2014, April 11). "After Six Woodson High Suicides, a Search for Solace

and Answers." *The Washington Post*. https://www.washingtonpost.com /local/crime/after-woodson-high-suicides-a-search-for-solace-and-answers /2014/04/11/8dd2a3b4-7f1d-11e5-b575-d8dcfedb4ea1_story.html.

30 **Their go-it-alone style:** Fleith, Denise de Seuza. (n.d.). "Suicide among Gifted Adolescents: How to Prevent It." The National Research Center on the Gifted and Talented. Spring 2001. Accessed October 18, 2023. https://nrcgt.uconn.edu/newsletters/spring012.

30 **Based on journals:** Fleith, "Suicide among Gifted."

Chapter Three: Down on the Farm

33 **No one is immune, but:** "Suicide Statistics." (2019). American Foundation for Suicide Prevention (AFSP). Accessed May 19, 2023. https://afsp.org/suicide-statistics.

33 **The largest number:** AFSP, "Suicide Statistics."

33 **In rural areas:** "Americans in Rural Areas More Likely to Die by Suicide." (2017, October 5). CDC. https://www.cdc.gov/media /releases/2017/p1005-rural-suicide-rates.html.

34 **America's farmers are dying:** Wedell, Katie, Lucille Sherman, and Sky Chadde. (2020, March 9). "Midwest Farmers Face a Crisis. Hundreds Are Dying by Suicide." *USA Today*. https://www.usatoday.com /in-depth/news/investigations/2020/03/09/climate-tariffs-debt-and -isolation-drive-some-farmers-suicide/4955865002.

34 **Farmers have been among:** Snee, Tom. (2017, June 12). "Long After '80s Farm Crisis, Farm Workers Still Take Own Lives at High Rate." *Iowa Now*. https://now.uiowa.edu/news/2017/06/long-after-80s -farm-crisis-farm-workers-still-take-own-lives-high-rate.

34 **farmers killed themselves:** Snee, "Long After '80s."

34 **Today, the suicide rate of farmers:** Turner, Brock E. W. (2022, January 7). "Suicide Rates Are 6 Times Higher among Farmers and COVID Is Making It Even Worse." Indiana Public Media, News. https://indiana publicmedia.org/news/new-program-aims-to-turn-tides-of-suicide -rates-among-farmers.php.

35 **"The farm has become the most stressful setting:** Wedell, Katie, "Midwest Farmers Face a Crisis."

38 **Farm debt has increased:** Key, Nigel, Christopher Burns, and Greg Lyons. (2019, October). "Financial Conditions in the U.S. Agricultural Sector: Historical Comparisons." USDA Economic Research Service. https://www.ers.usda.gov/publications/pub-details/?pubid=95237.

38 **Profit margins are low:** Semuels, Alana. (2019, November 27). "'They're Trying to Wipe Us Off the Map.' Small American Farmers Are Nearing Extinction." *Time.* https://time.com/5736789/small -american-farmers-debt-crisis-extinction.

39 **One big reason:** Semuels, "'They're Trying to Wipe Us.'"

39 **Banks foreclosed on 12,000:** Semuels, "'They're Trying to Wipe Us.'"

43 **In rural counties in America:** "Is There a Shortage of Mental Health Professionals in America?" (2019). Good Therapy. Updated March 26, 2020. https://www.goodtherapy.org/for-professionals/personal-develop ment/become-a-therapist/is-there-shortage-of-mental-health-profes sionals-in-america.

43 **That's a fraction of those available:** Buche, Jessica, Phillip M. Singer, Kyle Grazier, et al. (2016, August). "Primary Care and Behavioral Health Workforce Integration: Barriers and Best Practices." Health Workforce Policy Brief. August 2016. Behavioral Health Workforce Research Center, University of Michigan. https://behavioralhealth workforce.org/wp-content/uploads/2016/09/UM-FA2P3_Team-Based -Care-Policy-Brief_FINAL.pdf.

43 **Another factor is that rural:** Buche et al., "Primary Care and Behavioral Health."

45 **In the months following their:** Chung, Daniel Thomas, Christopher James Ryan, Dusan Hadzi-Pavlovic, et al. (2017). "Suicide Rates after Discharge from Psychiatric Facilities: A Systematic Review and Meta-analysis." *JAMA Psychiatry* 74(7): 694–702. https://doi.org /10.1001/jamapsychiatry.2017.1044.

45 **Experts are unsure why:** Chung et al., "Suicide Rates after Discharge."

49 **To counter it, the Federal Reserve:** Lawton, Kurt. (2016, August 22). "Taking a Look Back at the 1980s Farm Crisis and Its Impacts." Farm Progress. https://www.farmprogress.com/marketing/taking-look -back-1980s-farm-crisis-and-its-impacts.

50 **More land was needed:** Lawton, "Taking a Look Back."

50 **Farm foreclosures soared:** Lawton, "Taking a Look Back."

Chapter Four: The Ballad of Greg Whitesell, Part Two

54 **From there they'd be transferred:** Brockman, Courtney. (2015, May 20). "Reaching Out: A Conversation on Mental Health Evolves on the Flathead." Native News Project 2017, University of Montana. https://nativenews.jour.umt.edu/2017/reaching-out-flathead.

55 **They are "protective factors":** Henson, Michele, Samantha Sabo, Aurora Trujillo, and Nicolette Teufel-Shone. (2017). "Identifying Protective Factors to Promote Health in American Indian and Alaska Native Adolescents: A Literature Review." *Journal of Primary Prevention* 38 (1–2): 5–26. https://doi.org/10.1007/s10935-016-0455-2.

55 **They improve emotional health:** Henson et al., "Identifying Protective Factors."

56 **They have never seen:** Tang, Samantha, Natalie M. Reily, Andrew F. Arena, et al. (2022, January). "People Who Die by Suicide without Receiving Mental Health Services: A Systematic Review." *Frontiers in Public Health* 9. https://doi.org/10.3389/fpubh.2021.736948.

59 **This population passed on:** Pember, Mary Annette. (2017, October 3). "Trauma May Be Woven into DNA of Native Americans." *Indian Country Today.* Updated September 13, 2018. https://indian countrytoday.com/archive/trauma-may-be-woven-into-dna -of-native-americans.

59 **They consist of elevated risks:** Sandoiu, Ana. (2022, July 11). "The Impact of Historical Trauma on American Indian Health Equity." *Medical News Today.* https://www.medicalnewstoday.com/articles /the-impact-of-historical-trauma-on-american-indian-health-equity.

60 **Between 1819 and the 1970s:** "Federal Indian Boarding School Initiative." (n.d.). U.S. Department of the Interior, Bureau of Indian Affairs. https://www.bia.gov/service/federal-indian-boarding -school-initiative.

60 **Their goal was to culturally assimilate:** Bureau of Indian Affairs, "Federal Indian Boarding School."

60 **At fifty-three schools and counting:** Bureau of Indian Affairs, "Federal Indian Boarding School."

Chapter Five: Fire in the Brain

69 **Serotonin is a neurotransmitter:** "What Is a Psychological Autopsy?" (2013). Forensic Psychology Online. https://www.forensicpsychology online.com/what-is-a-psychological-autopsy.

69 **Serotonin is the Swiss Army knife:** "Serotonin: What Is It, Function & Levels." (n.d.). Cleveland Clinic. Last updated March 18, 2022. https://my.clevelandclinic.org/health/articles/22572-serotonin.

70 **The rest is made:** Cleveland Clinic, "Serotonin."

70 **Excessive serotonin activity:** Cleveland Clinic, "Serotonin."

73 **PET scans can measure:** "Metabolism." (2019). Nemours TeensHealth. https://kidshealth.org/en/teens/metabolism.html.

74 **Ketamine quickly reduces:** "Ketamine Rapidly Improves Cognitive Function Making Those in Suicidal Crisis Less Likely to Harm Themselves." (2021, November 2). Columbia University Department of Psychiatry. https://www.columbiapsychiatry.org/news /ketamine-rapidly-improves-cognitive-function-making-those -suicidal-crisis-less-likely-harm-themselves.

74 **But it has not been tested:** Mann, J. John, Christina A. Michel, and Randy P. Auerbach. (2021). "Improving Suicide Prevention through Evidence-Based Strategies: A Systematic Review." *American Journal of Psychiatry* 178 (7): 611–24. https://doi.org/10.1176/appi.ajp.2020 .20060864.

77 **These findings back up other research:** "A Few Simple Questions Can Help Prevent Suicide." (2022, August 2). Pew Charitable Trusts. https:// www.pewtrusts.org/en/research-and-analysis/fact-sheets/2022/08/02 /a-few-simple-questions-can-help-prevent-suicide.

77 **It's no coincidence:** Siegel, Michael, and Emily F. Rothman. (2016). "Firearm Ownership and Suicide Rates among US Men and Women, 1981–2013." *American Journal of Public Health* 106 (7): 1316–22. https://doi.org/10.2105/AJPH.2016.303182.

78 **isolation and loneliness are major risk factors:** Pew, "A Few Simple Questions."

78 **The annual Twins Days Festival:** Wheeler, Mark. (2004, November 1). "Twin Science." *Smithsonian Magazine.* https://www .smithsonianmag.com/science-nature/twin-science-98910961.

78 **Between 1812 and 2006:** Wheeler, "Twin Science."

78 **The majority found:** Voracek, Martin, and Lisa Mariella Loibl. (2007). "Genetics of Suicide: A Systematic Review of Twin Studies." *Wiener Klinische Wochenschrift* 119 (15–16): 463–75. https://doi.org/10 .1007/s00508-007-0823-2.

78 **That means these twins:** Casselman, Anne. (2008, April 3). "Identical Twins' Genes Are Not Identical." *Scientific American.* https://www .scientificamerican.com/article/identical-twins-genes-are -not-identical.

80 **Not only that:** "Largest Genetic Study of Suicide Attempts Confirms Genetic Underpinnings That Are Not Driven by Underlying Psychiatric Disorders." (2021, November 29). Mount Sinai Health System press

release. https://www.mountsinai.org/about/newsroom/2021/largest
-genetic-study-of-suicide-attempts-confirms-genetic-underpinnings
-that-are-not-driven-by-underlying-psychiatric-disorders.

Chapter Six: Fonda Bryant

84 **Fonda's father was:** Wikipedia contributors. (2023, May 30). "Johnnie Taylor." Wikipedia, The Free Encyclopedia. https://en.wikipedia.org /wiki/Johnnie_Taylor.

85 **They can become angry:** Rivara, Frederick, and Suzanne Le Menestrel, eds. (2016). *Preventing Bullying Through Science, Policy, and Practice.* Washington, DC: National Academies Press. https://doi.org/10.17226/ 23482.

85 **They can also suffer:** Rivara and Le Menestrel, *Preventing Bullying.*

85 **For reasons that are not yet clear:** Rivara and Le Menestrel, *Preventing Bullying.*

86 **The natural daily production:** Thau, Lauren, Jayashree Gandhi, and Sandeep Sharma. (2019, February 15). "Physiology, Cortisol." StatPearls Publishing. https://www.ncbi.nlm.nih.gov/books/NBK538239.

86 **Cortisol elevates blood sugar:** Thau et al., "Physiology, Cortisol."

86 **This abnormality has been:** Minkove, Judy F. (2015, December 14). "Combining Genes, Epigenetics and Stress Responses to Study Suicide and PTSD." Johns Hopkins Medicine. https://www.hopkinsmedicine .org/news/articles/combining-genes-epigenetics-and-stress-responses- to-study-suicide-and-ptsd.

87 **"That's traumatizing":** Ryu, Jenna. (2023, February 17). "A 14-Year-Old's Suicide, the Video That Was Posted and the Dangers of Sharing Graphic Content." *USA Today.* https://www.usatoday.com/story/life /health-wellness/2023/02/16/adriana-kuch-nj-teen-bullying-video -sparks-outrage-concern/11255672002.

88 **Social media consumers experience:** "Fear of Missing Out (FOMO): Potential Problems and Solutions." (2023, January 27). Better Help. https://www.betterhelp.com/advice/current-events/fear-of-missing-out -social-media-effects-and-solutions.

88 **Between 2000 and 2007:** Curtin, Sally C. (2020). "State Suicide Rates among Adolescents and Young Adults Aged 10–24: United States, 2000–2018." National Vital Statistics Reports 69 (11). https://stacks .cdc.gov/view/cdc/93667.

88 **By 2018, suicides:** Curtin, "State Suicide Rates."

88–89   **An economic crisis darkened:** "Do You Feel Like a Financial Burden?" (n.d.). The Student Room. Accessed August 30, 2023. https://www .thestudentroom.co.uk/showthread.php?t=5495018.

89   **In the past ten years:** Dean, Brian. (2023, March 27). "Social Network Usage & Growth Statistics: How Many People Use Social Media in 2023?" Backlinko. https://backlinko.com/social -media-users.

89   **In 2018 an academic review:** Memon, Aksha M., Shiva G. Sharma, Satyajit S. Mohite, and Shailesh Jain. (2018). "The Role of Online Social Networking on Deliberate Self-Harm and Suicidality in Adolescents: A Systematized Review of Literature." *Indian Journal of Psychiatry* 60 (4): 384–92. https://doi.org/10.4103/psychiatry .IndianJPsychiatry_414_17.

89   **In 2019 the American Academy of Pediatrics:** Barbaro, Michael. (2022, August 30). "Inside the Adolescent Mental Health Crisis." *The Daily*, produced by Michael Simon Johnson and Rikki Novetsky, podcast. https://www.nytimes.com/2022/08/30/podcasts/the-daily /teens-mental-health-crisis.html.

89   **That same year the United States:** Barbaro, "Inside the Adolescent Mental Health Crisis."

89   **A ten-year study of five hundred teens:** Brigham Young University. (2021, February 9). "10-Year Study Shows Elevated Suicide Risk from Excess Social Media Time for Teen Girls." *Newswise.* https://www .newswise.com/articles/10-year-study-shows-elevated-suicide-risk -from-excess-social-media-time-for-teen-girls.

89   **An independent survey of US teens:** Burstein, Brett, Holly Agostino, and Brian Greenfield. (2019). "Suicidal Attempts and Ideation among Children and Adolescents in US Emergency Departments, 2007–2015. *JAMA Pediatrics* 173 (6), 598–600. https://doi.org/10.1001/jama pediatrics.2019.0464.

89   **Teens who spent more time:** Twenge, Jean M., Thomas E. Joiner, Megan L. Rogers, and Gabrielle N. Martin. (2018). "Increases in Depressive Symptoms, Suicide-Related Outcomes, and Suicide Rates among U.S. Adolescents after 2010 and Links to Increased New Media Screen Time." *Clinical Psychological Science* 6 (1): 3–17. https://doi.org /10.1177/2167702617723376.

90   **Self-harm generally consists of:** Twenge et al., "Increases in Depressive Symptoms."

90 **However, those who engage in:** Mitchell, A. J., and M. Dennis. (2006). "Self Harm and Attempted Suicide in Adults: 10 Practical Questions and Answers for Emergency Department Staff." *Emergency Medicine Journal* 23 (4): 251–55. https://doi.org/10.1136/emj.2005 .027250.

90 **Online help-seeking:** Memon et al., "Role of Online Social Networking."

90 **In 2021, *The Wall Street Journal*:** Wells, Georgia, Jeff Horwitz, and Deepa Seetharaman. (2021, September 14). "Facebook Knows Instagram Is Toxic for Teen Girls, Company Documents Show." *The Wall Street Journal* (Eastern Ed.). https://www.wsj.com/articles /facebook-knows-instagram-is-toxic-for-teen-girls-company -documents-show-11631620739.

90 **They found that Instagram:** Wells et al., "Facebook Knows."

91 **Another internal report showed:** Wells et al., "Facebook Knows."

91 **According to their suit:** Wayt, Theo. (2022, August 7). "'Victims of Instagram': Meta Faces Novel Legal Threat over Teen Suicides." *New York Post*. https://nypost.com/2022/08/07/meta-faces-lawsuits-over-teen -suicides-and-self-harm.

91 **As Englyn interacted:** Wayt, "'Victims of Instagram.'"

91 **Her parents' suit alleges:** Wayt, "'Victims of Instagram.'"

91 **psychic damage brought on by her compulsive use of social media:** 60 Minutes Overtime. "Teen Watched Simulated Hanging Video on Instagram before Suicide." (2022, December 11). CBS News. https:// www.cbsnews.com/news/instagram-hanging-video-suicide-60-minutes -2022-12-11.

93 **Averaging all ages:** "Mental and Behavioral Health: African Americans." (n.d.). Office of Minority Health. Accessed August 30, 2023. https://www.minorityhealth.hhs.gov/omh/browse.aspx?lvl=4& lvlid=24.

94 **In the United States in 2019:** OMH, "Mental and Behavioral Health."

94 **However, in recent years:** Xiao, Yunyu, Julie Cerel, and J. John Mann. (2021). "Temporal Trends in Suicidal Ideation and Attempts among US Adolescents by Sex and Race/Ethnicity, 1991–2019." *JAMA Network Open* 4 (6): e2113513. https://doi.org/10.1001/jamanetworkopen .2021.13513.

94 **On average, suicide rates:** Alessandrini, Kyra Aurelia. (2021, May 11). "Suicide among Black Girls Is a Mental Health Crisis Hiding in Plain Sight." *Time*. https://time.com/6046773/black-teenage-girls-suicide.

95 **West Virginia University's Ian Rockett:** Novak, Sara. (2022, June 6). "Suicides among Black People May Be Vastly Undercounted." *Scientific American.* https://www.scientificamerican.com/article/suicides-among -black-people-may-be-vastly-undercounted.

95 **According to his 2010 study:** Novak, "Suicides among Black People."

95 **Consequently, black people:** Novak, "Suicides among Black People."

95 **"This leads to suicide misclassification":** Novak, "Suicides among Black People."

95 **That would make suicide:** Dokoupil, Tony. (2013, May 23). "Why Suicide Has Become an Epidemic—and What We Can Do to Help." *Newsweek.* https://www.newsweek.com/2013/05/22/why-suicide -has-become-epidemic-and-what-we-can-do-help-237434.html.

95 **In another recent study, Rockett:** Rockett, Ian R. H., Michael D. Regier, Nestor D. Kapusta, Jeffrey H. Coben, et al. (2012). "Leading Causes of Unintentional and Intentional Injury Mortality: United States, 2000–2009." *American Journal of Public Health* 102 (11): e84–92. https://doi.org/10.2105/ajph.2012.300960.

97 **A rough definition of sexual addiction:** Fong, Timothy W. (2006). "Understanding and Managing Compulsive Sexual Behaviors." *Psychiatry (Edgmont)* 3 (11): 51– 58. https://www.ncbi.nlm.nih.gov/pmc /articles/PMC2945841/.

97 **Studies about compulsive sexual activities:** Fong, "Understanding and Managing."

97 **Sexual addiction begins:** "Sex Addiction, Hypersexuality and Compulsive Sexual Behavior." (n.d.). Cleveland Clinic. Updated April 5, 2022. https://my.clevelandclinic.org/health/treatments/22690-sex -addiction-hypersexuality-and-compulsive-sexual-behavior.

97 **Some 88 percent of sexual addicts:** Cleveland Clinic, "Sex Addiction, Hypersexuality."

98 **In the United States, women attempt suicide:** Tucker, Raymond P. (2020, May 22). "The Gender Paradox of Suicide: How Suicide Differs between Men, Women, and Transgender/Gender-Diverse Individuals." CAMS-Care. https://cams-care.com/resources/educational-content /the-gender-paradox-of-suicide-how-suicide-differs-between-men -women-and-transgender-gender-diverse-individuals.

98 **About 60 percent of men use a gun:** Tucker, "Gender Paradox of Suicide."

99 **Around 62 percent of men die:** Isometsä, Erkki T., and Jouko K. Lönnqvist. (1998). "Suicide Attempts Preceding Completed Suicide."

British Journal of Psychiatry 173 (6): 531–35. https://doi.org/10.1192
/bjp.173.6.531.

103 **I thought this was hyperbole:** Windsor, Liliane C., Alexis Jemal,
and Edward J. Alessi. (2015). "Cognitive Behavioral Therapy: A
Meta-Analysis of Race and Substance Use Outcomes." *Cultural
Diversity and Ethnic Minority Psychology* 21 (2): 300–313.
https://doi.org/10.1037/a0037929.

103 **Black people are killed by police:** Jordan, Ayana, Aza Stephen Allsop,
and Pamela Y. Collins. (2021). "Decriminalising Being Black with
Mental Illness." *The Lancet: Psychiatry* 8 (1): 8–9. https://doi.org
/10.1016/s2215-0366(20)30519-8.

103 **A vast majority of the black people:** "Every Fatal Police Shooting
since 2015." (2022, June 2). *The Washington Post.* Updated June 1,
2023. https://www.washingtonpost.com/graphics/investigations/police
-shootings-database.

104 **Regarding black men:** *The Washington Post,* "Every Fatal Police
Shooting.

104 **A 2022 *Washington Post* investigation:** Gerberg, Jon, and Alice Li.
(2022, June 22). "When a Call to the Police for Help Turns Deadly."
The Washington Post. https://www.washingtonpost.com/investigations
/interactive/2022/police-shootings-mental-health-calls/.

104 **According to a study by the national nonprofit:** "People with
Untreated Mental Illness 16 Times More Likely to Be Killed by Law
Enforcement." (n.d.). Treatment Advocacy Center. https://www
.treatmentadvocacycenter.org/key-issues/criminalization-of-mental
-illness/2976-people-with-untreated-mental-illness-16-times-more
-likely-to-be-killed-by-law-enforcement-.

104 **None of these callers expressed concerns:** Treatment Advocacy
Center, "People with Untreated Mental Illness."

104 **"Until we reform the public policies":** Treatment Advocacy Center,
"People with Untreated Mental Illness."

104 **A recent survey by the Police Executive Research:** Lowery, Wesley,
Kimberly Kindy, Keith L. Alexander, Julie Tate, et al. (2015, June 30).
"Distraught People, Deadly Results." *The Washington Post.* https://www
.washingtonpost.com/sf/investigative/2015/06/30/distraught-people
-deadly-results/?utm_term=.a263183cf8bc.

105 **But in recent years:** Lowery, "Distraught People."

105 **The 988 initiative:** Chatterjee, Rhitu. (2022, July 16). "The New 988
Mental Health Hotline Is Live. Here's What to Know." NPR. https://

www.npr.org/sections/health-shots/2022/07/15/1111316589/988-suicide
-hotline-number.

105 **At the federal, state, and local levels:** "988 Lifeline Performance
Metrics." (n.d.). SAMHSA. https://www.samhsa.gov/find-help
/988/performance-metrics.

105 **September calls increased:** SAMHSA, "988 Lifeline Performance
Metrics."

106 **In some cases:** Schimelpfening, Nancy. (2021, March 25). "How
Involuntary Hospitalization for Depression Works." verywell mind.
Updated November 8, 2022. https://www.verywellmind.com
/involuntary-hospitalization-for-depression-1067261#citation-1.

107 **Do they display unusual anger:** "Risk Factors, Protective Factors, and
Warning Signs." (n.d.). American Foundation for Suicide Prevention.
Accessed August 30, 2023. https://afsp.org/risk-factors-protective
-factors-and-warning-signs.

108 **You may say something like:** "Talk Away the Dark: How to Start (and
Continue!) a Conversation about Mental Health." (n.d.). American
Foundation for Suicide Prevention. Accessed August 30, 2023. https://
afsp.org/story/how-to-start-and-continue-a-conversation-about-mental
-health-a-realconvo-guide-fr.

109 **Isolation or lack of connectedness:** "How and Why the 5 Steps Can
Help." (n.d.). #BeThe1To. Accessed August 30, 2023. https://www
.bethe1to.com/bethe1to-steps-evidence.

109 **Encourage them to think:** #BeThe1To, "How and Why the 5
Steps."

110 **For this reason, barriers on bridges:** Harvard T.H. Chan School of
Public Health. (n.d.). "Bridges and Suicide." Means Matter. Accessed
August 30, 2023. https://www.hsph.harvard.edu/means-matter/bridges
-and-suicide.

110 **If the individual does not have a counselor:** "What to Do When
Someone Is at Risk." (2020, January 5). American Foundation for
Suicide Prevention. https://afsp.org/what-to-do-when-someone-is-at
-risk.

111 **Studies have shown that talking:** "The Lifeline and 988." (n.d.). 988
Suicide & Crisis Lifeline. Accessed August 30, 2023. https://988lifeline
.org/current-events/the-lifeline-and-988.

111 **Though you'll want to do:** Falcone, Giulia, Adele Nardella, Dorian A.
Lamis, Denise Erbuto, Paolo Girardi, and Maurizio Pompili. (2017).
"Taking Care of Suicidal Patients with New Technologies and

Reaching-out Means in the Post-Discharge Period." *World Journal of Psychiatry* 7 (3): 163–76. https://doi.org/10.5498/wjp.v7.i3.163.

112 **Many employers offer EAP:** Wooll, Maggie. (2021, June 23). "What Is an EAP? A Guide to Employee Assistance Programs." BetterUp. https://www.betterup.com/blog/what-is-an-eap.

112 **Fonda also got involved:** "About Us." (n.d.). Mental Health America. Accessed August 30, 2023. https://mhanational.org/about.

113 **NAMI is active:** "Home." (n.d.). National Alliance on Mental Illness. Accessed August 30, 2023. https://www.nami.org/Home.

Chapter Seven: The Interpersonal Theory of Suicide

116 **With a team of researchers:** Heller, Dave. (2016, November 15). "FSU Professor: New Approach Needed to Improve Suicide Prediction." Florida State University News. https://news.fsu.edu/news/health-medicine/2016/11/15/fsu-professor-new-approach-needed-to-improve-suicide-prediction.

116 **"That was a wake-up call":** Heller, "FSU Professor: New Approach."

116 **Yet in 2008:** Anderson, Scott. (2008, July 6). "The Urge to End It All." *The New York Times.* https://www.nytimes.com/2008/07/06/magazine/06suicide-t.html.

116 **And between 2007 and 2018:** American Foundation for Suicide Prevention, "Risk Factors."

116 **and about 57 percent for young people:** Brueck, Hilary, and Shayanne Gal. (2020, September 12). "Suicide Rates Are Climbing in Young People from Ages 10 to 24. Here's How to Support the People You Love." *Insider.* https://www.insider.com/cdc-suicide-rate-in-young-people-10-24-continues-climb-2020-9.

117 **Today you are much more likely:** Florida State University. (2016, November 15). "FSU Professor: 50 Years of Research Fails to Improve Suicide Prediction." Newswise. https://www.newswise.com/articles/fsu-professor-50-years-of-research-fails-to-improve-suicide-prediction.

117 **He achieved this status:** Dokoupil, Tony. (2013, May 23). "Why Suicide Has Become an Epidemic—and What We Can Do to Help." *Newsweek.* https://www.newsweek.com/2013/05/22/why-suicide-has-become-epidemic-and-what-we-can-do-help-237434.html.

118 **He recalibrated his academic focus:** Dokoupil, "Why Suicide Has Become an Epidemic."

118 **When he and a colleague:** Allman, Rachel. (2021, January 5). "Profile: Thomas Joiner and the Study of Suicide." *Psychology Tools.* https://www

.psychologytools.com/articles/profile-thomas-joiner-and-the-study-of
-suicide/.

118 **Academically, this was interesting:** Allman, "Profile: Thomas Joiner."

118 **And the patterns:** Allman, "Profile: Thomas Joiner."

120 **When none of this is true:** Joiner, Thomas. 2007. *Why People Die by Suicide* (Cambridge: Harvard University Press), p. 98.

121 **These individuals may view:** Joiner, *Why People Die*, pp. 100–101.

121 **Senicide is connected:** Joiner, *Why People Die*, p. 102.

121 **Military history records:** Joiner, *Why People Die.*

121 **Joiner's theory holds:** Joiner, *Why People Die*, p. 96.

122 **What's more, those interactions:** Joiner, *Why People Die*, p. 97.

123 **And about her childhood:** Team Lehren. (2021, February 11). "Marilyn Monroe—I Often Felt Lonely and Wanted to Die." Lehren. https://lehren.com/entertainment/hollywood/marilyn-monroe-i-often -felt-lonely-and-wanted-to-die/76531/.

123 **"I am lonely":** Severson, Kim. (2022, September 27). "The Last, Painful Days of Anthony Bourdain." *The New York Times.* https://www .nytimes.com/2022/09/27/dining/anthony-bourdain-biography.html.

123 **Generally speaking, being pregnant:** Joiner, *Why People Die,* pp. 125–26.

124 **multiple births are more likely:** Villines, Zawn. (2018, May 14). "Parents of Twins More Likely to Have Anxiety or Depression." *GoodTherapy* (blog). https://www.goodtherapy.org/blog/parents-twins -more-likely-have-anxiety-or-depression-0514181.

124 **It helps explain why:** Joiner, Thomas E., Danniel Hollar, and Kimberly Van Orden. (2006). "On Buckeyes, Gators, Super Bowl Sunday, and the Miracle on Ice: 'Pulling together' Is Associated with Lower Suicide Rates." *Journal of Social and Clinical Psychology* 25 (2): 179–95. https://psycnet.apa.org/record/2006-04084-003.

124 **For 180 days after the 9/11:** Ahmad, Farida B., and Robert N. Anderson. (2021). "The Leading Causes of Death in the US for 2020." *Journal of the American Medical Association* 325 (18): 1829–30. https:// jamanetwork.com/journals/jama/fullarticle/2778234.

124 **Dr. David Jobes, who created the:** Jobes, David A., and Thomas E. Joiner. (2019). "Reflections on Suicidal Ideation." *Crisis* 40 (4): 227–30. https://doi.org/10.1027/0227-5910/a000615.

126 **"They do this in various ways":** Joiner, *Why People Die*, pp. 20–21.

126 **But as we'll see:** Joiner, *Why People Die*, p. 75.

127 **Studies have shown that people:** Joiner, *Why People Die*, p. 76.

127 **Even preschoolers who have displayed:** Joiner, *Why People Die*, p. 76.

127 **Joiner reports that rock icon:** Joiner, *Why People Die*, p. 81.

127 **He was reportedly afraid:** Joiner, *Why People Die*, p. 81.

128 **The theory's major achievement:** Wikipedia contributors. (2022, August 19). "Interpersonal Theory of Suicide." Wikipedia, The Free Encyclopedia. https://en.wikipedia.org/w/index.php?title =Interpersonal_theory_of_suicide&oldid=1105359669.

129 **Interestingly, of all the links:** Ma, Jennifer, Philip J. Batterham, Alison L. Calear, and Jin Han. (2016). "A Systematic Review of the Predictions of the Interpersonal–Psychological Theory of Suicidal Behavior." *Clinical Psychology Review* 46 (June): 34–45. https://doi.org/10.1016 /j.cpr.2016.04.008.

Chapter Eight: Stabilization and Suicide-Focused Intervention

133 **CCBHCs are required to provide:** "What Is a CCBHC?" (2021). National Council for Mental Wellbeing. https://www.thenationalcoun cil.org/wp-content/uploads/2021/12/What_is_a_CCBHC _UPDATED_8-5-20.pdf.

133 **Currently, there are 480 CCBHCs:** DeVoursney, David. Phone conversation with the author. March 16, 2023.

134 **This has made it hard:** DeVoursney conversation, March 2023.

134 **It's called the Safety Planning Intervention:** Stanley, Barbara, and Gregory K. Brown. (2012). Safety Planning Intervention: A Brief Intervention to Mitigate Suicide Risk. *Cognitive and Behavioral Practice* 19 (2), 256–64. https://doi.org/10.1016/j.cbpra.2011.01.001.

134 **A 2017 study concluded:** Chung, Daniel Thomas, Christopher James Ryan, Dusan Hadzi-Pavlovic, et al. (2017). "Suicide Rates after Discharge from Psychiatric Facilities: A Systematic Review and Meta-Analysis." *JAMA Psychiatry* 74 (7): 694–702. https://doi.org /10.1001/jamapsychiatry.2017.1044.

134 **A 2019 study showed that:** "Emergency Department Study Reveals Patterns of Patients at Increased Risk for Suicide." (2019, December 13). National Institute of Mental Health press release. https://www .nimh.nih.gov/news/science-news/2019/emergency-department -study-reveals-patterns-of-patients-at-increased-risk-for-suicide.

135 **At a conference table in the department of psychiatry:** The details of this case are taken from actual cases, but they are not true for Ron Joss, who is an actor. Ron Joss is not his real name. Due to privacy concerns, clinicians like Dr. Stanley often use actors instead of real

patients when they are demonstrating protocols such as the safety plan. This category of actor is called Standardized Patient, or SP for short. They are in high demand in medical schools across the country.

139 **Some have a greater disposition:** Broerman, Rebecca. (2018). "Diathesis-Stress Model." In Zeigler-Hill, V., Shackelford, T. (eds) *Encyclopedia of Personality and Individual Differences*, pp. 1–3. Springer, Cham. https://link.springer.com/referenceworkentry/10.1007/978-3 -319-28099-8_891-1.

143 **Advil and Tylenol are trade names:** Cummings, Emily. (2017, March 15). "5 Common, Over-the-Counter Medicines That Could Kill You If You Take Too Much." WGBA NBC 26 in Green Bay. https://www .nbc26.com/news/health/5-common-over-the-counter-medicines -that-could-kill-you-if-you-take-too-much.

145 **DBT is frequently the best:** Wilhelm, Mark. (2019, October 15). "CBT vs. DBT: When Is Each Type of Therapy Most Effective?" Cummins Behavioral Health Systems. https://www.cumminsbhs.org /cbt-vs-dbt/.

146 **A quick method called the Crisis Response Plan:** "About the Crisis Response Plan." (n.d.). Crisis Response Planning for Suicide Prevention. Accessed August 30, 2023. https://crpforsuicide.com/about.

146 **About 47,000 of those individuals:** Jobes, David A., and Thomas E. Joiner. (2019). "Reflections on Suicidal Ideation." *Crisis* 40 (4): 227–30. https://doi.org/10.1027/0227-5910/a000615.

148 **Maggie was a student in her early twenties:** The details of this case are taken from actual cases, but they are not true for Maggie, who is an actor. Maggie is not her real name. Due to privacy concerns, clinicians often use actors instead of actual patients when they are demonstrating protocols such as CAMS. This category of actor is called Standardized Patient, or SP for short.

153 **In a 2014 study:** Crane, Catherine, Thorsten Barnhofer, Danielle S. Duggan, et al. (2014). "Comfort from Suicidal Cognition in Recurrently Depressed Patients." *Journal of Affective Disorders* 155: 241–46. https://doi.org/10.1016/j.jad.2013.11.006.

Chapter Nine: Is the Future of Suicide Prevention Digital?

159 **Logistic regression is often used to:** Lawton, George, Ed Burns, and Linda Rosencrance. (2022, January). "Logistic Regression." TechTarget. https://www.techtarget.com/searchbusinessanalytics/definition/logistic -regression.

166 **Until now, suicidal ideation:** Kleiman, Evan M., Brianna J. Turner, Szymon Fedor, et al. (2018). "Digital Phenotyping of Suicidal Thoughts." *Depression and Anxiety* 35 (7): 601–8. https://doi.org /10.1002/da.22730.

166 **These assumptions came about:** Kleiman et al., "Digital Phenotyping."

167 **Participants who had more severe:** Kleiman et al., "Digital Phenotyping."

167 **Will therapists achieve the clinicians' Holy Grail:** Kleiman et al., "Digital Phenotyping."

170 **Epic's anonymized data included:** "Predicting Suicide Risk with Machine Learning." (2018, August 6). Epic. https://www.epic .com/epic/post/predicting-suicide-risk-machine-learning.

171 **"Predictions don't replace a clinical assessment":** Epic, "Predicting Suicide Risk."

171 **That's no better than flipping a coin:** Heller, "FSU Professor: New Approach." Florida State University News. https://news.fsu.edu/news /health-medicine/2016/11/15/fsu-professor-new-approach-needed-to -improve-suicide-prediction.

172 **a note he wrote:** "Veteran Suicide Stories." (n.d.). Once a Soldier. Accessed August 30, 2023. https://www.onceasoldier.org/Veteran -suicide-stories.

172 **In contrast, during the same twenty-year period:** DeSimone, Danielle. (2022, June 27). "Military Suicide Rates Are at an All-Time High; Here's How We're Trying to Help." United Service Organizations. https://www.uso.org/stories/2664-military-suicide-rates -are-at-an-all-time-high-heres-how-were-trying-to-help.

172 **AWP claims as many as forty-four veterans:** America's Warrior Partnership. (n.d.). Operation Deep Dive. Accessed August 30, 2023. https://www.americaswarriorpartnership.org/deep-dive.

172 **The AWP report is contested:** Lemle, Russell B. (2022, October 25). "VA Gets It Right on Suicide." MDedge. https://www.mdedge .com/fedprac/article/258954/health-policy/va-gets-it-right-suicide.

172 **Ironically, medical improvements:** Myers, Meghann. (2021, June 21). "Four Times as Many Troops and Vets Have Died by Suicide as in Combat, Study Finds." *Military Times.* https://www.militarytimes .com/news/your-military/2021/06/21/four-times-as-many-troops-and -vets-have-died-by-suicide-as-in-combat-study-finds.

174 **"The problem is that the data":** Werman, Marco, and Sarah Childress. (2012, December 20). "Military Suicide among Soldiers

Who Haven't Deployed." *The World*. https://theworld.org/stories
/2012-12-20/military-suicide-among-soldiers-who-havent
-deployed.

174   **For instance, 53 percent of service members:** Werman and Childress,
"Military Suicide."

174   **Because of the demand for personnel after 9/11:** Cardona, Robert
Andrew, and Elspeth Cameron Ritchie. (2007). "U.S. Military Enlisted
Accession Mental Health Screening: History and Current Practice."
Military Medicine 172 (1): 31–35. https://doi.org/10.7205/milmed
.172.1.31.

174   **interestingly, the same thing happened:** Cardona and Ritchie, "U.S.
Military Enlisted Accession."

175   **The trauma caused by sexual assault:** Shpancer, Noam. (2021, July 1).
"Why Are US Soldiers Killing Themselves?" *Psychology Today*. https://
www.psychologytoday.com/us/blog/insight-therapy/202107/why-are-us
-soldiers-killing-themselves.

175–76   **According to Department of Defense data:** Moyer, Melinda Wenner.
(2021, August 3). "'A Poison in the System': The Epidemic of Military
Sexual Assault." *The New York Times*. https://www.nytimes.com/2021
/08/03/magazine/military-sexual-assault.html.

176   **For 2021, the latest year on record:** "Suicide Statistics." (2022,
February 17). American Foundation for Suicide Prevention. https://
afsp.org/suicide-statistics.

176   **Active-duty military suicides were almost:** Garamone, Jim. (2022,
October 20). "Active Duty Suicide Rate Drops; Austin Says More Work
Needed." U.S. Department of Defense, DoD News. https://www
.defense.gov/News/News-Stories/Article/Article/3195429/active-duty
-suicide-rate-drops-austin-says-more-work-needed.

176   **Veteran suicides were about:** Miller, Matthew. (2021, September 8).
"2021 National Veteran Suicide Prevention Annual Report Shows
Decrease in Veteran Suicides." VA News. https://news.va.gov/94358
/2021-national-veteran-suicide-prevention-annual-report-shows-decrease
-in-veteran-suicides.

176   **The likelihood that a suicide attempt:** Shpancer, "Why are U.S.
Soldiers."

177   **Reach Vet (Recovery Engagement:** Carey, Benedict. (2020, November
23). "Can an Algorithm Prevent Suicide?" *The New York Times*. https://
www.nytimes.com/2020/11/23/health/artificial-intelligence-veterans
-suicide.html.

177 **"That is, they were forty times more likely":** Carey, "Can an Algorithm Prevent Suicide?"

178 **"I decided, you know, okay":** Carey, "Can an Algorithm Prevent Suicide?"

178 **A recent study of Reach Vet:** US Government Accountability Office. (2022, September). "Veteran Suicide: VA Efforts to Identify Veterans at Risk through Analysis of Health Record Information." GAO Report to Congressional Committees. https://www.gao.gov/assets/gao-22 -105165.pdf.

178 **Reach Vet decreased documented suicide attempts:** McCarthy, John F., Samantha A. Cooper, Kallisse R. Dent, et al. (2021). "Evaluation of the Recovery Engagement and Coordination for Health–Veterans Enhanced Treatment Suicide Risk Modeling Clinical Program in the Veterans Health Administration." *JAMA Network Open* 4 (10): e2129900. https://doi.org/10.1001/jamanetworkopen.2021.29900.

178 **However, when compared:** McCarthy et al., "Evaluation of Recovery Engagement."

179 **Furthermore, the 0.1 percent:** Carey, "Can an Algorithm Prevent Suicide?"

Chapter Ten: Systems Approaches: The United States Air Force

185 **"In the spring of 1996":** Garamone, "Active Duty Suicide Rate Drops."

185 **Fewer than a third of those:** Garamone, "Active Duty Suicide Rate Drops."

186 **the Air Force suicide rate was only a little more:** Shane, Leo, III. (2022, September 17). "Veterans Suicide Rate May Be Double Federal Estimates, Study Suggests." *Military Times.* https://www.military times.com/veterans/2022/09/17/veterans-suicide-rate-may-be-double -federal-estimates-study-suggests.

187 **All were taught warning signs:** Ramchand, Rajeev, Joie D. Acosta, Rachel M. Burns, et al. (2011). *The War Within: Preventing Suicide in the U.S. Military.* Santa Monica: Rand. https://www.rand.org/pubs /monographs/MG953.html.

187 **Planners focused extra resources:** Knox, Kerry L., Steven Pflanz, Gerald W. Talcott, et al. (2010). "The US Air Force Suicide Prevention Program: Implications for Public Health Policy." *American Journal of Public Health* 100 (12): 2457–63. https://doi.org/10.2105/AJPH.2009 .159871.

187 **There are about 800 active US Air Force bases:** Vine, David. (2015). "Where in the World Is the U.S. Military?" *Politico.* https://www .politico.com/magazine/story/2015/06/us-military-bases-around-the -world-119321.

187 **with a total population of about 330,000:** Wikipedia contributors. (2019, February 12). "United States Air Force." Wikipedia, The Free Encyclopedia. https://en.wikipedia.org/wiki/United_States_Air _Force.

187 **Travis Air Force Base in California:** Wikipedia contributors. (2023, June 6). "Travis Air Force Base." Wikipedia, The Free Encyclopedia. https://en.wikipedia.org/w/index.php?title=Travis_Air_Force_Base& oldid=1158800624.

188 **For eleven years after launch:** "A Comprehensive Approach to Suicide Prevention." (n.d.). Suicide Prevention Resource Center. Accessed August 30, 2023. https://www.sprc.org/effective-prevention /comprehensive-approach.

188 **Through 2008, with the exception of 2004:** University of Rochester Medical Center (URMC). (2010, May 19). "Air Force Prevention Program Reduces Suicide Rates Significantly." URMC Newsroom. https://www.urmc.rochester.edu/news/story/air-force-prevention -program-reduces-suicide-rates-significantly.

188 **In the program's heyday:** URMC, "Air Force Prevention Program."

190 **The USAF's strategy for preventing suicide:** Knox et al., "The US Air Force Suicide Prevention Program."

194 **While the Army's suicide rate increased:** Myers, Meghann. (2022, October 20). "Active Duty Suicides Dropped 15% in 2021, but Overall Trend Is Upward." *Military Times.* https://www.militarytimes.com /news/your-military/2022/10/20/active-duty-suicides-dropped-15-in -2021-but-overall-trend-is-upward.

195 **Studies have shown that Wingman Connect:** Wyman, Peter A., Anthony R. Pisani, C. Hendricks Brown, et al. (2020). "Effect of the Wingman-Connect Upstream Suicide Prevention Program for Air Force Personnel in Training." *JAMA Network Open* 3 (10): e2022532. https://doi.org/10.1001/jamanetworkopen.2020.22532.

196 **He said the Air Force seeks immediate:** Burns, Robert. (2020, February 10). "Air Force Suicides Surged Last Year to Highest in 3 Decades." ABC Action News Tampa Bay (WFTS). https://www .abcactionnews.com/news/national/air-force-suicides-surged-last -year-to-highest-in-3-decades.

Chapter Eleven: Systems Approaches: Denmark

199 **Staff members also follow up:** Miller, Greg. (2019, August 22). "Three Suicide Prevention Strategies Show Real Promise. How Can They Reach More People?" American Association for the Advancement of Science. https://www.science.org/content/article/three-suicide -prevention-strategies-show-real-promise-how-can-they-reach-more -people.

199 **However, in the program's first nine years:** Coffey, M. Justin, C. Edward Coffey, and Brian K. Ahmedani. (2015). "Suicide in a Health Maintenance Organization Population." *JAMA Psychiatry* 72 (3): 294–96. https://doi.org/10.1001/jamapsychiatry.2014.2440.

199 **Henry Ford aims to provide:** Miller, "Three Suicide Prevention Strategies."

200 **"It just makes sense":** Miller, "Three Suicide Prevention Strategies."

203 **But college and university students:** Taub, Deborah J., and Jalonda Thompson. (2013). "College Student Suicide." *New Directions for Student Services* 2013 (141): 5–14. https://doi.org/10.1002/ss.20036.

204 **The majority of students:** Cerel, Julie, Mary Chandler Bolin, Melinda M. Moore. (2013). "Suicide Exposure, Awareness and Attitudes in College Students." *Advances in Mental Health* 12 (1): 46–53. https://doi .org/10.5172/jamh.2013.12.1.46.

204 **About one-fifth:** "Digest of Education Statistics, 2016: Table 204.75d." (n.d.). National Center for Education Statistics. Accessed August 30, 2023. https://nces.ed.gov/programs/digest/d16/tables/dt16_204.75d.asp.

204 **Women in college are two to three times:** "Why Is Suicide So Common Among College Students?" (n.d.). Governors State University. Accessed August 30, 2023. https://www.govst.edu/suicide-prevention.

204 **For students of color:** Laidler, John. (2020, October 28). "COVID's Triple Whammy for Black Students." *The Harvard Gazette.* https:// news.harvard.edu/gazette/story/2020/10/covid-carries-triple-risks-for -college-students-of-color/#:~:text=College%20students%20of %20color%20not.

204 **and LGBTQIA+ students:** Green, Amy E., Myeshia Price-Feeney, and Samuel H. Dorison. (2020). *Implications of COVID-19 for LGBTQ Youth Mental Health and Suicide Prevention.* New York: The Trevor Project. https://www.thetrevorproject.org/wp-content/uploads/2020/04 /Implications-of-COVID-19-for-LGBTQ-Youth-Mental-Health-and -Suicide-Prevention.pdf.

205 **They learn the warning signs:** MacPhee, John, Kamla Modi, Sara Gorman, Nance Roy, Erica Riba, Diana Cusumano, John Dunkle, et al. (2021). "A Comprehensive Approach to Mental Health Promotion and Suicide Prevention for Colleges and Universities: Insights from the JED Campus Program." *NAM Perspectives*, June. https://doi.org /10.31478/202106b.

205 **Professional services such as crisis management:** MacPhee et al., "A Comprehensive Approach."

205 **Campuses must fight the stigma:** MacPhee et al., "A Comprehensive Approach."

206 **Restricting the availability of poisons:** MacPhee et al., "A Comprehensive Approach."

206 **In 1980 it was 38 per 100,000:** Nordentoft, Merete, and Annette Erlangsen. (2019). "Suicide—Turning the Tide." *Science* 365 (6455): 725. https://doi.org/10.1126/science.aaz1568.

206 **That's more than a 30 percent:** Nordentoft and Erlangsen, "Suicide—Turning the Tide."

206 **In 2007 the US suicide rate:** National Institute of Mental Health (NIMH). "Suicide," n.d. https://www.nimh.nih.gov/health/statistics /suicide.

206 **Between 1999 and 2006:** Centers for Disease Control and Prevention: National Center for Injury Prevention and Control. Web-based Injury Statistics Query and Reporting System (WISQARS). https://www.cdc .gov/injury/wisqars/index.html.

207 **A shortage of beds in psychiatric units:** Leyenaar, JoAnna K., Seneca D. Freyleue, Amy Bordogna, et al. (2021). "Frequency and Duration of Boarding for Pediatric Mental Health Conditions at Acute Care Hospitals in the US." *Journal of the American Medical Association* 326 (22): 2326–28. https://doi.org/10.1001/jama.2021.18377.

207 **Leyenaar estimates that between:** Richtel, Matt. (2022, May 8). "Hundreds of Suicidal Teens Sleep in Emergency Rooms. Every Night." *The New York Times*. https://www.nytimes.com/2022/05/08/health /emergency-rooms-teen-mental-health.html.

207 **in the some four thousand US emergency departments:** Leyenaar et al., "Frequency and Duration of Boarding."

208 **While the United States, with a population:** There are no hospitals or clinics in the United States that are specifically designated as suicide-specific facilities that I'm aware of. However, there are many hospitals

and clinics that offer specialized treatment for individuals at risk of suicide or who have attempted suicide. It's also worth noting that many general hospitals and clinics have protocols in place for managing patients who are at risk of suicide or who have attempted suicide. Are these equivalent to Denmark's "crises clinics"? I don't think so because in practice they do not attract practitioners who specialize in suicide but more typically employ practitioners familiar with suicide treatment. And as we've discussed, vital follow-up therapy is complicated and inconsistent.

209 **According to research led by:** Johns Hopkins Bloomberg School of Public Health. (n.d.). "Research Review: Suicide Risk Falls Substantially after Talk Therapy." *Social Work Today.* Accessed August 30, 2023. https://www.socialworktoday.com/news/rr_112514_05.shtml.

209 **Patient Thea Pedersen:** The facts of Thea Pedersen's case are taken from actual cases, and her name has been changed. She is a Standardized Patient. In real life she is an actress, and in demand at medical schools for her talent at portraying patients with psychological disorders.

211 **In the group receiving therapy:** Johns Hopkins Bloomberg School of Public Health, "Suicide Risk Falls Substantially."

213 **At the same time, the intervention:** Wikipedia contributors. (2022, October 23). "Good Behavior Game." Wikipedia, The Free Encyclopedia. https://en.wikipedia.org/wiki/Good_Behavior_Game.

213 **Misbehaving, and earning points:** Wikipedia, "Good Behavior Game."

213 **Earlier studies with shorter:** Kellam, Sheppard G., Amelia C. L. Mackenzie, C. Hendricks Brown, et al. (2011). "The Good Behavior Game and the Future of Prevention and Treatment." *Addiction Science & Clinical Practice* 6 (1): 73–84. https://www.ncbi.nlm.nih.gov/pmc/articles/PMC3188824.

215 **Additionally, the Danish charitable group:** Bioethics Observatory. (2019, November 26). "Suicide Continues to Be a Devastating Public Health Problem. After Decades of Prevention Programs, It Is Still Far from Being Controlled." Bioethics Observatory, Institute of Life Sciences, Catholic University of Valencia. https://bioethicsobservatory.org/2019/11/suicide-public-health-problem/33246.

Chapter Twelve: Facing Suicide
221 **Add to that a high population:** Castro, Joseph. (2013, March 29). "Where Is the Suicide Belt?" Live Science. https://www.livescience.com/34470-suicide-belt.html.

221 **While 80 percent of suicide deaths:** "Preventing Suicide." Includes information about at-risk populations. (n.d.). SAMHSA. https://www.samhsa.gov/suicide/at-risk.

222 **Adolescence is a time of important social:** Ho, Tiffany C., Anthony J. Gifuni, and Ian H. Gotlib. (2022). "Psychobiological Risk Factors for Suicidal Thoughts and Behaviors in Adolescence: A Consideration of the Role of Puberty." *Molecular Psychiatry* 27: 606-623. https://doi.org/10.1038/s41380-021-01171-5.

222 **These emotions can lead:** Ho et al., "Psychobiological Risk Factors."

222 **According to the CDC:** Curtin, Sally C. (2020). "State Suicide Rates among Adolescents and Young Adults Aged 10-24: United States, 2000–2018." *National Vital Statistics Reports* 69 (11). https://www.cdc.gov/nchs/data/nvsr/nvsr69/NVSR-69-11-508.pdf.

222 **It is plausible that the early onset:** Curtin, Sally C., and Melonie Heron. (2019, October). "Death Rates Due to Suicide and Homicide among Persons Ages 10–24: United States, 2000–2017." NCHS Data Brief No. 352. https://www.cdc.gov/nchs/products/databriefs/db352.htm.

222 **Almost 50 percent of Americans:** Cutler, David. (2020, May–June). "The World's Costliest Health Care." *Harvard Magazine*. https://www.harvardmagazine.com/2020/05/feature-forum-costliest-health-care.

223 **These lobbies aggressively fight:** Cutler, "World's Costliest Health Care"; and Moreno, Sabrina. (2022, October 28). "Health Care Industry Spending on Federal Lobbying Surged 70% over 20 Years." *Axios*. https://www.axios.com/2022/10/28/health-care-industry-spending-on-federal-lobbying-surged-70-over-20-years.

223 **This tells us that unvarnished:** Cooper, Zack, Stuart V. Craig, Martin Gaynor, and John Van Reenen. (2019). "The Price Ain't Right? Hospital Prices and Health Spending on the Privately Insured." *The Quarterly Journal of Economics* 134 (1): 51–107. https://doi.org/10.1093/qje/qjy020.

223 **Survival rates for heart disease:** Cutler, "World's Costliest Health Care."

223 **One recent study of young people:** Melillo, Gianna. (2022, November 22). "Mental Health Care Provider Shortage Linked with Increased Youth Suicide Rates: Study." *The Hill*. https://thehill.com/changing-america/well-being/mental-health/3746317-mental-health-care-provider-shortage-linked-with-increased-youth-suicide-rates-study/.

223 **About 20 percent of children in the US:** Mann, Denise. (2022, November 23). "Mental Health Care Shortage Could Play Role in U.S.

Youth Suicides." *U.S. News & World Report.* https://www.usnews.com
/news/health-news/articles/2022-11-23/mental-health-care-shortage
-could-play-role-in-u-s-youth-suicides.

224 **To lower the risk of suicide:** "Facts about LGBTQ Youth Suicide."
(n.d.). The Trevor Project. Accessed August 30, 2023. https://www
.thetrevorproject.org/resources/article/facts-about-lgbtq-youth-suicide.

224 **The suicide rate for persons seventy-five and older:** "Disparities in
Suicide." (2021, October 14). Centers for Disease Control and
Prevention. https://www.cdc.gov/suicide/facts/disparities-in-suicide
.html.

227 **That homemade video:** "Jordan Lefler (@JordanLefler): Landscape
Photographer Based in the US." Nomadict. https://nomadict.org
/jordan-lefler-jordanlefler-landscape-photographer-based-in-the-us.

228 **People trained in the methods of QPR:** "QPR Institute: Practical and
Proven Suicide Prevention Training." (n.d.). QPR Institute. Accessed
August 30, 2023. https://qprinstitute.com.

INDEX